About Island Press

Island Press is the only nonprofit organization in the United States whose principal purpose is the publication of books on environmental issues and natural resource management. We provide solutions-oriented information to professionals, public officials, business and community leaders, and concerned citizens who are shaping responses to environmental problems.

In 1994, Island Press celebrated its tenth anniversary as the leading provider of timely and practical books that take a multidisciplinary approach to critical environmental concerns. Our growing list of titles reflects our commitment to bringing the best of an expanding body of literature to the environmental community throughout North America and the world.

Support for Island Press is provided by Apple Computer, Inc., The Bullitt Foundation, The Geraldine R. Dodge Foundation, The Energy Foundation, The Ford Foundation, The W. Alton Jones Foundation, The Lyndhurst Foundation, The John D. and Catherine T. MacArthur Foundation, The Andrew W. Mellon Foundation, The Joyce Mertz-Gilmore Foundation, The National Fish and Wildlife Foundation, The Pew Charitable Trusts, The Pew Global Stewardship Initiative, The Philanthropic Collaborative, Inc., and individual donors.

Placing Nature

Placing Nature

Culture and Landscape Ecology

EDITED BY

JOAN IVERSON NASSAUER

ISLAND PRESS

Washington, D.C. • Covelo, California

ISLAND PRESS is a trademark of The Center for Resource Economics.

COVER PHOTOS

Top: Clearing, the New Gated Community, Des Moines, Iowa (April 1993).

Bottom: Fen with Creek, Shakopee, Minnesota (March 1996).

Library of Congress Cataloging-in-Publication Data

Placing nature: culture and landscape ecology / edited by Joan
    Iverson Nassauer
      p.   cm.
    ISBN 1-55963-559-2 (pbk.)
    1. Landscape ecology.   I. Nassauer, Joan Iverson.
    QH541.15.L35P58   1997
    577.5´5—dc21   97-14842
                                                        CIP

Printed on recycled, acid-free paper ♳

Manufactured in the United States of America

10   9   8   7   6   5   4   3   2   1

This book is dedicated to the memory of Hildegard Binder Johnson,
who saw culture in the landscape and helped us to see.

Contents

Acknowledgments

Each of the authors whose work is included in this book engaged in a process of discussion and mutual review of each other's work, exemplifying the possibilities for working across boundaries in landscape ecology. I am most grateful to my colleagues for their endeavor in writing this book. I learned a great deal from them and from our process of working together.

The Graduate School of the University of Minnesota made this book possible by awarding a grant to Deborah Karasov and me to organize a multidisciplinary project about culture and landscape ecology. I thank Dean Mark Brenner and Associate Dean Charles Louis for their faith in the project throughout its evolution.

The topic of our exploration grew out of the conclusions of the Blue Ribbon Panel at the ninth annual United States landscape ecology symposium. I thank Tom Crow for organizing the panel and all of my colleagues in the International Society for Landscape Ecology (IALE) for their work, from which I have learned so much. I also thank Margaret Moore, IALE program chair, with whom I worked as local program chair to organize the tenth annual national landscape ecology symposium, "Working in a World Dominated by Humans." The symposium allowed the authors of these essays to practice a multidisciplinary critique of applied landscape ecology. Special thanks to David Tilman, who first suggested our symposium theme, and to Lucinda John-

son, who suggested that we begin critical analysis of case studies as part of the national symposium. Those case studies became important touchstones that allowed us to communicate across disciplines by reference to real places. I thank Don Wyse and Helene Murray of the Minnesota Institute for Sustainable Agriculture, and Dan and Muriel French for allowing us to visit and review their farm and for participating in our critical review of applied landscape ecology. I also thank Sherri Buss, director of the Phalen Watershed Project; the Board of the Project; and Cliff Aichinger, director of the Ramsey-Washington Metro Watershed District, for generously organizing our visit and participating in our critical review of the Phalen Watershed.

I am also grateful to the McKnight Fund for the Arts and Humanities of the University of Minnesota, which made a pivotal contribution to the symposium. In addition, the USDA Forest Service; USDA Natural Resources Conservation Service; the USDI Fish and Wildlife Service; the University of Minnesota's Colleges of Agriculture, Natural Resources, and Architecture and Landscape Architecture, and the Center for Urban Affairs; and the Minnesota Institute for Sustainable Agriculture all joined in sponsoring this symposium.

The central activities leading to this book were seminars for scholars and graduate students in the humanities; design; and biological, physical, and social sciences in the winter and fall of

1995. Deborah Karasov and I organized these two experiences, where we shared, developed, and tested our ideas about landscape ecology. Special thanks go to Deborah for her work in organizing that first seminar, teaching the associated graduate course, and organizing the weekend and summer retreats for authors and visiting critics—all of which were essential to the authors' work.

Among those whose names do not appear as authors in this book but whose insights and questions were critical to its evolution are the students in geography, landscape architecture, architecture, and philosophy who participated in the seminar and retreats. Each of the authors is also indebted to our colleagues in the arts, sciences, humanities, and design, whose thoughtful participation in the discussion brought and tested important ideas. I thank Kinji Akagawa, Julie Bargmann, John Carmody, Roger Clemence, Edward Cushing, Susan Galatowitsch, Harrison Fraker, Mierle Ukeles Laderman, Roger Martin, Lance Neckar, Patrick Nunnally, David Pitt, Peter Reich, Earl Scott, Robert Sykes, and John Tester. Finally, Richard Forman and Frank Golley visited and participated in discussions at critical times in the project. Their insights as scholars and as fathers of landscape ecology provided important tests of the cultural principles for landscape ecology that we discussed, and their experience energized our work.

All of the authors hope that this book will speak to you if you are, or are preparing to be, a citizen who can speak for ecological health in your own community. We also hope it will speak to you if you are, or are preparing to be, a landscape ecologist—ecologist, ecosystem manager, watershed manager, conservation biologist, land developer, designer, planner, or engineer—who will directly make future landscapes. If this book does speak to you, it will be largely because of the skillful editing of Mary Keirstead, who worked with me on the final manuscript of the book. I am extremely grateful to her for her clear thinking and professionalism.

A Note about the Photographic Essay by Chris Faust

Chris Faust's photographs, which begin on the cover and appear throughout this book, were important catalysts in the discussion among the contributors to this book. In the project, experts in disciplines ranging from art to ecology and from geography to philosophy worked together to understand how culture can be activated as part of landscape ecology. Learning to listen to the languages of other disciplines and learning to recognize what each of us noticed when we looked at the landscape were essential to the way that we worked. Looking at real places as portrayed in Faust's photographs helped us talk and make common discoveries about the effects of culture. In his travels around the world to photograph landscapes, Faust finds that his photography punctuates the continuum of what he sees. The photographs he makes by this way of seeing remind us of places that we all can recognize. At the same time, they point out what Faust sees in particular. The son of a historian and a watercolor painter of landscapes, he captures the landscape at key points in the process of change. In the photographs that follow, look for reminders of your own experiences and also look for ways in which the combinations of these photographs speak to aspects of landscape ecology discussed in the written essays. This is what the authors of the essays did as we worked together.

JOAN IVERSON NASSAUER

Culture and Landscape Ecology: Insights for Action

JOAN IVERSON NASSAUER

Allee of Trees, on the Way to Warsaw, Poland (September 1994).

THOUGHTFUL OBSERVERS of global ecosystems cannot fail to see that we live in a world dominated by humans. We cannot stand apart from nature, and now nature as we know it cannot stand apart from us. Faced with dawning clarity about this new relationship, we are uncertain of what to do. What is our appropriate role in nature? How might the tremendous momentum of postindustrial technology and global economics be channeled or transformed in response to ecological fundamentals? How can ancient assumptions of Western culture and ingrained traditions be placed in a new context of ecological knowledge? What should our goals be? What should our strategies be? How should we live?

The authors of the essays in this book asked themselves these questions. Our different backgrounds in ecology, philosophy, art, literature, geography, landscape architecture, and history—and our varied experiences with nature and the landscape—led us to look for answers in different spheres of human experience. Jane Smiley was awarded the Pulitzer prize for her novel *A Thousand Acres*,[1] which revealed the overpowering necessity of an Iowa farm family's relationship to the land. In this volume, she probes the assumptions of agriculture, concluding that "agriculture not only has the ability to make civilization, it has the power to un-make it." As a child, Eville Gorham loved the peat bog landscapes of his native Nova Scotia. Today he is known around the world for his research on boreal wetland ecology and the effects of acid rain. Here, he brings his wealth of ecological knowledge to bear on what he sees as the more complex problem of restraining human impacts on ecosystems. Judith Martin, as a geographer, has analyzed urban settlements across the northern hemisphere and, as a planning commissioner, has directly affected the urban pattern of Minneapolis, the largest city in a metropolitan area of 2.5 million people. Her essay with urban historian Sam Bass Warner probes the dynamics of development decisions that in the past have rarely been evaluated for their landscape ecological

3

effects. Chris Faust's photographs are informed by his experience as a biologist. His photographic essay, which runs throughout the book, aptly juxtaposes the most crass and mundane details of using the land with the poetic power of all landscapes.

Together these essays, with the others in this book, suggest widely varied approaches for bringing human-dominated landscapes into intentional relationships with nature. However, all of the essays hinge on a shared assumption: we must use culture to advance ecological health, or we risk removing ourselves altogether from the ecosystems we know. Our shared recognition that new relationships with nature are necessary to human survival brings an urgency to our exchange.

Landscape Ecology: An Amalgam of Many Disciplines

Landscape ecology drew the authors of these essays together to discuss what we know and what we need to know about culture. Within landscape ecology, knowledge of biological and physical phenomena has grown rapidly, so rapidly that many landscape ecological solutions to landscape-management problems have been offered only to be impeded or disregarded because they did not fit their cultural context. As both federal and state resource-management agencies across the United States have striven to implement a new, more holistic approach, ecosystem-management stories accumulate of good science that has been submerged in conflict for lack of cultural knowledge. Whether the issue has been logging of old-growth forests in the Pacific Northwest, selecting cultivated fields for habitat reserves, or creating habitat corridors across a metropolitan landscape, ecological solutions have been realized to the extent that they fit culture. The authors of these essays recognize that cultural insights have not kept pace with the clear need for understanding human per-

ceptions, behavior, and communities, even when such insights have been critical to achieving ecological health.

From its beginnings in Europe, landscape ecology was conceived as an approach to understanding landscapes that drew upon both cultural and ecological knowledge.[2] The first president of the International Association for Landscape Ecology, the Dutch ecologist I. S. Zonneveld, answered the question "Who is a landscape ecologist?" this way:

> Any geographer, geomorphologist, soil scientist, hydrologist, climatologist, sociologist, anthropologist, economist, landscape architect, agriculturist, regional planner, civil engineer—even general, cardinal, minister, or president, if you like, who has the "attitude" to approach our environment—including all biotic and abiotic values—as a coherent system, as a kind of whole that cannot be really understood from its separate components only, is a landscape ecologist.[3]

The authors of the essays that follow are persuaded by our work together that landscape ecology must be a disciplinary amalgam cemented by the attitude that Zonneveld described. The defining concepts of landscape ecology set our course as we met together with other colleagues over the duration of a year. Landscape ecology opened ecological thought for critical discussion across disciplines because it goes beyond investigation of pristine ecosystems and beyond concerns for habitat restoration to consider the entire landscape of human settlement in all its sullied complexity. Landscape ecology investigates landscape structure and ecological function at a scale that encompasses the ordinary elements of human landscape experience: yards, forests, fields, streams, and streets. From the beginning, it has included the insistent and frequently destructive behavior of human beings as essential to understanding.[4]

Landscape ecology forced the authors to recognize the incompleteness of ecological knowledge and to confront the primary effect of culture in determining ecological function. The key landscape ecology concept that human beings and the land-scapes we make are influential parts of ecosystems led us to re-alize that we could not prescribe what future landscapes should be without consulting human values. Every possible future land-scape is the embodiment of some human choice. Science can in-form us; it cannot lead us.

When the German geographer Carl Troll coined the term *landscape ecology* in 1939, he was responding to a new technology, aerial photography, which displayed patterns of fields, forests, streams, and roads from a distance.[5] Aerial photographs made the landscape look like an enormous puzzle, and Troll believed that the shapes, sizes, and arrangement of the pieces made a difference in the overall ecology of the landscape. Although people did not make the landscape, they did craft much of the pattern. Today landscape ecology questions the effect of the pattern and looks to culture as one means of change. The authors of these essays struggled to find the ideas that could activate culture as part of a constructive working system of landscape ecological principles.

Urgent Realities: Population, Energy, Biodiversity

To view humans solely as a cause of ecological problems is to surrender to the most damaging aspects of culture. However, ex-amining culture for solutions did lead some of us to underscore the urgent need to reexamine cultural assumptions and to reject some pervasive elements of Western culture. Curt Meine works from his knowledge of environmental history to conclude that the parceling of land in the United States by the rigid rectilin-ear geometry of the Public Land Survey has altered the patterns and processes of biological diversity within the landscape and continues to undermine our perceptions of those patterns and processes. Eville Gorham, working from his knowledge of eco-system function, and Jane Smiley, working from her observations

of farming in the Midwest, each describe how contemporary agriculture can overtake the ecological capacities of the land-scape. This critique is not one that matters only if you live on a farm. Gorham describes the radical enhancement of the nitrogen cycle through the atmosphere by modern fertilizer manufactur-ing and the high proportion of energy inputs required for pro-duction of crops in industrial agriculture. Smiley believes that "What will or can be done with farming goes to the heart of what will or can be done with the rest of the earth."

Gorham's essay emphasizes the conclusion of many ecologists and observers that population growth is the fundamental global ecological challenge. Paired with postindustrial economic systems and proliferating Western consumer expectations, our soaring human population may already have exceeded the capacity of the global ecosystem to support it. Gorham describes the ecological effects of humanity's relatively new cultural habits of using fossil fuels, synthetic fertilizers, and pesticides and herbicides. He shows that the mammoth scale of earth moving and habitat destruction that accompany human settlement at the turn of the millennium casts a shadow over the entire planet and threatens the biodiver-sity necessary to human existence. Smiley sets these phenomena firmly in the context of culture and delves into the unexamined habits that reflect our Western concept of civilization. That the detached intelligence of a great ecologist, Gorham, and the syn-thetic intelligence of a great novelist, Smiley, both clearly envi-sion ecological catastrophe in the absence of profound cultural reform injects a convincing urgency into the ideas that follow. They must be ideas that can launch us into action.

The Place of Nature: In Culture and on the Land

Where nature *should be* in settled landscapes to improve their ecological function is a critical question for which landscape ecology suggests answers.[6] Where nature *can be* in the enormously complex but fundamentally pragmatic cultural process of making places is equally fundamental. Science may give us normative criteria for new landscape patterns, culture will give us the realized design. The essays in this book work from scientific knowledge of ecological function to posit cultural ideas about landscapes so that concrete ecological function and tangible human experience can simultaneously make a place for nature on the land.

Ecological Concepts

In his essay, ecologist William H. Romme summarizes landscape ecology concepts related to biodiversity, energy and material flows, disturbance, and cultural systems, applying each of these to investigate the place of nature in his home landscape, La Plata County, Colorado. The concepts he describes have direct implications for landscape patterns in any settled landscape. We are likely to maintain greater biodiversity if large patches of native ecosystems are protected and if additional large patches are restored. The plants and animals that depend on these ecosystems are more likely to survive if these patches contain a variety of related types of ecosystems and if the patches are connected. Large patches are increasingly rare because human settlement nearly always fragments large native ecosystems into smaller parcels. While large patches are often essential to ecological health, smaller patches also can support the movement and survival of species.[7]

Not only native ecosystems have ecological value. Different types of fields, yards, and even parking lots can support ecological health to different degrees depending on their function. For example, the pioneering landscape architecture practice of Andropogon Associates showed that parking lots can be designed to infiltrate or store rainwater rather than sending it to flood down-

stream.[8] Residential sites and farm fields can be designed to prevent soil from eroding, to require little or no addition of water or nutrients or use of pesticides or herbicides, and to prevent pollutants from moving off the site. They can even be designed to include relatively diverse habitats that connect to the surrounding landscape pattern.

Cultural Conceptions

Whether the opportunity is to protect the pristine or restore some aspect of ecological function to the settled landscape, as Romme describes, we live with the very real artifacts of cultural conceptions in the landscapes that make up our everyday experience. Every park, shopping center, field, or highway connotes our cultural conception of nature. Landscape patterns begin in the mind.

Gorham reminds us of Donald Worster's insight that even ecologists, who have scientific knowledge of ecosystems, hold widely varied views of nature, ranging from an unspoiled paradise to a resource for exploitation. The authors of the essays in this book see—and, to a degree, embody—this same spectrum of views in North American culture. While they agree with the landscape ecology concept that humans are a part of nature, they differ on the question of how humans, settlement, and economic activity fit into nature.

The landscape patterns that now are familiar to us in North America tend to isolate nature from settlement. Gorham advocates that nature should be protected separate from settlement and builds upon Eugene Odum's four compartment zoning model of landscapes, including urban–industrial, productive, protective, and compromise environments. Gorham insists on the ethical and biological necessity of protective environments but also describes the cleansing functions that compromise environments can perform. He also finds value in nature in the city, describing urban wetlands as "the closest approach to wild nature that the city can offer," and suggests that they "deserve protection as a reminder of the natural world."

In contrast, Smiley's essay evokes the possibility of a wholly new landscape pattern, one in which nature is not protected because it is not isolated. Instead nature dominates. She questions whether civilization as we know it can support nature and calls for radically new models for living on the earth. Continuing with our civilization as exemplified by agriculture "will undermine rather that enhance the landscape's capacity to support itself and us," she asserts.

A third view expressed in several of the essays is that nature can be more completely integrated with settlement than zoning or a wholly new landscape pattern implies. While pristine landscapes must be protected, zoning alone may divide the landscape into patterns too discrete to accommodate its overall ecological function. Romme suggests many strategies for integrating ecological function within development patterns of rural communities. Warner and Martin, and I too, report possibilities for, and recent experiments in, integrating ecological function back into the city.

Integrating nature into settlement increases contact and friction between people and ecologically rich landscapes. People threaten streams, lakes, wetlands, woodlands, and prairies by changing the flow of energy or material into these habitats and by actually encroaching on them with development. These flows may be as apparently innocuous as a pet cat prowling a nearby meadow, as invisible as the flow of herbicides carried in rainwater from lawns to lakes, or as dramatic as a massive fish kill in a poisoned stream. In a way that demonstrates the subtle power of culture to shape landscapes, people sometimes feel threatened by natural habitats as well. Where plants or wildlife are perceived to be out of control, whether by virtue of a messy appearance or by

real losses—of homes to fire or of desired plants to weeds or hungry wildlife—nature is not wanted.

The Culture of Nature

Nearly every aspect of culture affects ecological health. For example, diet, childbearing, public health, and transportation by private cars all affect human consumption of resources in momentous ways. While the discussion among the authors of these essays recognized these fundamental effects, it focused on Western cultural assumptions about nature, not because the culture of nature is more important than resource consumption, but because the culture of nature may be an immediately tractable means of affecting landscape ecological function. Where landscape patterns are the products of our cultural norms of the landscape, probing cultural images may suggest strategies to finesse apparent conflicts, which may be as much the product of unrecognized cultural norms as of different ecological goals. Several essays in this book describe how aesthetic experience, ecological knowledge, or landscape care are at the heart of cultural images of nature.

Aesthetic Experience

Aesthetics is explicitly about nature. Representations of landscapes decorated ancient Roman homes, preoccupied the wealthy in eighteenth-century England, and span the range from high art to kitsch in North America today. Equally important as representations of landscapes, whether in poetry, painting, or environmental art, is the fact that landscape viewing is a popular pastime. Whether the everyday aesthetic value of the landscape is expressed by a pause to look out the window of your house or by a drive to see fall leaves, varieties and levels of connoisseurship abound in landscape aesthetics. As Marcia Eaton and Eville Gorham tell us, even scientists experience nature aesthetically. Because aesthetic experience has so deeply and persistently influenced nearly every culture's conception of nature,[9] thinking about aesthetic experience can provide penetrating insights into why people make certain landscape patterns. As Eaton describes, aesthetic experience is of the moment. We know what we like. In the landscape, we act on what we like. For this reason, aesthetics may give landscape ecology a strategic lever for changing landscape patterns. Eaton and I detail how art, design, and planning that incorporate the deep aesthetic satisfaction people find in nature can help to overcome problems of perception that obstruct applications of landscape ecological knowledge. We see aesthetic tradition as the embodiment of community values and, consequently, the basis for a language that can be used to provoke change and sustain ecological quality.

Ecological Knowledge

Several authors suggest that greater ecological knowledge will promote cultural change. Gorham, Eaton, and Meine each describe how understanding of nature will not only change the landscape but enrich human experience. Eaton analyzes how ecological knowledge will help to sustain aesthetic attention to landscapes over time and continually motivate a desire for more ecological knowledge. Ecological knowledge will also lead to more discerning human experiences, in which ecologically destructive phenomena are not mistaken for beautiful nature. Deborah Karasov, Gorham, and I describe how the landscape itself can be a means of environmental education, exemplifying aspects of more pristine places or portraying the ecological functions of even the most densely settled landscapes. Romme's and Karasov's accounts of cases of land-planning dilemmas and their

potential resolution support the possibility that people can make nature part of human settlement if they know how.

Landscape Care

Gorham begins by telling us that "during early human history, caring for the land was unnecessary; as a part of the natural world it took care of itself." But now, he says, "human societies must care, and care deeply, for the planetary ecosystem as an integrated whole if they are to survive." Smiley has a different view, that "our goal should be not to care for the earth but to enable it to have sufficient complexity that it can care for itself." The difference may lie in how we interpret care. I have emphasized the beneficence of landscape care as a cultural attitude despite its frequently damaging ecological effects in the form of clean, weed-free lawns, fields, and forests.[10] Care is beneficent when it means watching over a landscape and intervening in change rather than asserting absolute control, because, as I say in chapter 4, "landscapes require tending not making." Settled landscapes are enjoyed, and the people who inhabit them are judged, to the degree that landscapes exhibit care. We can take advantage of the ready-made cultural necessity of care by attaching ecological health to its lawlike aesthetic conventions, and if we combine greater ecological knowledge with our cultural need to display care, we can provoke new forms of intelligent gardening and farming.

Traditions of Land Ownership and Development

Cultural traditions that may appear to have little relationship to ecology may actually have profound cumulative or insidious effects. Meine tells us that "exploration of the new requires assimilation of the past." He suggests that the grid land-division pattern of the Public Land Survey is emblematic of our blinkered cultural attitudes about land ownership and concludes that it is our attitudes that must change. Smiley's lesson of the medieval Scandinavian settlement in Greenland, related to her novel *The Greenlanders*,[11] warns that we may have difficulty achieving sufficient distance from our own cultural condition to see its consequences. By questioning our means of agriculture, she digs at the roots of our own cultural condition and sees traditions that obscure destructive ecological realities.

To both Meine and Smiley, the omnipresent, inflexible pattern of land ownership and the driving exigencies of market economics pose profound obstacles to change. As vivid evidence, Romme describes the tragic contradiction between the wish to be closer to nature that is evident in hundreds of new householders living on large lots in the unincorporated areas of La Plata County, Colorado, and the effect of those same large lots as barriers to the migratory paths of elk and mule deer. Karasov describes the way in which conceptions of private-property rights have underpinned virtually all discussions of the future of a suburban trout stream. She says, "most state regulatory agencies understand that developers who purchase property and act in accordance with zoning and environmental regulations have a right to pursue development of their property."

I argue that in our culture, where land ownership fragments ecological patterns, owning land has also been the only reliable way to protect it. Meine describes how Thomas Jefferson prescribed the Public Land Survey to embody his ideal of a democratic populace of small land holders. While land ownership in the United States is increasingly concentrated among fewer owners, the ideal of land ownership retains enormous cultural power. I describe how only ownership by the public or by a wealthy, enlightened family has protected the last remaining large patches of indigenous habitats in the most urbanized county in Minnesota. As Smiley points out, decades of warning about the damage caused by soil erosion on private land has not stopped soil erosion. Despite widespread knowledge and massive incentives to conserve, in our system only individual farmers can decide to prevent erosion. Similarly in metropolitan areas, only public or private owners of land, homes, and businesses can decide to design and manage their landscapes to contribute to ecological quality. Romme tells us that private landowners and developers play a pivotal role in the future biodiversity of La Plata County. I suggest that our landscape ecology strategies should use the cultural power of ownership to achieve ecological ends.

Judith A. Martin and Sam Bass Warner Jr. describe how limitations imposed by public regulations, as well as developers' perceptions of market demands, may prevent individuals from having the choice of more ecologically sound landscapes. Perceptions of what people want and will buy may be more limiting than what they would actually find attractive if they were given the choice. Martin and Warner relate developers' perceptions that the market for environmentally innovative residential development is very limited. Developers feel restrained by the market rather than by their own abilities to imagine more ecologically appropriate development patterns. In the words of one developer, "What we have is what we are." Whether for reasons of perceived real estate market or for short-term gain in production agriculture, or simply for reasons of tradition, change to increase the ecological health of the land has not come easily. The question looms large: How do we act to change landscape patterns?

How to Act

Acting with Humility

All of us who contributed to this book agree that our ability to act is severely limited by our knowledge. The intelligent tending that I advocate requires that we see each new adjustment in our landscapes as experimental, and that we remain watchful for the response. Smiley argues that we should draw from knowledge rather than belief when we consider actions on the land, because "knowledge tends . . . toward putting the knower in his or her rightful, and limited, place." She warns that "as our millennium ends and our population grows, the margin once allowed for survival by the abundance of nature and the expanse of geography grows smaller and smaller. Mistakes, even sincere mistakes of sincere belief, have ever more serious consequences."

In the seminars that led to this book, Gorham frequently reminded participants of Aldo Leopold's dictum: "To keep every cog and wheel is the first precaution of intelligent tinkering."[12] Gorham himself adds the following, even more succinct watchwords, "If you don't know, go slow." The contributors to this book, some of whom have spent their careers learning about ecology, agree that we generally do not know—at least not enough to keep up with the accelerated rate and landscape scale at which human-induced change has overtaken familiar places and creatures over the past century.

Acting across Scales

Carl Troll discovered essential characteristics of landscapes by looking at them at a new scale made apparent by a new technology, aerial photography. Landscape ecology opened the door to the discussion recorded in these essays partly because it directs our view of nature to a new scale. Meine calls for us to "somehow achieve the capacity to step away from the artificial order in which our lives are embedded. We must appreciate the varied scales of time and space in which we exist. We must read well the character of the earth and know how culture has influenced the view from within."

The authors of these essays have come to agree that we must work across scales as we anticipate the effects of our actions. Working across scales means considering global effects like climate warming, consulting the ecology of the watershed, and noticing patterns of species movement before we change a single site. It also means consulting the cultural interpretation of the larger landscape before designing a single site. Cultural interpretation begins with looking *at* the landscape to see the way we ordinarily look through it, in precisely the way that Meine demonstrates by looking at the land-ownership grid. Cultural interpretation is coming to grips with our attachment to life inside our automobiles in the way that Martin and Warner describe. It is using cultural meaning strategically to provoke awareness of ecological health in the way that Eaton and I describe. Finally, working across scales means critically examining the time scales of our own immediate experience. Romme's work in fire ecology has vividly demonstrated the ecological consequences of past obliviousness to the time scales of natural disturbance by fire in the landscapes of the mountain West.[13] In this book, he details how cultural blindness to annual migration paths may threaten the elk population in La Plata County.

In addition to working across scales, we must match scales of ecological and cultural phenomena. That means tuning our actions in the landscape to time and space scales that operate beyond everyday experience. As a strategy for bringing ecology into our conscious awareness, Eaton lays out categories for matching ecological scales with aesthetic experience in design. Gorham concludes that "imbalance in the pace of technological and social change may become . . . the cause of . . . ecological catastrophe." Acknowledging the disjuncture between ecological and cultural scales encourages us to look ahead and should provoke us to act.

Insights for Action

These essays are intended to be part of an accreting framework for landscape ecology. They mix the thinking that characterizes philosophy, design, or history with the strong foundations established by science. These essays also inevitably invoke a call for action beyond disciplinary knowledge and even beyond landscape ecology. Each of the authors offers insights about how we can live with nature. Many suggest strategies that move us toward a culture that is attentive to ecological health, in which we behave in response to nature. Some describe the ecological parameters that could begin to limn reformed landscape patterns. Each of us has the attitude to see the landscape as a whole and to see the regenerative potential of human action.

Notes

1. J. Smiley, *A Thousand Acres* (New York: Knopf, 1991).

2. K. Schreiber, "The History of Landscape Ecology in Europe," in *Changing Landscapes: An Ecological Perspective*, I. S. Zonneveld and R. T. T. Forman, eds. (New York: Springer-Verlag, 1990), pp. 21–35.

3. I. S. Zonneveld, Presidential Address, *International Association for Landscape Ecology Bulletin* 1 (1982): 1.

4. P. G. Risser, "Landscape Ecology: The State of the Art," in *Landscape Heterogeneity and Disturbance*, M. G. Turner, ed. (New York: Springer-Verlag, 1987).

5. Schrieber, "The History of Landscape Ecology in Europe."

6. See, for example, G. K. Meffe and C. R. Caroll, *Principles of Conservation Biology* (Sunderland, Mass.: Sinauer, 1994); W. E. Dramstad, J. D. Olson, and R. T. T. Forman, *Landscape Ecology Principles in Landscape Architecture and Land-Use Planning* (Washington, D.C.: Island Press, 1996).

7. R. T. T. Forman, *Land Mosaics: The Ecology of Landscapes and Regions* (New York: Cambridge University Press, 1995).

8. F. Steiner and T. Johnson, "Fitness, Adaptability, Delight," *Landscape Architecture* 80 (1990): 96–101.

9. Y. Tuan, *Topophilia* (Englewood Cliffs, N.J.: Prentice-Hall, 1974).

10. J. I. Nassauer, "The Aesthetics of Horticulture: Neatness As a Form of Care," *Hortscience* 23 (1988): 973–977.

11. J. Smiley, *The Greenlanders* (New York: Knopf, 1988).

12. A. Leopold, *A Sand County Almanac and Sketches Here and There* (New York: Oxford University Press, 1949, 1963).

13. W. H. Romme and D. G. Despain, "Historical Perspective on the Yellowstone Fires of 1988," *BioScience* 39 (1989): 695–699.

Recommended Reading

Forman, R. T. T. 1995. *Land Mosaics: The Ecology of Landscapes and Regions*. New York: Cambridge University Press.

Forman, R. T. T., and M. Godron. 1986. *Landscape Ecology*. New York: Wiley.

Naveh, Z. 1995. "Interactions of Landscapes and Cultures." *Landscape and Urban Planning*. 32: 43–54.

Naveh, Z., and A. S. Liebermann. 1984. *Landscape Ecology: Theory and Application*. New York: Springer-Verlag.

Risser, P. G. 1987. "Landscape Ecology: The State of the Art." *Landscape Heterogeneity and Disturbance*. M. G. Turner, ed. New York: Springer-Verlag.

Risser, P. G. 1995. "The Allerton Park Workshop Revisited: A Commentary." *Landscape Ecology*. 10: 129–132.

PART I
Urgent Realities

1 | Human Impacts on Ecosystems and Landscapes

EVILLE GORHAM

OVERLEAF

Top: Outside Cheryl's Window, SOHO district, New York City (November 1994).

Bottom: The Bad River, Copper Falls State Park near Mellen, Wisconsin (April 1993).

EVILLE GORHAM is an ecologist at the University of Minnesota who specializes in studies of acid rain, aquatic chemistry, and the ecology and biogeochemistry of wetlands. A member of the National Academy of Sciences and a fellow of the American Academy of Arts and Sciences and the Royal Society of Canada, he has served on numerous national and international committees concerning acid rain, wetlands, and global warming.

We are essentially inseparable from the earth, from its creatures, and from each other. We are they, and they are us, and when any one person, species, or ecosystem is impoverished, we are all impoverished.
—Donella Meadows, "A Reaction from a Multitude"

DURING EARLY HUMAN HISTORY, caring for the land was unnecessary; as a part of the natural world it took care of itself. Later, with the development of agriculture, caring for the land meant the maintenance of soil fertility by farmers. Later still we added the prevention or mitigation of local water and air pollution to our evolving concept of care. Now it is becoming increasingly clear that human societies, if they are to survive and prosper, must care, and care deeply, for the planetary ecosystem as an integrated whole.

Human Impacts on the Biosphere

The planetary ecosystem, often called the biosphere, forms a thin envelope about 10 miles deep around the outer part of the earth's crust, where solid, liquid, and gaseous phases (the lithosphere, hydrosphere, and atmosphere) are intermingled. The rea-

sons for our concern about the health of the biosphere are not far to seek. When we look at other species of large mammals, such as the various kinds of seal, deer, and dolphin, we see that their populations worldwide do not exceed a few millions or at most tens of millions. Before the development of agriculture, the global human population was of a similar magnitude, perhaps 5 million, so that its impact on the life-supporting capacity of the biosphere was very small. Now, with the human population increased a thousand-fold and exceeding 5 billion, supplemented by more than 4 billion large domesticated mammals—cows, pigs, sheep, goats, camels, and water buffaloes—that impact has become so large that it threatens to disrupt and degrade the biosphere in a number of important ways.[1] Indeed, we are now at a point where some scientists believe that we have already exceeded considerably the capacity of the global ecosystem to maintain for all its different peoples a reasonably adequate (i.e.,

Western) standard of living. Arthur Westing, for instance, of the International Peace Research Institute in Oslo, has estimated that carrying capacity to be about 2 billion people, much less than the more than 5 billion present inhabitants and the 8 billion or so projected by the year 2020.[2] At the average living standard of the Third World, the carrying capacity might be about 10 times higher, 20 billion—based on per capita energy use as an index of environmental impact.

The effects of population growth have been greatly enhanced by a vast increase in the per capita use of energy—for industry, agriculture, and transport—by people in developed countries such as the United States. They use hundreds of times as much energy per capita as people in the poorest countries of the world, for instance, Ethiopia and Nepal, whose consumption is, nevertheless, much greater than that in the most primitive hunter-gatherer societies. Because that energy is derived largely from fossil fuels, we have seen a toxification of our environment by acid rain, mercury, and other trace elements abundant in coal and oil, and we face the prospect of severe "greenhouse" warming of the climate by carbon dioxide released to the atmosphere following the combustion process.

Humans have also become great earthmovers, so that collectively they must now be regarded as a major geological agent, causing immense destruction of habitats. For example, tremendous transformations have been wrought in landscapes as American agribusiness has displaced the family farm. In this connection, industrial production of nitrogenous fertilizers from the nitrogen present in the atmosphere has doubled the nitrogen circulating through the biosphere, which is affecting in major ways nitrogen cycles—and other ecological processes—far from the farm fields to which the fertilizer is applied. Likewise, toxic pesticides and herbicides, several of them molecules so newly invented by agricultural chemists that microbial decomposers have

not yet evolved metabolic techniques to destroy them effectively, have been spread widely throughout the biosphere. Chlorofluorocarbons, an industrial class of molecules also newly invented as refrigerants and spray-can propellants, have been even more widely dispersed, reaching the stratosphere and destroying a part of the ozone layer that protects us from damaging ultraviolet radiation.

Humans have transported, often inadvertently, so many plants and animals around the globe that substantial fractions of the species in a given region have been introduced. In the eastern United States, for example, the proportion of nonnative plants is 20 percent. Such introductions have often caused serious disruption in local ecosystems, as is currently the case with invasion of North American wetlands by the European purple loosestrife and of waterways by the zebra mussel. Largely through destruction of habitats, humans are causing a holocaust of species extinction seen only five times in the history of the earth, the last of them about 65 million years ago in response to a massive asteroid impact at the boundary between the Cretaceous and the Tertiary periods. We also face dangers from the obverse of species extinction, that is, from genetic engineering and its applied offshoot biotechnology, which is just now beginning a phase of rapid expansion. Many scientists believe that adequate safety measures have yet to be devised for the release of genetically altered organisms into unconfined environments.[3]

Finally, if we look with Stanford ecologist Peter Vitousek and his colleagues at the terrestrial production of organic material by plant photosynthesis, we find that a large part of it (40 percent) is now either used directly as food, fodder, and wood products by humans (3.5 percent), lost owing to human activities such as conversion of forests to agriculture and desertification (12 percent), or co-opted by altering natural communities for human purposes such as agriculture and forestry (24 percent).[4] Such activities often have a strong impact on the cycles of carbon, nitrogen, phosphorus, sulfur, and other elements whose balanced interactions are essential to maintaining the smooth functioning of the biosphere. They also lessen considerably the diversity of plants and animals that is equally essential to biospheric function. It is clear from a consideration of these and many other impacts, including inadvertent, indirect, synergistic, and cumulative effects of the activities mentioned, that human beings are altering the structure and function of the biosphere very significantly in many ways that scientists have only recently been able to measure and understand (figure 1).[5]

Land Use and Its Regulation

What does all this mean for our stewardship of the biosphere? First and foremost it means that we must reconsider many of the social and economic policies that have contributed to ecological degradation. Having done so, we must craft new policies that

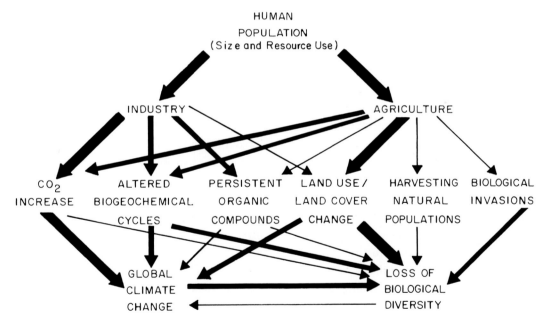

Figure 1. The influence of human populations, operating through their agricultural and industrial activities, on ecosystems and landscapes. (Copyright New Zealand Ecological Society. Reproduced with permission from Vitousek et al.)

will preserve, insofar as possible, the life-support systems of the biosphere. Whether we can in fact have "sustainable development" worldwide or will eventually find it to be a facile and cruelly deceptive oxymoron remains to be seen; certainly the policies that will bring it about in a politically acceptable manner are far from evident.[6] The underlying basis for such policies is, however, clear: We must regulate, or "zone," the uses of landscapes (and seascapes) for specific purposes far more rigorously and effectively than has hitherto been possible. We do, of course, practice such zoning regularly in our cities; in addition, we pass open-space and greenbelt legislation and set aside land for national and state forests, parks, wildlife refuges, and wilderness areas. On the other hand, current political trends in many parts of the world are strongly opposed to the philosophy behind such zoning policies, which are taken to interfere with individual property rights, and they will be very difficult to expand until the need becomes much more apparent. That it is likely to do so within the coming century seems obvious to many ecosystem and landscape ecologists.

In a prescient article published more than a quarter-century ago, Eugene Odum, the doyen of American ecology in the years after World War II, offered a useful approach to land-use regulation by proposing a four-compartment model of the landscape divided into urban-industrial, productive, protective, and compromise ecosystems, the last type being responsible for both productive and protective functions.[7] He argued for a model in which towns and cities occupying a given amount of space would require for their sustenance a certain amount of land to trap solar energy for food production. They would also require a certain amount of protective landscape, such as national parks and wilderness areas, to provide those basic services of air and water purification, soil formation, temperature control, and protection of biological diversity that nature provides to us at no cost. To be effective, Odum's global categories would of course require re-

finement and division into subcategories on both regional and local scales to take into account different sorts and areas of croplands, forests, grasslands, wetlands, and other ecosystems.

Let us focus on the importance of productive and protective ecosystems and the value of the services they provide. As a crude indication of what the costs of those services might be were it to become necessary for us to pay for them, consider the case of Biosphere 2 (earth being Biosphere 1). Biosphere 2, conceived as an ecotechnological model for exploring and colonizing space, is a futuristic "greenhouse" of glass and steel engineered to be a self-sustaining landscape without exchange of materials (including atmospheric gases) with the outside world. It did, however, require substantial inputs of fossil-fuel energy costing about a million dollars a year to drive a variety of engineering systems that enhanced the life support provided by the almost 4,000 species of plants and animals inhabiting individual tropical rain forest, marsh, desert, savanna, stream, and agricultural ecosystems. The cost of building and maintaining the closed system that was designed (but failed) to support eight "Biospherians" on three acres of totally enclosed land through two years of operation was about $150 million, or almost $19 million per person.[8] With costs such as these, can we really afford to overpopulate and toxify the planet at the same time that we severely decimate the rich array of millions of species engaged in providing our (and their) life support free of charge?

It is worth pointing out here that the inhabitants of Biosphere 2 made great efforts to recycle wastes effectively and efficiently and to avoid wherever possible the use of toxic chemicals. Unfortunately, this is not the case in our agricultural and urban-industrial systems where much of the waste is discharged to the air and water to pollute and degrade adjacent and even far distant ecosystems. Moreover, toxic chemicals are in widespread use, and many are discharged to the environment. Both wastes and toxins are treated as "externalities" in economic terms, uncounted in the balance sheet of credits and debits and left for others to pay now or in the future. Fortunately, a new breed of ecological economists is teaching us not only the true costs of these and other externalities but also how to include them in the balance sheet, so that their costs will be paid by those responsible for generating them.[9]

The life-support activities of protective ecosystems can, fortunately, be assisted in large part by those that Odum designated as compromise, or multiple-use, ecosystems, which are designed to provide us with goods as well as services. These are the forests, grasslands, waters, and other ecosystems that we maintain in a semi-natural condition to help in cleansing our air and water and in maintaining the hydrologic cycle and other ecosystem functions while we harvest wood, cattle, fish, and other useful things on what we hope will be a sustainable basis. They may vary in scale from a woodlot or a small pond to a national forest or the Great Lakes.

Much forest land is managed in this way to allow the harvest of trees, deer, fish, and other resources while meeting the needs of hikers, campers, boaters, bird-watchers, and others. How successful forest management has been depends, as is often the case, on whom one asks. The failure of our management practices is, unfortunately, not at all uncommon. A recent and dramatic example is the cod fishery on the Grand Banks of Newfoundland, which, through overfishing (aided probably by shifts in oceanic temperatures) has undergone a catastrophic decline in the last decade, after centuries of harvest, thereby destroying the livelihood of thousands of fishermen.

Odum has estimated recently that 70 percent of the land in the United States is maintained in protective and semi-natural compromise status; 24 percent is cultivated, often with nonnative species; and 6 percent is developed as urban-industrial space. He estimated further that in producing crops for human uses cultivated land requires about twice the energy input captured from the sun by protective and compromise ecosystems. The added energy comes from fossil fuels and is used to produce and spread fertilizers, herbicides, and pesticides; supply irrigation water; and power tractors. Nowadays, American agribusiness expends about 2.5 calories of fossil-fuel energy to produce 1 calorie of food, 50 to 100 times as much energy as expended by preindustrial farmers. Moreover, to bring that food calorie to the table requires, through processing, packaging, storage, and transport, another 5 calories. Refrigeration in the home and cooking add another 2.5 calories, so that the final ratio of energy input to output is an astonishing 10 to 1.[10] The energy requirement of urban-industrial ecosystems, also supplied by fossil fuels, is about 10 times that of the natural systems.

Whether the landscape proportions characteristic of the United States are those best suited to long-term sustainable support of its present human population is a question not yet resolved, and one that will become moot as the population continues to increase both in numbers and energy use. The question must, moreover, be considered on a broader global basis, given the interdependence of all countries of the world for their supplies of food, energy, and raw materials. Major environmental problems such as the dust bowl of the 1930s and the ozone hole of the present, regional in their extent, or impending problems such as the increasingly likely greenhouse warming of the climate, global in its extent, will help to focus our minds on the essential point—that we humans are now operating not only locally but on regional and global scales as well, and largely as "sorcerer's apprentices" ignorant of the likely consequences for human welfare and, ultimately, for human survival.

The Values of Wilderness

It is legitimate to ask at this point: Cannot all of the necessary life-support systems be provided by managed compromise ecosystems without any need for the protective category of national parks (often themselves partly compromise systems) and true wilderness areas? The answer is that although compromise systems can indeed carry out many of the life-support functions of cleansing and detoxifying our air, land, and water while helping to maintain the natural cycles of nutrients, atmospheric gases, and so on, wilderness areas have their own unique values.

For some, wilderness preservation is a matter of ethics, dictating that we not knowingly cause the extinction of other creatures that inhabit the earth. This concern may have its roots in an inborn tendency to "biophilia," or love of the plants and animals that share the planet with us, although the concept of such a genetic bias is quite controversial at present.[11] Whether or not it is genetic, it is widely demonstrated by gardeners, pet keepers, animal watchers, and even—in debased form—by those who purchase plastic flowers and lawn flamingos. For others, such as my fellow ecologist and environmentalist Herbert Wright, it is an aesthetic question, with pristine ecosystems analogous to original works of art; no connoisseur will accept that a copy—however good—can truly substitute for the real thing. Wilderness has the additional aesthetic appeal that it often gives us an accurate picture of the landscape as it was when Europeans came to it as settlers, providing us, as it were, with a living museum.

In more practical terms, wilderness is the best possible baseline against which to assess the effects that we humans have had on the land. In addition, because those human effects are absent, it is easier to work out how diverse plant and animal communities have responded over time to the interacting environmental factors of climate, topography, and soil. Wilderness is, moreover, the ultimate protector of biodiversity, which includes not only the millions of species of plants, animals, and microbes but also the genetic diversity within each species. Biodiversity is under severe threat from habitat destruction and fragmentation, particularly in the tropical rain forests. Wilderness must, therefore, be preserved

on a very broad scale, particularly where large mammals with extensive and often migratory ranges are important elements in the landscape.

Consider in this connection the number of little-known wild species, some of them increasingly endangered, that have provided us with a wide variety of antibiotics (various fungi), drugs acting against cancer (Pacific yew, Madagascar periwinkle) and heart disease (foxglove), models for the study of injured heart muscle (Mexican salamander) and diseases such as leprosy (armadillo) and diabetes (monkfish), and for the study of heredity (fruitfly, breadmold).[12] We must realize that only a small part of the world's flora and fauna has been tested for usefulness in these and manifold other ways, and thereby be persuaded that wilderness is not a luxury for elites in the developed countries but a vital resource for all the world's people. Indeed, if the world's food supply, now largely provided by a very few strains of a handful of cereals and other major crop species chosen initially by very primitive peoples, is to be protected against the stresses of evolving new diseases and of global warming, it will be necessary to seek out and preserve with great care all of their wild relatives, in which genes for resistance to disease, drought, and other stresses still reside. That also means protecting the ecosystems in which they can flourish. A further benefit of biodiversity, recently discovered by my colleagues David Tilman and Shahid Naeem, is that it mitigates the losses of productivity in natural ecosystems that are caused by environmental stresses such as drought.[13] In the final analysis, as the journalist Donella Meadows has written, "Biodiversity contains the accumulated wisdom of nature and the key to its future."[14]

We must recognize, however, that the term *wilderness* is relative. Few if any regions have entirely escaped the influence of aboriginal humans, and none have escaped deposition from the atmosphere of at least traces of pesticides, heavy metals from the combustion of fossil fuels, and radioactive fallout. Likewise, the threat of global warming hangs over all ecosystems. Paradoxically, our present wilderness must often be managed, for instance, to substitute prescribed burning for wildfires that threaten inhabited areas or to remove exotic introduced species. Lastly, we must realize that all ecosystems go through natural processes of disturbance, such as fire, flood, drought, and storm. They also exhibit natural patterns of change, whether cyclic as in the case of recurrent forest fires or directional as, for example, when floating mats of vegetation colonize the margin of a pond and convert it gradually into a wetland. Preservation is, therefore, a relative concept. What we must strive for is to preserve the dynamics of wilderness ecosystems, free as far as possible from the influence of human perturbation; we cannot possibly "freeze" them forever in time, nor would it be right to do so.

Applying Ecological Knowledge to Environmental Problems in Natural and Urban Ecosystems

At the opposite end of the spectrum from wilderness lie the cities and metropolitan areas of civilized societies. As Judith A. Martin and Sam Bass Warner Jr., (chapter 6) point out, these areas have largely been neglected by ecologists—and yet they are indeed ecosystems, elements of the biosphere that can be examined in just the same way that scientists investigate other, more natural ecosystems, whether they be forest, grassland, wetland, lake, or desert.[15] Unless we understand such systems, we cannot possibly manage and preserve them as required for human welfare.

Natural ecosystems are often easily recognizable, that is, more or less clearly bounded as a forest, a stream, a bog, or a watershed that contains all three. They need not, however, exhibit such clear boundaries. It is, for instance, perfectly legitimate to take a specific, arbitrarily defined block of prairie and treat it as an ecosystem representative of the grassland that surrounds it. One might equally well take a city block and do the same. Or one might examine a city, a metropolitan area, or a specific county, as William Romme (chapter 8) has done, and treat it as an ecosystem, or rather a series of ecosystems linked by their interactions into a landscape. At the extreme one can go much farther and treat earth itself as a planetary ecosystem, in a new subdiscipline recognized as global ecology. In all these cases an ecologist studies the properties of ecosystems: their structure, function, regulation, and development over time.

Energy Flow along Food Chains

Ecosystem function is similar in both natural and urban ecosystems. Energy comes in from outside, in the first case as radiation from that giant nuclear reactor, the sun, and in the second case as coal and oil, which are really two different kinds of fossil sunlight. The energy is then used in both systems to serve a variety of functions such as building, organizing, and maintaining different kinds of structures, and developing systems for storage and transport. In the process energy is transformed from its original state and is reradiated away ultimately as heat.

In natural ecosystems solar energy is captured by green plants, locked as stored energy in their tissues, then flows along food chains and webs from green plants to herbivore consumers and then to primary, secondary, and, occasionally, tertiary carnivores. Opportunistic omnivores, among them human beings, exploit several levels of the food chain. At each step most of the energy—often 90 percent or more—is dissipated in food gathering, body maintenance, and excretion, which explains why food chains seldom go beyond five links. It also explains why we shall be forced into vegetarianism if we do not control human population growth; a ton of grain will support many more people if eaten directly than if first converted by cattle into beef.

Biological magnification is an important property of food

chains. Just as energy is largely dissipated at each step, so are materials—such as carbohydrates and fats—that are broken down to carbon dioxide and water that are given off to the atmosphere, where they are again available for photosynthesis. However, elements of radioactive fallout, or complex, resistant molecules of DDT, are not readily broken down or excreted. They are conserved at each step and increase in concentration, sometimes to harmful levels. That is why such toxic substances are most hazardous to organisms at the end of the food chain, whether they be bald eagles, caribou-eating Inuit, or consumers of fish from midwestern lakes and rivers.

Useful materials, whether they be compounds of carbon, nitrogen, iron, or calcium, are processed along food chains and recycled in various forms to and from both natural and urban ecosystems, just as are toxins such as lead or DDT. A city can, therefore, be examined exactly as an ecologist would study a forest, a prairie, or a wetland, and comparative analysis of the flows of energy and materials through different cities could well help to lead us in the direction of more efficient and sustainable urban design.[16]

Often the closest approach to wild nature in cities and suburbs is in their scattered wetlands. These deserve protection if for no other reason than as a reminder of the natural world from which we have come and upon which we still rely. Reconstruction of vanished wetlands, grasslands, and woodlands within metropolitan areas could serve a valuable educational purpose, particularly for children, and deserves greater consideration by planners and landscape architects.

Ecosystem Regulation

Ecosystems, and their component populations of individual species, are regulated by competition for space and resources such as light, water, and nutrients, and by the nature of species interactions, for instance, as plants and pollinators, hosts and parasites, or predators and prey. The numbers of organisms, and the factors controlling them, are therefore of vital concern in our picture of ecosystem regulation. The main regulators of populations have always been the four horsemen of the apocalypse—famine, pestilence, war, and death. Human endeavor has ameliorated their influence and so created at compound interest a human population explosion, which we see as an upward sweeping curve when the population of earth is plotted versus time. It might better be termed a population implosion because it occurs largely by overcrowding more and more a limited number of major metropolitan centers. Ecologists, more than most others, know that a species cannot survive forever on the slippery slope of a compound-interest curve. If we do not employ more effectively—and where possible improve—our present methods of population control, the four horsemen will return with increased fury to carry out their age-old task of pruning back the overabundance of shoots on the tree of life.

The difficulties of managing species and regulating ecosystems and landscapes are well illustrated by the troubles of Biosphere 2, whose oxygen concentrations fell to dangerous levels (14 percent by volume) and had to be replenished from the outside.[17] The unforeseen cause was the uptake—by calcium in the concrete structure—of carbon dioxide produced from atmospheric oxygen by microbial oxidation of soil carbon. At the same time, concentrations of the trace gas nitrous oxide rose to possibly toxic levels. Nutrient overload polluted the aquatic habitats, and both air temperatures and light levels could not be maintained at the levels anticipated. Along with failure of these physical systems came various failures of the biological support systems; for instance, vines overran food plants despite active weeding, and all pollinating insects went extinct, as did 19 of 25 vertebrate species.

All in all, it is clear that humans are far from being able to maintain a closed life-support system for any appreciable length of time, even with the best ecological advice. They should therefore protect with all their might the diverse resources—physical, chemical, and biological—that the planet now provides free of charge, while continuing to support research of the kind continuing in Biosphere 2, which can contribute new and fascinating insights into how ecosystems and landscapes function to support life.

Ecosystem Interactions

It is essential to recognize that the ecosystems composing a landscape, whether it be urban or rural, interact by exchanging energy, materials, and organisms with one another. These exchanges occur on time scales that may vary from days, weeks, or months in, for example, the case of animal migration, to millennia as, for example, in the weathering of calcium and potassium from the rocks and soils underlying a forest and their eventual transport into the sediments of an adjacent lake or into streams, rivers, and eventually the ocean.

The interactions among ecosystems are most likely to cause problems when humans disturb them in various ways. When, for instance, a developer cuts down the trees adjacent to a small headwater stream in order to expand suburban housing, that action will inevitably alter what goes on in the stream. If it is a cool, spring-fed trout stream, removing the tree canopy over the stream may warm the water in summer beyond the limits that trout can tolerate and to levels more suitable for other kinds of fish. The absence of an autumnal influx of leaf litter from the trees may mean the end of subsistence for the small invertebrate animals that rely on it for food, whereas the increase of sunlight may allow a variety of photosynthetic algae to thrive and form the base of a quite different food chain. That, too, will affect the trout. Developers and planners, like ecologists, are becoming

much more aware of such problems, but all too seldom do the three groups work closely together to deal effectively with the problems.

Elsewhere the use of pesticides and herbicides in agroecosystems leads inevitably to their transport by wind and water to other, more natural ecosystems, sometimes with disastrous consequences that have included massive fish kills and the deaths of top predators such as eagles and peregrine falcons. Modern industrialized agriculture, as Jane Smiley (chapter 2) points out, is also extremely destructive of biodiversity through its alteration of the diverse natural habitats within ecosystems and landscapes. Moreover, as Curt Meine (chapter 3) remarks, agriculture has often been imposed in a geometric grid on much less orderly landscapes, particularly in the midcontinent. The consequences of the grid for the remaining uncultivated portions of the prairie landscape must be severe, especially in disrupting physical patterns of water flow and biological patterns of animal foraging, dispersal, and migration across ecosystems and landscapes. These consequences have not, however, been given adequate study.

Urban-industrial areas likewise release a variety of materials to other systems, ranging from sewage to toxic metals (lead, mercury, cadmium, and the like) and the carbon dioxide that threatens to alter the climate and hence to disturb all ecosystems. Indeed, scaling up our ecological knowledge from small plots to whole ecosystems, then to landscapes, and ultimately to the entire global ecosystem is one of the most daunting tasks for ecologists today. Another is to carry out studies, including whole-ecosystem and whole-landscape experiments, over the time scale of decades that is required for a thorough understanding of ecosystem responses to stress. Yet another is to bring to bear cooperatively the knowledge and experience of specialists in the natural sciences, social sciences, and humanities to solve the problems consequent upon human manipulation of ecosystems and landscapes. The perspectives of the humanities and social sciences are particularly important for landscape ecologists, who as students are trained rigorously in the sciences but often have little appreciation of the ways in which cultural concepts and values impinge on landscape-management practices. Those in the humanities and social sciences, on the other hand, often fail to appreciate the subtleties of species and ecosystem interactions that are vital to the maintenance of the biosphere, but of which scientists know far too little to be truly effective managers.

Environmental and Cultural Factors That Affect Ecosystems and Landscapes

Ecosystems of various kinds are linked into landscapes, heterogeneous areas on the scale of acres to hundreds of square miles and comprised of clusters of different types of interacting ecosystems that are repeated in similar form throughout the area.[18] Differentiation of the world's diverse ecosystems and landscapes rests on the interaction of several partially independent environmental factors acting over time: climate, soil parent material, topography, biota, and fire. The major limiting factor on a regional or continental basis is climate. It is no accident that in the midcontinent of North America tall forests are found in the east, where rainfall exceeds evaporation. There the plants project much farther above than below ground. In arid western prairies, on the other hand, the tops of the grasses may be inconspicuous and only a few inches tall whereas the roots reach down several feet into the soil beneath, to where water is available.

Another factor of great importance is nutrient supply, which is related to the quality of the soil. Where plants are isolated from the soil and nutrients must come from rain, snow, and dustfall, plants face a difficult situation. Dwarf trees on deep peat bogs, decades old but only a few feet tall and unable to root deeply in the waterlogged, anaerobic peat, may send roots laterally 30 feet because of the scarcity of available mineral nutrients caused by their isolation from the soils around and beneath the bogs.

Fire is also a highly significant factor in some ecosystems. Without it, prairies can turn slowly into savanna and woodland as hazel and bur oak invade and conquer the prairie grasses. The even-aged pine stands of the Boundary Waters Canoe Area Wilderness in northern Minnesota are also a result of periodic fires, leading to the conclusion that prescribed burning must be a vital tool in the preservation of the northern wilderness. Paradoxical as it may seem, we must manage the wilderness; it cannot be left alone because we cannot risk letting natural fires burn and perhaps get out of control, threatening the settled landscape beyond the wilderness borders.

Along with environmental factors, various cultural factors alter ecosystems and landscapes, creating managed farms, forests, lakes, streams, wetlands, and human settlements out of pristine wilderness areas and, in the process, sometimes degrading or even destroying their productivity. As figure 2 shows, these cultural factors operate at various levels through the policies of sovereign states (and the world bodies to which they belong), the public and private agencies that serve those policies, and the public officials who are directly responsible for how the policies are carried out. The agents who ultimately carry out the policies may operate at the scale of whole landscapes as do, for instance, some landscape architects, or at the level of individual ecosystems within landscapes that are converted to human use by—among others—farmers, foresters, fishermen, and miners.

Ecologists are not shown in figure 2, but they have the very important role of studying the structure, function, development, and regulation of ecosystems and landscapes—natural and managed—to provide the knowledge necessary both to use and to preserve them. That knowledge may be transmitted to public agencies such as the federal Environmental Protection Agency

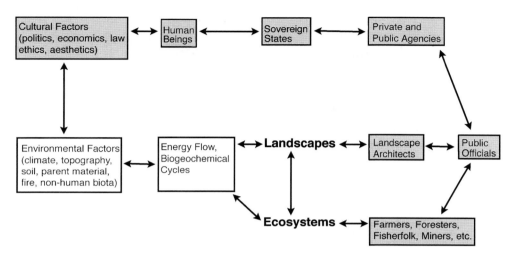

Figure 2. The interrelationships of ecosystems and landscapes with the environmental and cultural influences on them.

and state departments of natural resources; to private organizations such as The Nature Conservancy, the Environmental Defense Fund, and the Natural Resources Defense Council; or to the public via newspapers and magazines. Action may be taken at a variety of levels, from the individual farmers and homeowners who alter their use of fertilizers and pesticides to the sovereign states that sign international agreements such as the Montreal Protocol regulating the phaseout of ozone-destroying chemicals.

We must recognize that these environmental and cultural influences are not entirely independent. Culture is undoubtedly a product—in some measure—of the landscapes and natural resources available to a given population, so that the culture of Massachusetts fisherfolk is likely to be different from that of Minnesota farmers for environmental as well as purely ethnic and cultural reasons. Contrariwise, fisherfolk in different parts of

the world will exhibit certain cultural similarities based on the way in which they obtain their livelihood and the environmental resources that they exploit. Cultural factors can also alter the nature of the environment itself, as is currently the case with acid rain, chemical toxification by trace metals and organic compounds, and global warming.

The Influence of Cultural Concepts and Values

Our views of nature, and thus how we should treat the biosphere, are colored inevitably by our different backgrounds and by our education. As Donald Worster, a leading environmental historian, has pointed out so eloquently in his book *Nature's Economy*, two antithetical views have been held even by ecologists trained in scientific rationality.[19] On the one hand are the arcadians, who look at nature in an aesthetic (but also a practical) light as an unspoiled paradise where we should try, insofar as it is possible, to live in harmony with all the other inhabitants. On the other hand are the utilitarians, who see nature simply as a resource to be used for human benefit.

These alternative cultural values can be further subdivided, as described recently by the social scientist Bryan Norton.[20] He divides the utilitarians into two classes: one class—we may call them here exploiters—believes that all resources, including even renewable resources such as forests, grasslands, and aquatic ecosystems, are either available in abundance or infinitely substitutable through advances in science and technology and can therefore be used up in the pursuit of economic and material goals. Most land developers probably fall in this group, along with a number of economists. Their guiding principle might be, in the words of Wilkins Micawber, "Something will turn up," and they are the group least likely to be concerned about soil erosion, pollution damage to ecosystems, and losses of biodiversity. The other class—call them conservative users—believes that renewable resources are not infinitely substitutable and should not, therefore, be used up. They do believe, however, that such resources can be managed effectively and in perpetuity for maximal sustainable use by and benefit to human society. This group includes many economists and resource managers, and their watchwords would seem to be "I know what I'm doing, and it's all for the best."

Norton also distinguishes two categories of arcadians. One class—call them the naturalists—would include most ecologists (including this author), many environmentalists, and a new breed of resource managers who believe that because of our lack of ecological knowledge and understanding, the management of renewable resources solely for human benefit is likely to interfere, often suddenly and unexpectedly as thresholds of stress are crossed, with other ecosystem functions that support—free of charge—human as well as other life. Such management can,

therefore, lead eventually to loss of ecosystem integrity, degradation, and failure to support its inhabitants. Failure will be especially likely in times of severe environmental stress, often brought on by human activities both locally and elsewhere. Their watchwords, embodying cautious, adaptive management of ecosystems with continual monitoring and feedback modification of objectives and practices, might well be "If you don't know, go slow." A recent book, *Barriers and Bridges to the Renewal of Ecosystems and Institutions*, describes six interesting case studies of adaptive management; Gordon Baskerville's lengthy and somewhat disheartening historical account of forestry in the Canadian province of New Brunswick illustrates very clearly the need for such management and the diverse problems encountered in attempting to put it into practice.[21] The second category of arcadians would include some ecologists and many environmentalists, as well as many environmental philosophers and ethicists—we may call them preservers. Preservers believe that all species have a right to exist, and that human beings do not have the right knowingly to cause their extinction, particularly in the pursuit of short-term economic and material ends. For words to live by they might quote the Golden Rule: "Do unto others as you would have them do unto you."

Both naturalists and preservers advocate extensive set-asides of natural wilderness or semi-wilderness (national park) areas in order to maintain the protective functions of the biosphere and, in particular, its biodiversity. As Marcia Eaton (chapter 5) and Joan Nassauer (chapter 4) have noted, these functions are often invisible and inaccessible to aesthetic appreciation until linked by education to visible cues in the landscape. As an example consider the nation's wetlands, more than half of which (in the conterminous states) have been lost to development of one kind or another since European settlement.[22] Unfortunately, wetlands have generally been regarded as wastelands suitable only for "reclamation," a word that is anathema to wetland ecologists (among them this author). Only a few hydrologists, ecologists, and biogeochemists appreciate that wetlands serve a variety of functions in the biosphere, among them the mitigation of flood peaks, the trapping in sediments of excess nutrients and toxins, and the participation in unique and important ways in cycles of carbon, nitrogen, and sulfur—elements vital to living organisms and to the worldwide control of atmospheric temperature. They also provide significant habitats for waterfowl and furbearers and serve as nurseries for a variety of fishes. No wonder that the late Edward Deevey, one of the most distinguished American ecologists, titled his 1970 presidential address to the Ecological Society of America "In Defense of Mud."[23]

The four widely different human views of nature just described are not held by individuals immutably. We all know (perhaps unwillingly) from our own behavior that humans can subscribe comfortably, at different times and in different circumstances, to contrary principles.

There are many other cultural concepts and values that influence our view of nature and of the land in particular. In *Changes in the Land*, William Cronon has shown in considerable and fascinating detail how the European settlers' attitude toward land as the exclusive property of individuals clashed violently with its communal use by Native Americans and thereby changed dramatically the landscapes of New England.[24] Likewise, individualist views of land management are now taking over, gradually, from the collectivist views that were predominant in the former Soviet Union. Curt Meine (chapter 3) has demonstrated how the grid concept of the early land surveyors has influenced the flat agricultural landscapes of the American midcontinent. Ideas of social hierarchy also color our use of the land, as William Romme (chapter 8) makes clear to us in his discussion of landscape development in the mountains of Colorado. Interestingly enough, the concept of stewardship, which is related to the concept of sustainability and implicit in the views of conservative users, naturalists, and preservers alike, has been shown by Joan Nassauer to require for its acceptance—in both urban and rural settings—evidence of care. As she points out, care is most readily demonstrated by signs of neatness and order, such as fences and mown borders, in otherwise much less orderly landscapes. Probably the most eloquent case for environmental stewardship is presented in Aldo Leopold's "land ethic," as set out in *A Sand County Almanac*.[25]

The Place of the Human Species in the Biosphere

Some exploiters, and even some ecologists, might argue that the environmental concerns expressed heretofore in this chapter merely reflect the nature of competition among organisms, which drives evolution by natural selection toward ever "higher" forms of life. So why worry? After all, other species—like humans—exploit one another in food chains; manage other species, as do ants tending their colonies of fungi or aphids; and transport other organisms and introduce them to new habitats, as do birds. Likewise, other species overuse resources and move on, as do locusts; disperse chemical toxins into the environment, as do the fungi that produce antibiotics; build artificial and crowded social environments, as do bees, termites, and ants; use tools, as do some birds as well as primates; and communicate by sound with others of their species, as do most higher animals. Moreover, our ability to alter the planetary environment pales beside that of the most primitive photosynthetic organisms, whose introduction of free oxygen into the water and the air changed in a most fundamental way the entire suite of chemical reactions taking place at the surface of the earth. In this view, humans can be regarded merely as members of one species among millions, working out their destiny just as the members of other species do, with the world of nature almost infinitely resilient and capable of adjustment to whatever a given species may do.

On the other hand, I and many others will argue that the human species is unique—its role in the biosphere is not strictly comparable to that of the other species with which it shares the planet—and, therefore, deserves a different sort of consideration. As noted earlier, the human population has grown to be a thousand times larger than that of most other large mammals and has become able to use a variety of energy resources that vastly exceed simple muscle power (including that of domestic animals). We have also developed an unmatched capacity to learn, think consciously, and communicate that has far outstripped that of other animals and that has endowed us with a unique sense of history and the possibility of rapid cultural (as opposed to slow biological) evolution. We have, moreover, developed a sense of compassion that has caused many of us to reject the laissez-faire social Darwinism that would allow the wholesale destruction of habitats and a holocaust of species extinctions in the pursuit of short-term material gain, at the expense not only of other species but of our own descendants. We have also learned enough to realize that although nature may be almost infinitely resilient, her mechanism of natural selection—the "struggle for existence"—has victims as well as victors. Without a great deal of restraint in matters of population growth, resource use, and habitat destruction, we may indeed—through our own hubris—be among those victims.

To avoid such victimization we are in great need of creative ideas. First, we must speed the demographic transition to zero (or negative) population growth in the developing countries, perhaps most effectively by increasing the participation of women in their educational systems and in their decision-making processes. Second, we must increase conservation and recycling while lessening pollution, either by the economics of scarcity or by regulation, most particularly in the developed countries. Third, we must reverse habitat destruction in both the developed

and less-developed countries. We also need to rethink our patterns of settlement in ways that will allow greater protection of ecological functions in the landscape.

Looking Forward

We can see that maintaining the biosphere's capacity to sustain life as we know it, in the face of mounting threats from human population growth, increasing per capita use of energy and materials, and ever more rapid technological innovation, is a daunting task that promises to tax our abilities to the utmost.[26] It seems to me as a scientist that the overriding problem we face lies in the contrast between the relative simplicity of the physical sciences and the extreme complexity of the social sciences.

Rapid advances in technology, based on physics and chemistry, continually pose new threats to the integrity of ecosystems, which have increased in scale very recently—on the order of decades—to the point where the entire planetary ecosystem is now at risk from chemical toxification, ozone depletion, global warming, and loss of biodiversity. That is not to say that technological advances cannot benefit the environment. For instance, scrubbers developed to remove sulfur dioxide from smokestacks, and other new technologies, have reduced acid rain appreciably in Europe and eastern North America, and substitutes for chlorofluorocarbons have greatly reduced the threat to the ozone layer. The ever increasing efficiency with which we use energy, land, and water for human ends has also slowed the rate of environmental degradation. Unfortunately, however, in most cases it is far easier to calculate the benefits of a new technology than to estimate its environmental costs or to assess its risks, particularly over the long term. In any case, far less effort is devoted to such matters.

Advances in the enormously complex social sciences that undergird economics, politics, law, and management have necessarily come much more slowly than advances in technology, and so far have been largely—though not entirely—unsuccessful in devising policies and procedures to arrest and ameliorate the ever-increasing ecological degradation caused by technological change. This imbalance in the pace of technological and social change, which we should seek far more actively to address, may well become, if it is not already, the chief limit to progress in environmental protection and perhaps ultimately the cause of ecological catastrophe. Certainly a far greater infusion of ecological principles into the conduct of public affairs and much greater cooperation among scientists, planners, legislators, and other public officials at all levels from local to international will be necessary if catastrophe is to be averted.

There are, of course, those who take a far more optimistic view of the human prospect, believing that rapid cultural changes will bring about a reconciliation of technology and the environment in time to avoid ecological disaster.[27] Others take a less sanguine view of cultural flexibility, believing that wars and social conflicts are not amenable to technological solutions and that technological optimism is not enough.[28] Our children or grandchildren will, no doubt, learn who was right.

Acknowledgments

I am grateful to my coauthors, and to the other diverse participants in the seminar that preceded this book, for leading (and sometimes forcing) my thoughts in unaccustomed but facinating directions. I also thank Joan Nassauer and Deborah Karasov for inviting me to contribute this chapter, thereby encouraging me to put those thoughts in some sort of order. My friends Phillip Regal and Crawford "Buzz" Holling helped to educate me in these matters, and another friend, Debra Clemente-Amacher, typed—without a single complaint— seemingly endless drafts of the manuscript. Mary Keirstead was of great assistance in editing the manuscript. Peter Vitousek kindly allowed me to reproduce figure 1. Lastly, I am grateful to Donella Meadows for providing the epigraph for this chapter.

Notes

1. B. Freedman, *Environmental Ecology*, 2d ed. (San Diego: Academic Press, 1995); J. H. Ausubel, D. G. Victor, and I. K. Wernick, "The Environment Since 1970," Consequences 1, no. 3 (1995): 3–15.

2. A. H. Westing, "Our Place in Nature: Reflections on the Global Carrying Capacity for Humans," in *Maintenance of the Biosphere*, N. Polunin and J. H. Burnett, eds. (New York: St. Martin's, 1990), pp. 109–130.

3. P. J. Regal, "International Biosafety: A Global Imperative," *The Scientist* 9, no. 21 (1995): 13; T. B. G. Egziabher et al., *The Need for Greater Regulation and Control of Genetic Engineering* (Penang, Malaysia: Third World Network, 1995).

4. P. M. Vitousek, P. R. Ehrlich, A. A. Ehrlich, and P. A. Matson, "Human Appropriation of the Products of Photosynthesis," *BioScience* 36 (1986): 368–373.

5. P. M. Vitousek, C. M. D'Antonio, L. L. Loope, and R. Westbrooks, "Biological Invasions As Global Environmental Change," *American Scientist* 84: 468–478; P. M. Vitousek, C. M. D'Antonio, L. L. Loope, M. Rejmanek, and R. Westbrooks, "Introduced Species: A Significant Component of Human-Caused Global Change," *New Zealand Journal of Ecology* 21 (1997): in press.

6. D. Worster, "The Shaky Ground of Sustainable Development," in *The Wealth of Nature: Environmental History and the Ecological Imagination*, D. Worster, ed. (New York: Oxford University Press, 1993), pp. 142–155; B. Willers, "Sustainable Development: A New World Deception," *Conservation Biology* 8 (1994): 1146–1148; S. Lélé and R. B. Norgaard, "Sustainability and the Scientist's Burden," *Conservation Biology* 10 (1996): 354–365.

7. E. P. Odum, "The Strategy of Ecosystem Development," *Science* 164 (1969): 262–270.

8. J. C. Avise, "The Real Message from Biosphere 2," *Conservation Biology* 8 (1994): 327–329.

9. R. Repetto, *World Enough and Time* (New Haven, Conn.: Yale University Press, 1986).

10. M. E. Clark, *Ariadne's Thread* (London: Macmillan, 1989), pp. 104–105.

11. S. R. Kellert and E. O. Wilson, eds., *The Biophilia Hypothesis* (Washington, D.C.: Island Press, 1993).

12. P. F. Torrence, "The Endangered Species Act," *Science* 269 (1995): 1803–1804.

13. D. Tilman and J. A. Downing, "Biodiversity and Stability in Grasslands," *Nature* 367 (1994): 363–365; S. Naeem, L. J. Thompson, S. P. Lawler, J. H. Lawton, and R. M. Woodfin, "Declining Biodiversity Can Alter the Performance of Ecosystems," *Nature* 368 (1994): 734–737.

14. D. H. Meadows, "A Reaction from a Multitude," in *The Earth in Transition: Patterns and Processes of Biotic Impoverishment*, G. M. Woodwell, ed. (New York: Cambridge University Press, 1990), pp. 513–521; see pp. 520–521.

15. Z. Neveh, "Landscape Ecology As an Emerging Branch of Human Ecosystem Science," *Advances in Ecological Research* 12 (1982): 189–237; see in particular pp. 204–209.

16. S. Boyden, *An Integrative Ecological Approach to the Study of Human Settlements*, (Paris: UNESCO, 1979); S. Boyden, S. Millar, K. Newcombe, and B. O'Neill, *The Ecology of a City and Its People: The Case of Hong Kong* (Canberra: Australian National Press, 1981).

17. J. E. Cohen and D. Tilman, "Biosphere 2 and Biodiversity: The Lessons So Far," *Science* 274 (1996): 1150–1151.

18. R. T. T. Forman, "Some General Principles of Landscape and Regional Ecology," *Landscape Ecology* 10 (1995): 133–142.

19. D. Worster, *Nature's Economy*, 2d ed. (New York: Cambridge University Press, 1994).

20. B. G. Norton, "Intergenerational Equity and Environmental Decisions: A Model Using Rawls' Veil of Ignorance," *Ecological Economics* 1 (1989): 137–159.

21. G. Baskerville, "The Forestry Problem: Adaptive Lurches of Renewal," in *Barriers and Bridges to the Renewal of Ecosystems and Institutions*, L. H. Gunderson, C. S. Holling, and S. S. Light, eds. (New York: Columbia University Press, 1995); see also C. Walters, *Adaptive Management of Renewable Resources* (New York: Macmillan, 1986).

22. W. E. Frayer, *Status and Trends of Wetlands and Deepwater Habitats in the Conterminous United States*, 1970s to 1980s (Michigan Technological University, 1991).

23. E. S. Deevey, "In Defense of Mud," *Bulletin of the Ecological Society of America* 51 (1970): 5–8.

24. W. Cronon, *Changes in the Land: Indians, Colonists, and the Ecology of New England* (New York: Hill and Wang, 1983).

25. A. Leopold, *A Sand County Almanac and Sketches Here and There* (New York: Oxford University Press, 1949).

26. E. Gorham, "An Ecologist's Guide to the Problems of the 21st Century," *The American Biology Teacher* 52 (1990): 480–483; S. A. Levin, ed., "Forum: Economic Growth and Environmental Quality," *Ecological Applications* 6 (1996): 12–32.

27. J. H. Ausubel, "The Liberation of the Environment," *Daedalus* 125, no. 3 (1996): 1–17.

28. C. Starr, "Sustaining the Human Environment: The Next Two Hundred Years," *Daedalus* 125, no. 3 (1996): 235–253.

Recommended Reading

Clark. M. E. 1989. *Ariadne's Thread: The Search for New Modes of Thinking*. London: Macmillan.

Cunningham, W. P., and B. W. Saigo. 1995. *Environmental Science: A Global Concern*. 3d ed. Dubuque, Iowa: W. C. Brown.

Forman, R. T. T. 1995. *Land Mosaics: The Ecology of Landscapes and Regions*. Cambridge: Cambridge University Press.

Freedman, B. 1995. *Environmental Ecology*. 2d. ed. San Diego: Academic Press.

Woodwell, G. M., ed. 1990. *The Earth in Transition: Patterns and Processes of Biotic Impoverishment*. Cambridge: Cambridge University Press.

2 | Farming and the Landscape
JANE SMILEY

OVERLEAF

Top: Freshly Seeded Field, near Ogallala, Nebraska (May 1995).

Bottom: Ortonville Elevator Detail, Ortonville, Minnesota (September 1995).

JANE SMILEY is the author of numerous books and short stories, including *The Greenlanders, Moo,* and the 1992 Pulitzer Prize winner *A Thousand Acres.* She is a Fellow of the American Academy of Arts and Sciences.

LET ME START WITH AN IMAGE that I see almost every day when I go to ride my horse, who lives on a farm in central Iowa. I drive up the interstate and get off on a country blacktop that heads due east. More or less flat black fields stretch ahead of me and to either side. Every mile I cross an intersection with a gravel road. The sky is enormous and imposing. The wind is often blowing 25 or 30 miles per hour. Small groups of buildings cluster beside the road, but I almost never see anyone who is not inside an automobile or a farm machine—and why should I? There is no place to walk. The fields run up to the road, and at corners, where the house has been taken down, are pens full of hogs. A walk would take you nowhere—things look the same from every point of view. The land looks stitched—in or out of the growing season, narrow lines of seedlings, plants, crops, then dead stalks turn the fields into an optical illusion, or a sheet of lined paper, or a bolt of cloth, but not anything earth-like. As the growing season progresses, the land disappears entirely. Corn passes into soybeans, soybeans into corn.

All discussions of landscape, whether of use, beauty, or health, must give the discussion of agriculture a central place, because not only has agriculture made civilization, it has the power to unmake it. Agriculture has transformed and is transforming the earth, and how people meet the land through farming is the single most important and consistent way that humans—urban and rural, mere eaters or actual farmers—have contact with nature, both the natural world and their own natures. The land that must bear the major burden of overpopulation is farmland, and how we farm determines most basic attributes of our human world, beginning with how many of us can be supported and ending with what sorts of lives the living will be able to have.

In north-central Iowa and in similar places, American farming has reached an ideal, an ideal that through multinational corporations and the General Agreement on Tariffs and Trade (GATT) treaty has been and is being exported to all parts of the globe— all of these farms are large, uniform, and productive. Even the hogs are large, uniform, and productive. This depopulated countryside produces an enormous amount of calories for human consumption, though, of course, it is not self-sufficient in food, except for someone who likes a diet of corn, soybeans, and pork. This ideal of largeness, uniformity, and productivity is pursued all over our culture and economic system, and while it is hard to see how largeness, uniformity, and productivity could go wrong in fast-food restaurants and churches, on farms, the ideal tells a different story.

The first thing the ideal says is that farming, as an activity, is not worth doing, that is, not worth expending *human* energy on. It says that as few humans as possible should be working in the fields—almost all other human activities are more desirable. The second thing it says is that if all land looks the same, then for all practical purposes it can be treated in the same way. Same with corn plants, bean plants, and hogs. If there are slight variations in the land, for example, small watercourses, patches of different soil types, small hillocks, these should either be ignored or, if necessary, made uniform. The third thing it says is that there is very limited room in all this expanse for any form of life that cannot be bought and paid for. There is no cover for game birds, rabbits, and rodents, no forage for deer, no prey for foxes and owls. There is no room in the soil for the germination of any but one or two species and varieties of plants. There is not even room in the soil for insects and plants formerly considered desirable, like ladybugs and wildflowers. This region is not only humanly depopulated, it is vastly, profoundly stripped of life-forms; and the soil is so conditioned with chemicals that varying the life-forms cannot easily be done.

The fourth item to be read out here is that the humans have closer relationships with their machines than they do with their land. The gridding of America that Curt Meine discusses in chapter 3 has had far-reaching effects on every aspect of farming and agricultural land use. Big square fields demand large planters, combines, and fertilizer applicators, which in turn confirm the need for big square fields, both to support their cost and to allow for their turning radii. The machines then create the landscape in their own image and mediate between the human and the land. Both land and human become machinelike.

These four qualities of our landscape are widely considered to be desirable. The solitary farmer is desirable because no one likes to farm anyway. Farming is hard, daylong, physical work, and sedentary work and recreational activities are preferred by the majority. For the farmer himself, isolation and solitude mean being answerable only to himself and, in many cases, being the sole owner of a great deal of land. It means that his community relationships are few and well defined, either by the marketplace or by clear parameters such as family ties. The uniformity of land and life-forms is desirable, too, because then inputs and outputs, which cost money, are predictable and easily understood. The fewer interactions that exist between the various parts of the living world, the fewer things there are to go wrong. Predictable production is good, because then markets are potentially more stable, facilitating steady investment. A machinelike landscape and a machinelike human are good because machines work and produce 24 hours a day and do only what they are designed to do. Let us call the Terminator, as portrayed by Arnold Schwarzenegger, the perfect machine. Broken down to parts, the Terminator took a licking and kept on ticking. That is the ideal.

What is wrong with these ideals? They have worked, they do work. Most people get fed, or could if the distribution system worked as predictably as the production system. So what if this most human of landscapes is boring, ugly, unhealthful, and promotes death over life? That is the way agriculture is. That is the way civilization is. That is the way we are.

It is clear by now that all of the world's past civilizations have had to come to terms with natural limits to agricultural production. According to Clive Ponting in *A Green History of the World*, Mesopotamian civilization succumbed to the rigors of declining agricultural production as a result of salinization of agricultural soils due to the effects of irrigation.[1] Others have destroyed themselves through deforestation of watersheds and severe depletion of soils, or through overtaxing a thriving agricultural base, which results in abandonment of farms and depopulation of the countryside—Hellenistic Greece is an example of this, according to classicist Victor Hanson Davis.[2] Similar lessons about agriculture are to be learned on Easter Island and in one of my own favorite outposts of civilization, Viking Greenland.

Greenland, I think, helps us understand two things—first, how easy it is for humans to inhabit and thrive in even the least hospitable places in the world (after all, the Greenlanders did manage to support 3,000 to 5,000 people over almost 500 years; to build 12 churches, a nunnery, and a monastery; to have a small literature; and to grow to a larger stature than their contemporary Europeans), and second, how easy it is to wreck one's home with bad agricultural practices. While I do not at all discount the Norse cultural convention of feuding as a significant factor in the demise of the Greenlanders, recent studies show that agricultural practices such as overgrazing eventually resulted in the invasion of sand into previously fertile pastures, reducing the number of animals that could be grazed and the amounts of forage crops that could be raised for winter use. Just think, it took the benighted Greenlanders almost 500 years to damage and

partly destroy a fragile subarctic ecosystem. With our knowledge and foresight, it has taken only 100 years for us to damage and partially destroy the much hardier and more diverse ecosystem that we have in the Midwest. What we do better than the Greenlanders is export our wealth at a cheap enough price so that we can impoverish ourselves and enrich others and think we are getting a good deal.

Another interesting thing about Greenland is that the Norse Greenlanders lived in more or less close proximity with the Inuit for several centuries; but for the most part, there is no evidence of much cultural cross-pollination. The Europeans continued to consider the Inuit children of Satan, to wear woven woolen European-style clothes, to eat a typical Norse diet based on cheese and milk, to live in European-style houses heated with fire (though they showed some ingenuity here), and to look to Europe for direction—at some archaeological sites in Greenland, items of clothing have been found that are imitations of French styles of the early fifteenth century, a time when there was very little contact between Greenland and Europe. Even so, the Hvalsey Fjorders wanted to emulate Parisians. Considering conditions in Greenland, especially after the onset of the Little Ice Age, they might have more profitably emulated the Inuit, who seemed to have impressed the Greenlanders with their hunting skills, their happy attitude, and their usual prosperity. Even though I suspect there were a few Norsemen who emulated Inuit hunting methods, Greenlandic society in general failed to survive the destruction of Scandinavian agricultural forms. No more cows, sheep, and goats, then no more Greenlanders, the final reward for not going native.

It has become clear in the last decade that our own agricultural base is seriously at risk. The warnings come to us in a host of ways. What subject is more boring than soil conservation? The very words call up the ennui of sitting in one's seventh-grade classroom and looking at a reproduction of Margaret Bourke-White's photograph "Contour Plowing" in the dog-eared text-book. And yet the soil is never conserved. Experts estimate that more soil is lost today to wind and water erosion than was lost during the dust-bowl years of the thirties. Everyone knows what soil erosion is and what it looks like—snowdrifts blackened with wind-borne particles, brown rivers, silted-up streams—but for the most part soil erosion has lost its power to enrage us.

How about the end of the family farm? A few years ago, there was a rash of articles about the fact that the average age of farmers was then about 60, and that these farmers, about to retire, had no one to leave their land to. Younger people interested in farming could not afford to buy in. Many were getting out, but others, determined to get in, were investing in machinery rather than land, planning on lives as tenant farmers. Why the family farm is the least of evils, farmwise, can be explained, and often is; but all the explanations have not prevented the acceleration of their decline. If you drive around Iowa or Minnesota, the desolation left in the towns and on the land by this process is clearly visible, but other problems seem, or must seem to most people, more significant, less inevitable. And the problem is not just that our countryside is turning into a habitation of ghosts. A depopulated countryside is more expensive for the rest of us. Most writers about farms cite the 1947 study by Walter Goldschmidt that compared towns in California's San Joaquin Valley.[3] The town surrounded by corporate farms was a sad, impoverished burden on the state welfare rolls (taxpayers supporting farmworkers so that farm owners did not have to), while the town surrounded by family farms boasted home ownership, hospitals, a PTA, small businesses, churches, and a newspaper.

Another harbinger of things to come is the shortened life expectancy of farmers and farmworkers and their families. It seems incontrovertible that those who apply pesticides, drink from pesticide-contaminated ditches and wells, and otherwise come into daily contact with the by-products of industrial farming are dying more quickly than the rest of us. Agriculture has become something that people do not want to do and, given a choice, should probably choose not to do for the sake of their own mental and physical health.

There are smaller indications, too, that agriculture is not working—our food, though abundant, is monotonous and flavorless. No self-respecting chef I have read about lately actually likes American chicken. The difference between carefully cultivated organic potatoes of unusual varieties and the average supermarket potato is startling, in price as well as in flavor and texture. The contamination of meat by salmonella and other organisms, a problem the USDA thought was licked, has emerged again as a by-product of massive chicken and pork farming. The fearsome emergence of antibiotic-resistant forms of bacteria can be blamed partly on the addition of antibiotics to animal feed, as can the harmful effects, not all of which are known, of the addition of estrogenlike growth hormones to animal feed. Soon, perhaps, eating itself will provoke the same distaste that farming does. In general, modern farming is coming to resemble more and more closely the tobacco industry—it is bad for the land, it produces a damaging product, those involved promote it anyway for the sake of shareholder profit and all the other varieties of greed, and it has to be supported through subsidies by the federal government.

This is the civilization we have, as expressed in our use of the land: It values efficient production above all things, and its perfect emblem is the flat field of tall corn plants, set like an ugly block in the middle of someplace no one wants to be. What will happen next is more of the same. Whereas farmers and farm writers who discussed these issues 10 years ago hoped to startle society into taking an interest in the agricultural base and changing it, writers today say things like this: "Much less is this book a tract for current political or agrarian reform, which, in any case, can do little now to save family agriculture in this country. The life of a farmer is increasingly Hobbesian—poor, nasty, and brutish, even if not always short."[4] Though some writers, like Gene Logsdon, see small organic farms rising like sprouts around the huge trunks of toppling agribusiness farms, the general mood is bleaker than it used to be, and 12 or 15 years ago it was already fairly dark.

BUT THE END OF THE FAMILY FARM is only the tip of the iceberg, only a symptom of what really endangers us. What will or can be done with farming goes to the heart of what will or can be done with the rest of the earth. One characteristic of farms is that almost all of them are privately owned, conferring on the owners the absolute right of doing with them as they please. Ownership of land simultaneously creates an object (the piece of land) and an ownership relationship. Both are false identities. A piece of land is really a living system closely connected to everything around it, and an "ownership relationship," carrying the intrinsic right to change, destroy, profit from, or sell the object, is really a betrayal of a different type of reciprocal relationship that is the only sort of relationship that one living being can actually have with another. Nevertheless, private ownership is so enshrined in our culture that every single desire of ecologists to preserve or protect something in nature must contend with it. We cannot save the farm, or the land, without enlisting, persuading, and educating the farmer to do it for himself, often against what he perceives to be his self-interest.

Another quality of the modern farm, that it is by definition not self-sufficient, is increasingly true of every ecosystem. All farms receive inputs and produce commodities. Almost all farm-

ers go to the store for their food. Most farms these days do not support every member of the farming family, so that the income from a family member's job in town is one of the farm inputs. How different from farms of even 80 years ago or less. The food of the farm was raised in the barn or the garden or the orchard; the work energy—draught horses—ate hay and oats from the farm's own fields and reproduced themselves. In earlier times, most farms also produced their own fibers and clothing, their own tallow and candles, and their own lumber, furniture, and cooking fuel. Where it was once the nature of a farm to be more or less self-sufficient and to sell off the excess, now it is the nature of a farm to be entirely subject to every aspect of the society and the economy. A farmer *must* borrow to plant the crop, *must* know the markets to sell the crops, *must* have a ready supply of Middle-East oil, *must* buy his hybrid seed, and *must* have lobbyists in Washington to look after his interests in the farm bill. The integrity of any one farm is perennially endangered by these connections, since the failure of any one of them can spell the end of that farm. Thus it is with the integrity of any ecological project. Everything that we would like to do has to be done from outside the location itself, either because the inhabitants, like the residents of the Galapagos Islands, would prefer not to remain ecologically pristine, or because the place, like many a wilderness area, cannot meet its own costs.

Related to this dependence is the simplicity of the modern farm—the soil and its chemical soup, the corn and beans, the hogs, the machines, the farmers and their pole buildings. The variety is so minimal that everything needs protection from the much wider variety of the surrounding natural world—weeds, insects, diseases, storms, weather change, deer, and other animals. A simple system must be cared for 24 hours a day. A more complex system, like a prairie, a rain forest, or a healthy middle class, takes care of itself. Its complexity assures that the decline or destruction of a single part of the whole will not greatly damage the overall health of the system, which can flexibly take advantage of the normal, and even abnormal, variety of circumstances that is usual in the natural world. An example of this might be the heavy rains of the flood year 1993—corn and bean monocultures in Iowa were unable to support so much rain, and much topsoil washed away in the floods. Remnants of the former prairie ecosystem in the same region throve—roots and living plant matter made a mat that protected the soil, and some plants that like moist conditions took the place of those that prefer dry conditions. The overall plant system handled the excess water far better than neighboring fields of yellowing and weakly corn and bean plants did. Just as beans rely on Atrazine, so also does farming rely on the public purse in the form of subsidies and banks. Our goal should be not to care for the earth but to enable it to have sufficient complexity that it can care for itself. And yet, farming is our most common way of thinking about and interacting with the earth. What farming shows me is that if we bring to the earth the model closest to hand, the garden or the farm, we will undermine rather than enhance the landscape's capacity to support itself and us.

The last problematic quality of the farm that I will discuss is familiarity. Because agriculture has made civilization, very few among us come to agriculture from a truly wild perspective, let us say a hunter-gatherer perspective, and those who do are rapidly dying out or being forced over to agriculture. In Minnesota, for example, we do not have to look far into the past to witness the enforced conversion of the Ojibway peoples from hunting and gathering around Lake Superior and other lakes to what the Bureau of Indian Affairs (BIA) liked to think of as farming. During the allotment period at the end of the nineteenth century, tribal members were given plots of land, though as hunters and gatherers they had little use for them. The BIA, I

suppose, liked to think that one rural occupation was much like another. Or else they did not. Perhaps they engineered the forcible transformation of hunter-gatherers into farmers as the intentional cultural genocide that it seems to be in retrospect. At any rate, the absence in our culture of those who are unfamiliar with agriculture means farms seem natural to us no matter how unnatural (fertilized, irrigated, herbicided and pesticided, plowed, planted, cultivated, graded, etc.) they are. The so-called naturalness of farms leads us into imposing farmness or gardenness, as a definition of beauty or use, on all of nature. I see the ill effects of this very familiarity in, for example, the development of hobby farms in the rural West, where a scarcity of water and problems of terrain mitigate against them. While we may rationally say that only some particular landscapes should be used for farms, as people spread over the landscape, they will prefer what they are familiar with, and for most people, what is countryside-like is farmlike. That means domestic plants and animals, grass, apple trees, and tomatoes as well as the re-creation in entirely unsuitable landscapes of the general European pattern of imposing the familiar on the native, until all is familiar and much is lost.

AGRICULTURE IS THE DILEMMA of civilization because it both separates us from nature and connects us to it; it both makes civilization possible and puts it at risk. But one might say that the earth has learned to live with agriculture. However, critics of agriculture in the 1990s hold the widespread view that the forms of agriculture that have been known for most of the history of civilization are ending, giving way to forms that will have many additional, unforeseeable consequences, but will certainly have the problematic qualities discussed here. One of the basic assumptions of the new agriculture is that humans can and should manipulate nature at its very foundations for the sake of feeding as many humans as possible. Agriculture is to be put to the service of population growth, as if unrestrained population growth has already been accepted as an unalloyed good. But I think that we should pause to contemplate civilization for a moment before we concede the old agriculture and welcome the new.

I think most people would agree that our historical period, beginning with the end of the Second World War, is strongly marked by all sorts of conflict. The battlefields have been small (the family) and large (Cambodia, the former Yugoslavia). The casualties have been abstract (our sense of what a family is) and horrifyingly real (a million Rwandans). To me, the underlying question in all of these conflicts, of decolonization and civil rights and feminism, is: Who shall and shall not be defined as civilized? In recent memory, those harbored by our civilization who were and are considered uncivilized have been women, children, people of color, Jews, gypsies, members of the working classes, people from non-European backgrounds, and tribal peoples. There is no arguing that the dispute is taking place, and that even while the definition of civilization is broadening, opposition to that broadening is growing sharper and more entrenched. Nevertheless, it is in this very conflict, in the incorporation of those hitherto considered "uncivilized," that our salvation lies.

Four basic questions of civilization now remain to be answered, or answered anew, in light of the dangers we find ourselves in as a result of overpopulation, the ozone hole, the greenhouse effect, and the decline of biodiversity. One of these, of course, is: What shall we eat? The simple annual monocrops—wheat, rice, corn, and soybeans—have created the costly and unnatural systems of farming that are in our day beginning to fail. If we cannot afford pork and corn, then must we eat, as The Land Institute in Salina, Kansas, suggests, Illinois bundleflower and eastern gama grass? Why not? The fact is, if we do not carefully consider what we are to eat, then our choice of the familiar simply because it is familiar may doom us.

The second question is: Who (or what) shall do the work? The example of women's work over the past 150 years demonstrates the scope of the change. Much of what women once spent all their lives doing—carding, spinning, weaving, sewing, washing, soap making, candle making, building fires, growing and preparing food, cooking it, and cleaning up after the eating—has devolved from women to machines, freeing women to become members of civilization—to be educated, to make laws, to write books, to pursue scholarship and research. But, of course, the costs of nonhuman energy have proved very high, and environmentalists look with horror at the rise into civilized consumer status of all the Chinese, Indians, and south Asians, not to mention the poor classes of the Americas. Many maintain that the earth's atmosphere, in particular, cannot bear the use of so much more carbon-based energy. Perhaps technology will find a cheaper and cleaner energy source, but at least the question must be asked—who, or what, will do the work? As a woman and the mother of daughters, I resist any answer that will attempt to "uncivilize" women, an answer proposed in some quarters. But—what then?

The only answer to the third question, which is: What do we know? has to be "Not much." The earth is still in many ways terra incognita, which of course has not prevented our species from assuming and asserting dominion over it. The imposition of agriculture is, I think, a nice example of how humans tend to work. Someone discovers or invents a technique, for example, plowing. The rush to apply this technique as "knowledge" is irresistible, and as it gets applied all over the place, experts come out of the woodwork and assert that they know something, though as the years pass, it becomes clear that they know only two things—how to apply that technique and how to charge others for it. In our country, technique is often mistaken for knowledge, but knowledge is a more difficult and more slowly

accumulating commodity. Technique accrues to ego, but knowledge more than likely does not. Technique is compounded of
successes—all you have to do is apply the technique; but knowledge is made up of mistakes—honest assessments of the many
outcomes of many techniques.

The other great mental activity that masquerades as knowledge is belief. We live in an era of increasing beliefs. All the absolute religious beliefs come to mind, because they are so loud,
insistent, and divisive, but all sorts of beliefs masquerade as
knowledge, too, like belief in the efficacy of the free market as a
way of deciding what has value. Belief drives the believer to action, while knowledge produces caution. One component of real
knowledge is the knowledge of the possibility of being wrong.
It is difficult to act on what you know because part of what you
know is that there is plenty you do not know that might be more
significant than what you do know. Like technique, belief tends
to be self-aggrandizing while knowledge tends the other way, toward putting the knower in his or her rightful, and limited, place.
When we ask, What do we know? what we mean is, Do we
know enough to act? Our world would be a better place if more
who had answered "Yes" to that question had instead answered
"No." As our millennium ends and our population grows, the
margin one is allowed for survival by the abundance of nature
and the expanse of geography grows smaller and smaller. Mistakes, even sincere mistakes of sincere belief, have ever more serious consequences.

A fourth question that needs to be asked is: Are we worth
saving? Not, Am I worth saving? because most of us would automatically say "Yes" or, Are *they* worth saving? (as in "those
strange, alien people whom I don't understand and can't relate
to, who might have hurt me and might yet do so") because we
all know that the answer to that question has often been "No."

Are we worth saving? No quick answers, because it is important
as our civilization changes to discuss what good we are, and why
we are worth saving. Our culture and our economy seem to act
out only one answer—we are worth saving because we want to
be saved. Desire to live, to prosper, to possess, and to expand
seems to be the unanswerable goal of all our economic and cultural activity, and its result seems to be the exploitation of every
corner of the earth with the resulting destruction as an insignificant side effect. Desire as a motivation seems to have produced
irresponsibility on a global scale. If responsible ways of seeing,
experiencing, and using the earth are the only things that will
save us, then perhaps pondering why we are worth saving as a
group and as individuals will produce a greater degree of responsibility toward our home.

Whether or not these questions are asked, they will be answered in some way or another, with more conflict or less, as the
definition of civilization gets worked out. And the answers to
these four questions will become more diverse, less uniformly
based in Western European perspectives, beliefs, aesthetics, and
ideologies. The European way, certainly since the Renaissance
and probably for far longer, has been to impose answers on the
landscape and on other peoples, with, of course, force but also
with persuasion and threats. The justification was always a Euro-
centered view of "civilization." It is only in our time that a Euro-
centered way of knowledge has begun to lose its grip, challenged, though perhaps not challenged enough, by other modes.

When we set agriculture in the center of the picture and ask,
How does this human activity make the land "beautiful,"
"healthy," and "useful"?, the ways of seeing beauty, knowing
health, and understanding use that come to us from non-European sources are essential to our ability to act wisely and in the
interests of future generations. One example of something that

has been learned from Native American farmers is the companion planting of corn, beans, and squash together in hills. The legume fertilizes the grain, the stalks of the grain serve as a frame for the vines of the squash, and each plant matures at a different rate. Such a planting regimen offers not only the benefits of a longer harvest but such other benefits as nutritional complementarity. Even more essential than our readiness to try different techniques, though, is our willingness to adopt a non-European, even an anti-European, sense of humility in the face of the alien other, be that nature or non-European human culture.

Agriculture has not only made civilization and ourselves, it has made and remade the surface of the entire globe. To ponder the usefulness, beauty, and health of even a tiny section of that globe, we must ponder agriculture deeply and at length.

Notes

1. C. Ponting, *A Green History of the World* (New York: St. Martin's, 1991).

2. V. D. Hanson, *The Other Greeks* (New York: Free Press, 1995).

3. W. Goldschmidt, "Agribusiness and the Rural Community," in *As You Sow: Three Studies in the Social Consequences of Agribusiness* (Montclair, N.J.: Allenheld, Osmun, 1978).

4. V. D. Hanson, *The Other Greeks*.

Recommended Reading

Bird, E. A. R., G. L. Bultena, and J. C. Gardner, eds., *Planting the Future: Developing an Agriculture That Sustains Land and Comment*. Ames, Iowa: Iowa State University Press, 1995.

Hanson, V. D., *The Other Greeks: The Family Farm and the Agrarian Roots of Western Civilization*. New York: Free Press, 1995.

Hanson, V. D., *Fields without Dreams: Defending the Agrarian Idea*. New York: Free Press, 1996.

Jackson, W., W. Berry, and B. Colman, *Meeting the Expectations of the Land: Essays in Sustainable Agriculture and Stewardship*. San Francisco: Northpoint Press, 1984.

Logsdon, G., *At Nature's Pace: Farming and the American Dream*. New York: Pantheon, 1994.

Ponting, C., *A Green History of the World: The Environment and the Collapse of Great Civilizations*. New York: St. Martin's, 1991.

Soule, J. D., and J. K. Piper, *Farming in Nature's Image: An Ecological Approach to Agriculture*. Washington, D.C.: Island Press, 1992.

3 | Inherit the Grid

CURT MEINE

CURT MEINE is a conservation biologist and writer with the International Crane Foundation in Baraboo, Wisconsin, and a lecturer in the Institute for Environmental Studies at the University of Wisconsin–Madison. He has worked as a consultant to various scientific and conservation organizations, including the National Academy of Sciences, the American Museum of Natural History, and the U.S.-based Biodiversity Support Program. His publications include the award-winning biography *Aldo Leopold: His Life and Work.*

The culture of a nation, by general consent, would, I suppose, be regarded as its greatest heritage, but a heritage perhaps equally worthy of being cherished is the land surface which a nation occupies. The culture to a large extent must have been influenced by the character of the land surface, and in any event culture and land surface are interwoven, and interact in countless directions difficult to unravel.
—Reginald G. Stapledon, *The Land: Now and Tomorrow* (1935)

Ecological design is the careful meshing of human purposes with the larger patterns and flows of the natural world and the study of those flows and patterns to inform human purposes. . . . When human artifacts and systems are well designed, they are in harmony with the larger patterns in which they are embedded.
—David W. Orr, *Earth in Mind* (1995)

WE FACE A SHARP BEND in the road. Behind us lies the landscape we inherit, before us the landscape that, in due time, we will bequeath. Looking back, we see important flaws in the relationship between the human-dominated landscape and the natural world. Looking ahead, we see a need to reform that relationship but find it hard to know just how we might alter our direction, shift our momentum, adjust our speed. We seek a more careful "meshing" (to use David Orr's word) of social and natural systems, but we have no sure map to guide us.

Lacking explicit directions, we peer ahead, advance with deliberation, and make forays. We ask, what kind of knowledge and experience do we need to blend in any given place to address issues of biodiversity conservation, environmental quality, landscape aesthetics, economic sustainability, social justice, and com-munity cohesion? We begin to integrate perspectives, ideas, and data from diverse fields—ecology, restoration ecology, conservation biology, environmental history and economics, geography, landscape ecology, landscape architecture, land-use planning and design, and architecture and the allied arts.

History contributes a caution: exploration of the new requires assimilation of the past. In particular, we need to be aware of and avoid the flaws that have placed us in our current bind. Conservation biologist Gary Meffe, in defining his own field's contribution, cites Albert Einstein on this point: "We cannot solve the problems that we have created with the same thinking that created them."[1]

Here we consider one of the key features of the thinking that created our problems: the perception of context. If, as Orr suggests, sound design requires that "human artifacts and systems" fit well with "the larger patterns in which they are embedded," then a clear view of those patterns is essential to successful design. Yet, our artifacts and systems have tended to cloud the view. Architectural historian Vincent Scully writes:

> The relationship of manmade structures to the natural world offers . . . the richest and most valuable physical and intellectual experience that architecture can show, [yet] it is the one that has been most neglected by Western architectural critics and historians. There are many reasons for this. Foremost among them, perhaps, is the blindness of the contemporary urban world to everything that is not itself, to nature most of all.[2]

Scully extends and responds to his own complaint:

> At present, most human beings of the developed nations live in an environment that is almost entirely manmade, or think they do so. Hence the major contextual questions of modern architecture have come to be those having to do with the modification of existing manmade environments by new structures. But underneath all the complexity of those urban situations *the larger reality* still exists: the fact of nature, and of humanity's response to the challenge—the threat, the opportunity—that nature seems to offer in any given place. It follows, therefore, that the first fact of architecture is the topography of a place and the way human beings respond to it with their own constructed forms.[3] (emphasis added)

In considering contextual questions of the past and future landscape, we need amend Scully's observation only slightly. Not only have our urban structures and situations been inattentive to "the larger reality," so too have patterns of settlement and land use throughout the human-dominated landscape. Subdivisions, suburbs, edge cities, towns, farms, ranches, managed forests, and semi-wild lands are also "manmade structures," though less compact or obvious than the skyscraper and city block. They too are constructed forms within the landscape. Recently, environmental historians and conservation biologists have even reexamined wilderness—or at least our received idea of wilderness—as a human construction.[4] Meanwhile, our understanding of "the larger reality" of nature has continued to expand and change. In recent years, ecologists have stressed the dynamics of natural systems and the need to take ecological processes into account in conservation and resource-management strategies.[5]

Here, then, is a task. We must somehow achieve the capacity to step away from the artificial order in which our lives are embedded. We must appreciate the varied scales of time and space in which we exist. We must read well the character of the earth and know how culture has influenced the view from within.

The lenses through which we see landscapes, and ourselves within them, vary from place to place and from culture to culture. In much of North America, we perceive—and modify—the landscape through the superimposed system of rectangular land surveys, with its grid of township and range lines, that was instituted in the late 1700s. In those places where the grid system predominates, it has profound impacts on the landscape and the patterns of life within it. But our obligation to inherit wisely the grid holds broadly applicable lessons. As a metaphor, the grid illustrates starkly the difficulties that can ensue when our land distribution and tenure systems are constructed without appreciation of their natural contexts.

Yet, the very pervasiveness of land-survey systems can hinder our appreciation of them. As Hildegard Binder Johnson notes in her important study *Order upon the Land*, "most Americans accept the survey system that so strongly affects their lives and perception of the landscape in the same way that they accept a week of seven days, a decimal numerical system, or an alphabet of 26 letters—as natural, inevitable, or perhaps in some inscrutable way divinely ordained."[6] In our present efforts to devise more sustainable land-management and landscape-design practices, we need to grasp fully the historical impact of land-survey systems and to consider the constraints and opportunities they offer in light of conservation biology, landscape ecology, and other emerging fields.

As WES JACKSON WRITES, "The grid and property lines and what they mean must be factored in, almost as immutable givens, as we begin our journey to become native to a place. Those lines are likely to last as long as there is a United States."[7] To factor in the grid—what it signifies, the impact it has had—we need first to place it in perspective.

We are drawn to places where the larger reality of the earth can be sensed. Those who dwell among mountains have ready access to such panoramic views. This access now draws us as desperately to the modern American West as the halt are drawn to Lourdes (and with much the same hope for healing).[8] Those who dwell near oceans and other wide waters are also blessed with built-in access to larger realities: the creatures of the deep, the visible arc of the horizon, the pull of the moon. Deep forest—even the threatened fragments that remain—can still lift us beyond the human scale and put us in our place.

For dwellers of flatlands and inlands, however, a sense of the enveloping order is harder to come by. No grand vistas, no swelling sea, no vaulting trunks and shafts of light to lift the eyes to greater proportions. Johnson writes that, in our most *extreme* Midwest of straight roads, furrows, and ditches, "all forms seem to be hardened into plane geometry. . . . Enthusiasm over nature's roundness can be stirred only by the spectacle of clouds under the dome of the sky."[9] In flatlands, the hints of magnitude, the feeling of ultimate context, must come to us through filters of rectangular corn and soybeans fields, straight county roads that meet at precise 90-degree angles, and strip developments that cling to the grid lines like detritus to storm grate. Yet, even

within neatly stitched, buttoned-down landscapes, we find ourselves inevitably confronting the larger reality of wild nature.

Where to find it? From one of its odd corners, memory whispers a hint: seventh-grade English class, Miss Fitch presiding. Or trying to, anyway. The suburban adolescents under her care were none too attentive to begin with, and she had begun to lose access to our minds. One afternoon, in an effort to strike a spark of critical thinking within us, Miss Fitch pulled out the classic brainteaser. "Listen again. You're standing in the door of your house at Point A. You walk a mile due south to Point B. Then you turn right and walk another mile due west to Point C. But then, suddenly you see a WILD BEAR! So you turn right and race one mile due north, where you arrive safely back at your house." Dramatic pause. "What color was the bear?" The expected bewilderment all around. I recall trudging my triangular way through those imaginary stations and somehow arriving at the answer. Distraction, however, ruled. It was not the logic of the problem that held me but the daydream vision of the great bear wandering through arctic mists. We walk with wildness, and within wildness, even if unawares. Before I could raise my hand, a classmate screamed from the southern latitudes of my consciousness: "WHITE!"

The ostensible point of discussion that afternoon had more to do with methods of deductive reasoning than with finding our place in the world or the role of mystery in illuminating reality. Yet, however unintended, the latter lessons snagged. "Nature is not a place to visit," Gary Snyder writes, "it is *home*."[10] Let the bear signify the presence of the wild in our home, and of our home in the yet larger wild place—the wild that we have banished to odd corners of our classrooms, our landscapes, our selves, the wild that provides guidance when we are ready for it. Aldo Leopold understood the fundamental cultural value of these wild presences and places. They "give definition and meaning to the human enterprise." We return to them again and again, he wrote, "to organize yet another search for a durable scale of values."[11] And when we turn back to the cultural enterprise, to the more humanized portion of the landscape, we find ourselves, and our place, changed. With pragmatic consequences. "The lessons we learn from the wild," Snyder observes, "become the etiquette of freedom."[12] The better we know the larger reality, the better we might know how to act within it.

WITH THE EXCEPTION of the 13 original American states, plus Maine, West Virginia, Kentucky, Tennessee, and Texas, the continental land mass of the United States is delineated politically according to the land-survey system developed originally in the Ordinances of 1784 and 1785 and the Land Act of 1796, and modified through later acts and policies. (Canada's land survey followed much the same system.)[13] Under the survey, all lands in the public domain were to be measured and divided according to a gridwork of survey lines whose coordinates would, in Johnson's words, "always run north-south and east-west with complete disregard of the terrain. This unconditional rule [made] it possible for the survey to be continuous not only in concept but in practice over thousands of square miles—the most extensive uninterrupted cadastral system in the world."[14]

Formalized under the influence of eighteenth-century rationalism and Enlightenment science, drawing upon (or at least resembling) diverse precursors, and applied and polished according to Thomas Jefferson's political vision, the survey system was well suited to its central task: the efficient distribution of lands, whose indigenous peoples had been dispossessed of their tenure, among newly arrived inhabitants for whom individual land possession was a bulwark against the inequities of European land tenure and a stabilizing keel for the embarking democracy. "It is not too soon," Jefferson wrote from France in 1785, "to provide by every

possible means that as few as possible shall be without a little portion of land. The small landholders are the most precious part of a state."[15] Among the "possible means" would be the survey system.

The land ordinances established the principles and methods of the survey: adoption of the nonvarying gridwork of survey lines as the fundamental model; subdivision of the western territories into square townships, first envisioned to be 10 miles square, later amended to 7, and finally 6 square miles; further subdivision of the 6-square-mile blocks into 36 square sections; consecutive numbering of the sections; reservation of one section of each township for maintenance of a public school; appointment of surveyors and geographers to undertake and direct the survey; and auctioning off of the lands so defined. Following strict Euclidean geometry and Cartesian coordinates, Gunter's chains in hand, the government surveyors began their work in the wild lands of eastern Ohio. The work would continue to the Pacific. "Across the public lands," Wallace Stegner wrote, "the General Land Office imposed a grid of surveys upon which the small freeholds of the ideal agrarian democracy could be laid out like checkers on a board."[16] "The result," John Hildebrand observes in *Mapping the Land*, a history of one of the millions of freehold farms to which the survey gave definition, "was the landscape as a work of political imagination."[17]

Not, that is, as a work of ecological or biogeographical realism, or as a foundation for socioeconomic and environmental sustainability. The scientific basis of the survey, after all, lay in mathematics and geometry, not in the natural sciences—much less in the *integrating* natural sciences of ecology, biogeography, and evolutionary biology, which were but faint premonitions in the Age of Enlightenment. The survey, in abstracting the earth, might indeed extend across the continent to the Pacific. There was nothing to stop it—not great rivers, or sweeping plains, or abrupt plateaus, or vast mountain ranges, or high deserts, or thick forests. For that matter, not civil wars, or native uprisings, or land speculators, or corrupt officials, or land rushes, or railroad barons. All fell before, within, and under the grid. Although perfection could not and would not be attained in the laying on of lines, the illusion of perfectibility and control could be maintained.

Up to a point.

For there was an inherent flaw in the methodology of the original U.S. Land Survey. The survey aimed to render square townships on the landscape, with the eastern and western boundaries laid out along parallel north–south longitudinal meridians. But (as English teachers and polar bears can teach us) meridian lines are not parallel; they converge as one moves closer to the earth's poles, where they intersect. In reality, the survey squares are not squares at all, but curved trapezoids in three-dimensional space. If the survey were carried out to the poles, the trapezoids would become triangles. In short, on a round earth one simply cannot construct and stack identical square townships along a north–south axis.

The convergence of the meridians could not be disregarded in the ideal grid system. The grid might extend unencumbered by climate, geology, hydrology, slope, aspect, soil type, flora, and fauna; resurveying might be required when waves washed away sands, rivers gained and lost oxbows, landslides reshaped landforms, or volcanoes created new land; corners might be cut through the fatigue, error, or bribery of the surveyors. None of these called into question the attempt to fit an artificial order upon the natural order. But this one ultimate "natural feature"—the curvature of our earthly orb—could not finally be ignored.

In the beginning, nonetheless, it was. The Ordinances of 1784 and 1785 did not address the problem, nor did the Land Act of 1796. Not until 1804 did the Surveyor General begin to work out not exactly a *solution,* but a *technique* to mask the flaw. The

problem was addressed not through reconstitution of the survey or reconsideration of its principles, but through a series of expedient steps described in the surveyors' field manuals over the first half of the 1800s. The key innovation was the establishment of regular "correction lines" that allowed the grid to be shifted slightly to take into account the earth's curvature. The geodetic technique could not solve the unsolvable problem; all it could do was institute a shift in order to compensate for it.

Johnson notes that this "grid shift," though important to surveyors, is "rarely noticed in the field." But across the broad actual landscape of the American earth, one may find what she calls "this right-angled curiosity." "Offsets through correction lines . . . can be seen from the air because of the sharp angles they produce on north–south running section roads. On the ground they make for awkward driving, even in the twentieth century. . . . On good modern roads, corners have often been replaced by a curve."[18] We might wish to protect some of these anomalies. They might remind us of our own imperfectibility. They might show us that the earth remains, despite the order imposed upon it, whole, round, and essentially wild—beyond, in the end, the willing impulse of immodest human intentions.

BEFORE ME LIES a sharp bend in the road. I pull off on the wide grassy shoulder, 50 yards before the narrow road takes a 90-degree dogleg turn to the east. A driving wind from the northwest carries the first serious chill of the fall. High pressure has also brought bright coherent clouds, behind which the falling sun shines resplendently. Defying the gusts, strewn flocks of mallards plummet from on high into the field on the west side of the road, joining those already feasting on the dross of the just-harvested corn. At least a thousand ducks forage in this field alone, moving methodically among the gaunt remains of the summer's crop, vacuuming waste kernels.

Leaving the car, I turn up my collar to the wind and stride north past the traffic sign, its black arrow against a yellow background, pointing east. Take heed, motorists, or carom among the solid oaks in the woodlot straight ahead.

Turn east. In the adjacent field to the south, the farmer combines his corn, moving in concentric rectangles; now he approaches the far corner. The road continues east for a hundred yards, where another sign directs the traveler to take a 90-degree left turn, due north again.

Proceed 100 yards to the second corner. At the bend, there is activity amid the branches of scrawny Chinese elms. The migrating juncos have arrived only recently. They have taken to this particular spot for food and shelter from the wind. A dozen of them flit from elm branch to ground, working just the thin strip of shoulder between the pavement and the roadside brambles. Like the mallards, they dine on waste corn. In this case, however, the corn has spilled over centrifugally from trucks negotiating the sharp curve. Closer inspection reveals that the laws of physics and ecology remain intact: the corn kernels, and hence the juncos, are predominantly in the shoulder of the outer, not the inner, curve of the road.

Pause. At the corner, off to the side of the road, a yellow stake is hidden amid the elms. A small sign mounted at its top reads:

WITNESS POST
Please do not
disturb nearby

S   M
U   A
R   R
V   K
E   E
Y   R

At the base of the post, a small aluminum shield marks the section corner.

Round the corner, face due north, and walk on a short way. The woodlot to the left is great with oaks. The brawniest, an expansive bur oak four feet wide at breast height, dates from a time before roads, corn, and survey markers arrived in the savannas, when the Sauk and Fox watched mallards fly to roost in interstitial wetlands.

Reverse course, and head back around the bend in the road.

Pass again the feasting mallards, one mass hopscotching another through the corn leavings.

Return to the initial point and, before moving on, face true north again.

THE FLAW IN THE SURVEY was obviously not fatal. For all practical purposes, the surveyor's makeshift correction lines sufficed. The grid triumphed. Where the grid was laid, we now see and live the world through it. It orders the streets of our cities and towns. It turns in on itself in our suburban subdivisions and cul-de-sacs. It dictates how we drive to work and walk to school. It guides ambulances, school buses, limousines, and hearses. It directs our backhoes, tractors, manure spreaders, plows, and combines. It drains water from some lands, spreads it out across others. It leads our cows to pasture, shows our neighbors where to stop, tells our politicians where to campaign. It fixes the borders of lands we deem sacred enough to include in national parks. It bounds our national forests and wildlife refuges. Ironically, even wilderness came to be defined by the grid: When in 1924 Aldo Leopold and his colleagues in the Forest Service traced the boundaries of the Gila Wilderness Area, the nation's first, they did so along survey lines.[19]

Although the grid's influence was and is ubiquitous, its triumph was not absolute. Johnson's *Order upon the Land* is an extended study of a region, the intricately dissected country along the Upper Mississippi River, where one may view "the tension between the efforts of surveyors to put a conceptual order upon the land and the country's natural configuration of hills and valleys."[20] Close examination of the grid's deviations in such areas might reveal precisely what angle of slope, what curve of river, what depth of wetland muck is required to give nature precedence.

One can observe other manifestations of such "tension": angled street corners where Chicago's diagonal thoroughfares, following ancient ridges and pre-European trails, meet the city's postsettlement latticework of streets; center-pivot irrigation systems on the high plains that, due to some wrinkle in the local topography, leave pie wedges of unwatered land during their circumambulations; the weird artificiality of the Four Corners of Arizona, New Mexico, Colorado, and Utah; the way Camelback Mountain blots out the otherwise uniform nighttime grid of streetlights in Phoenix.

Such places underscore the point. The triumph of the grid, and the tenacity with which the surveyors served the ideal, remains mind-boggling. The consequences, for biotic and human communities alike, are pervasive. In organizing the way Americans define, distribute, possess, and use land, the grid has profoundly modified the gene flows, populations, species, and communities of life in the landscape. No one has yet attempted to review the myriad ways in which the land survey has affected the continental biota. Even listing the mechanisms of influence would be exhaustive. The broader categories would include such factors as encouragement of urbanization; facilitation of habitat conversion and fragmentation; construction of roads, fences, and other barriers; segregation, concentration, and intensification of land uses; division of land jurisdictions and management plans; and hindrance of cooperative conservation efforts.

Examples of the grid's impact on biodiversity can be found at all levels of biological organization:

Genetic. Many of the structures that follow grid lines—roads, fences, ditches, hedges, shelterbelts—serve as corridors for (or, alternatively, barriers to) the dispersal of organisms and the exchange of their genetic material. Roads in particular have been shown to have differential impacts on spiders, insects, and small and large mammals, depending on road width, type, and frequency of traffic. One multiyear study in a Kansas grassland, for example, found that cotton rats and prairie voles rarely crossed a three-meter-wide dirt road.[21]

Population. By directing construction of roads and other landscape features, the grid has encouraged the spread of some plant and animal populations and restricted others. In the forests of the upper Great Lakes, for example, the density of gray wolves has been found to be inversely proportional to the density of roads. In this region, wolves rarely occur in areas where the density of roads exceeds 0.9 linear miles per square mile.[22]

Species. The grid has had lasting impacts on the distribution of many plants and animals. For example, during the decades following European settlement of the mixed grass prairie of Oklahoma, Kansas, and Nebraska, the osage orange was widely planted as a windbreak hedge plant (usually along field borders) beyond its original range. This in turn allowed the fox squirrel, which favors the osage orange's softball-sized fruits, to move beyond the wooded riparian zones where it originally occurred and into the uplands.[23]

Community. The composition and function of plant and animal communities have also been altered by the grid's demands. Each day, my route to work takes me along County Road A, which follows the section line. The road neatly dissects a small, shallow, circular pothole, less than an acre in size. To build the road around this tiny refuge for arrowheads and migrating buffleheads and grebes would have required a jog of 50 yards west or east. Now the road has become a lesson in disrupted hydrology. The compacted soils of the roadbed have altered the groundwater flow. The western half-moon of wetland drains a somewhat larger catchment than the eastern. The western half holds more water through the summer; the eastern half tends to dry up.

Landscape. The effects of the grid can be discerned in almost any landscape where it has influenced land use. For example, few factors have been so effective in galvanizing support for forestry reforms over the last two decades as published images of the stark borders between clear-cuts and wooded lands in the American West.[24] These borders often follow the survey lines dividing private and public forest lands and public-land jurisdictions (i.e., national parks and national forests). The impact of such habitat edges on the biodiversity of forest interiors has been a central focus of research in conservation biology since the early 1980s.

Biome. Entire biomes have been changed through the grid's influence. The tallgrass prairies and oak savannas of the North American interior are among the most extensively altered ecosystems on the continent, with the estimated losses exceeding 99 percent.[25] As William Cronon remarks in *Nature's Metropolis: Chicago and the Great West*, "Few other regions in the United States were better suited [to the survey system]. . . . By imposing the same abstract and homogeneous grid pattern on all land, no matter how ecologically diverse, government surveyors made it marketable. . . . The grid turned the prairie into a commodity, and became the foundation for all subsequent land use."[26]

In addition to its direct impacts, the grid, through the patterns of land use it facilitates, affects biodiversity by altering biological, ecological, and even physical processes, including migration, colonization, seed and spore dispersal, herbivory, parasitism, predation, fire, and flooding. William Romme, for example, describes how the migration of elk in La Plata County, Colorado, "is becoming more difficult and dangerous for both elk and humans as their traditional movement corridors become obstructed by subdivisions and strip development along highways" (chapter 8, this volume).

The grid's pervasive impact on human communities and the character of civic life in North America deserves separate discussion. We can say, in general, that the continuing evolution of the social and political landscape cannot be understood apart from the grid upon which it quite literally rests. The farming economy and community grew out of the grid; the grid, too, has fed the economies of scale that promote farm consolidation and the depletion of those same rural economies and communities. Many a Main Street was laid out along the grid line; many a Main Street has, in turn, declined through grid-abetted sprawl and rational calculations of, for example, optimal Walmart placement. Only in the last few years have commentators begun to consider the connections between the grid, the political economy it has engendered, and the fraying strands of community life.[27]

What can we say, in sum, of the enduring effects of the land survey and its consequent grid? The very pervasiveness of the survey trivializes any list of attributes. Let us consider, however, a few of the more far-reaching.

A tentative inventory would include many positive and long-celebrated features. The freeholding yeoman, keeping fertile the ground of American democracy, was, in Stegner's words, "a kind of Jeffersonian hope more than he was a Jeffersonian fact." Nonetheless, "the fact of free land had meant that a great many people acquired freeholds in the New World."[28] Concentration of land ownership, wealth, and political power might have been worse without the survey. Land disputes might have been pandemic in the new land. Ignoring for the moment the unignorable—the alienation of the native inhabitants—Americans have generally been able to avoid conflicts over land possession through the survey's clear definition of property.[29] The education provisions instituted through the survey, including the eventual establishment of the land-grant colleges under the Morrill Act, provided Americans with unprecedented educational opportunities. Moreover, the process of surveying gave us reliable records of what the land was like at the time of European settlement and a convenient basis for subsequent mapping, quantitative analysis, and restoration measures.

On the other side of the ledger are the forces that the grid directed, and with which conservationists, architects, landscape architects, and planners (among others) must contend. The survey imposed a standard scale and method, and drew attention away from the particular features, constraints, and opportunities found in any given place. "Too much rectilinearity, tied to efficiency, in our daily environment has been an American misfortune," Johnson concludes.[30] The survey promoted land fraud and speculation on a continental scale. It encouraged the adoption of the hard utilitarian view of land as commodity rather than (in Johnson's words) "a common good under the stewardship of its owners" or (in Leopold's words) "a community to which we belong."[31] The land survey by its very implementation emphasized and deepened the distinction between public and private land, and hence between public and private interest in the use of land. For our inability to bring into harmony these interests—not to mention those of the prior inhabitants, future generations, and other species—we continue to pay mightily. The grid, of course, did not breathe these forces into being. Economic doctrines, land policies, and traditions of faith, philosophy, and science have contributed as much, if not more. But the grid did give these forces exceptional opportunities to express themselves.

We inherit a grid that is simultaneously real and metaphorical. It has dictated our system of land use and our way of thinking about land—the natural, the wild, the human, the civilized. Our daily activity and our planning take place within it. At the same time, it signifies our adherence to, and imposition of, an abstract construction of the human mind. We have looked to the lines first, not to the land upon which the lines have been laid. In this light, we can see that one of the functions of our evolving national land ethic is to help us to read in between the lines.

AN INHERITANCE is, almost by definition, inescapable. We can neither uncritically celebrate nor deny the fact that the grid has helped make us who we are. If we unconditionally embrace what it has made of us and our society, we become thoughtless patriots. If we unconditionally denounce what it has made of us, we fall into self-hate, availing little.

We cannot return, in any case, to a pre-grid world. Moreover, there is no evidence that places that humans have occupied outside the formal North American grid are any more ultimately "fitted" or conducive to a sustainable future. Other humanized landscapes throughout the world developed, too, before the integration of the natural sciences provided us with an alternative view of the land, its "membership," and its workings. Many landscapes lacking the extensive grid have nonetheless been more thoroughly converted than North America's, leaving only small patches of wildness. We have inherited the grid, but recently enough that residual wildness yet remains. For now.

The grid was designed to allow land tenure to be modified quickly and efficiently, and it will allow for ever more intense economic land use unless we actively comprehend it and build wildness into and through it.[32] We are on a fast road to a wholly domesticated, extremely mechanized, and not necessarily civilized landscape. There is, however, still time to turn aside.

Our remaining option, then, and our self-defined task, is to accept the inheritance with grace. How can conservation biology, landscape ecology, and landscape design aid in this task? Part of the answer lies in understanding previous efforts to reconcile the dictates of the grid with a more humane and naturalistic vision. The tradition of such efforts is as old, if not as prominent, as the land survey itself. Historian Vernon Carstensen notes, for example, that in 1785, "Washington and other farmers foresaw and complained about" the control that the straight lines of quarter sections would exercise over the shape and size of fields and thus over tillage methods.[33]

In *Beyond the Hundredth Meridian*, his classic study of the life and career of John Wesley Powell, Stegner explores the most significant challenge that has been made to the primacy of the grid. During the latter half of the 1800s, as European settlement advanced into the arid lands west of the hundredth meridian, it became clear that the traditional 160-acre family homestead was poorly suited to such conditions. Stegner wrote:

> [The] firmly fixed pattern of settlement, of which the rectangular surveys and the traditional quarter-section of land were only outward manifestations, though in some ways determining ones, began to meet on the Great Plains conditions that could not be stretched or lopped to meet Procrustes' bed. . . . The rectangular grid of the General Land Office could easily leave all the water for miles within a few quarter-sections, and the man who obtained title to those quarters could control thousands of surrounding acres. Instead of rectangular parcels, therefore, Powell proposed surveys based on the topography, letting farms be as irregular as they had to be to give everyone a water frontage and a patch of irrigable soil.[34]

Through the 1870s and 1880s, Powell recommended a series of land reforms in the West based on the essential reality of arid-ity. These included proposals for political organization of the arid lands along natural watershed divisions and for cooperative management of the region's range and water resources. Such ideas sought to encourage a system of land tenure based not on the polarity but on the complementarity of public and private interest in land. The momentum, however, of the "fixed pattern of settlement" proved all but irresistible. Powell's visionary proposals fell dormant.

Yet, within a few short years the impetus behind Powell's recommendations began to counter history's momentum. The efficiency with which the grid—in alliance with market forces, land policies, and new technologies—allowed land resources to be exploited gave rise to the Progressive-era conservation movement. In particular, the heedless depletion of the pineries of the upper Great Lakes forests inspired the crusade to establish forestry as a profession in the United States and to organize national forests on the public domain. In this sense, one can argue that it was from within the grid itself that the seeds of its rejection as the *sine qua non* of land policy germinated. By fostering irresponsible land use on an epic scale, the grid made the conservation movement necessary.[35]

Even as forestry advocates, national park supporters, and game protectors were pursuing conservation in the nation's hinterlands, others were attempting amendments of the grid in urban settings. As early as 1869, Frederick Law Olmsted and Calvert Vaux introduced curvilinearity into the plans for the Riverside community near Chicago. In the decades that followed, according to Johnson, "the opposition against rectangular planning was tied to a back-to-nature movement that produced two major 'substitutes for nature' on the American scene, landscape parks and suburbs."[36] Even larger-scale projects were undertaken. For example, civic leaders in Chicago in the early decades of the twentieth century instituted the system of forest preserves that still rings the city (and that, ironically, protects some of the Midwest's most important remnants of prairie and savannah ecosystems).

The fundamental importance of the watershed as a landscape unit—in contrast to the superimposed importance of the section or township—was reaffirmed during the 1930s as the national movement for soil conservation gained force. The manifestations were both topographical, as contour plowing, terracing, and strip cropping introduced curves into the grid, and sociopolitical, as landowners organized themselves in soil conservation districts. Interest in conservation at the watershed scale flourished. At Coon Valley in western Wisconsin, 92,000 acres were included within the Coon Creek Erosion Control Demonstration Project, advertised from the roadside as "The First Watershed Project of the Nation."[37] Leopold, who supervised the wildlife-management component of the project, surmised from his experience there that "each of the various public interests in land is better off when all cooperate than when all compete with each other. . . . The crux of the land problem is to show that integrated use is possible on private farms, and that such integration is mutually advantageous to both the owner and the public."[38]

Leopold's own intellectual evolution can be interpreted, in part, through the grid. Through his training as a forester, he became accustomed to it. His early attempts to define the principles by which game populations could be managed were carried out in large part in a midwestern landscape where clean farming was monotonizing the biota of the typical farmstead. Leopold proposed to diversify the habitats of that landscape through what he called the "interspersion of types." Such interspersion of land uses created additional "edges" that could support populations of bobwhite quail, cottontail rabbits, and other farm game animals. He even reduced the technique to a neat formula: "The potential density of game of low mobility requiring two or more types is, within ordinary limits, proportional to the sum of the type peripheries."[39] By the late 1930s, Leopold's

faith in formulaic answers (though not in responsible science) was tempered by an increased appreciation of landscape-level ecological processes and the need for approaches to conservation that recognized land as more than a collection of isolated and independent "resources." One result would be his definition, in 1947, of a land ethic that "enlarges the boundaries of the community to include soils, waters, plants, and animals" and that "changes the role of *Homo sapiens* from conqueror of the land community to plain member and citizen of it."[40]

Leopold's quiet call would be lost in the din of postwar development fervor, but it would also gain a growing audience and help to inspire a movement. Coincident with the advent of environmentalism, Johnson notes, planners began to adopt land-use regulations that aimed to "loosen the hold of the survey pattern on real estate development and lessen the powerful influence that the existing cadastral system had on urban planning." She continues with an example:

> An architect in Barrington, Illinois, observed that subdivision based on soil information could "minimize a variety of problems which application of a rigid arbitrary gridiron system of design ignores or accentuates." At the time of these debates and observations much of the urban-rural fringe was already frozen into the survey pattern by streets, utility installations, and lots. As a countermeasure, town planners used soil maps, which follow the lay of the land, rather than the gridiron pattern.[41]

The same liberalization could be seen in the pioneering work of Ian McHarg, who in *Design with Nature* (1969) used overlay maps on soils, vegetation, and other biophysical features of the landscape in large-scale design and planning exercises.[42]

Broadly speaking, these and other past efforts to respond to the grid aimed to correct its perceived aesthetic, social, political, environmental, and even spiritual deficiencies. They addressed only peripherally issues of the diversity and larger patterns of life within the grid. They could not have done otherwise. As integrative as they often were, they still tended to address particular components of the landscape—soils, forests, parklands, rangelands, wildlife, suburban lots, urban neighborhoods—with only incidental attention to the total landscape mosaic or to the broad spectrum of living things and ecological processes implied in the term *biodiversity*. Even so welcome a concept as "greenspace" lacked a certain vitality, a sense of the evolutionary and ecological drama transpiring within and between those green spaces.

BY CONTRAST, new concepts in conservation biology, landscape ecology, restoration ecology, and other fields allow us to see these spaces differently. Built upon the premise that it is wiser to recognize, consult, and take direction from the order in the land than to impose an abstract order *upon* the land, these new concepts provide tools that we can apply in a selective and coordinated fashion to the management of urban space, suburb, farmstead, field, woodlot, forest, stream, watershed, and wild land. They attempt to build connectivity, dynamism, and wildness back into a landscape where fragmentation and control were not merely collateral results but purposeful goals.[43] They evoke a new aesthetic, one that may help us to overcome the century-old division between utility and beauty in conservation.[44]

Signs of progress toward these ends can be seen at various scales. At the scale of the building site, architects and designers are beginning to sketch the outlines of a "sustainable architecture." Drawing on proven traditions, but responsive to environmental realities, these efforts build upon the architectural innovations of the past several decades. New, however, is a strengthened emphasis on context. In *Designing with Nature: The Ecological Basis for Architectural Design*, Ken Yeang describes the need to see the project site as "more than just a spatial zone":

> At present, many designers tend to wrongly conceive the environment and its state as simply a physical and spatial zone (i.e., as a site and geographical location) on which the designed system is

erected. They are not fully aware of (or some prefer to ignore) the existing ecological and biological systems inherent in their project sites. Many of the current design approaches that claim to be "green" do not show a thorough understanding of the earth's ecosystems and their functioning. In an ecological design approach, the concept of the environment has to be regarded as much more inclusive, encompassing not only the physical (inorganic) milieu of the building but . . . the biological (organic) milieu as well. In most building projects, we find that the architect or the designer has completely omitted any consideration of the biological components of the project site's ecosystem.[45]

Recognition of this embeddedness is no small advance and calls for a new kind of genius. Even Frank Lloyd Wright's masterworks, for all their indebtedness to midwestern tallgrass prairies and Appalachian falling waters, dealt little with the actual prairie and stream ecosystems themselves.

At the landscape scale, landscape ecology offers new opportunities to understand how the spatial arrangement of land types affects their composition and function.[46] Similarly, one of conservation biology's central tasks since the early 1980s has been to investigate how biodiversity responds to the spatial arrangement and temporal dynamics of habitats. Increasingly this information is being used to devise conservation plans for both reserved and nonreserved lands. During this same period, the advent of geographic information systems (GIS) has extended McHarg's basic approach to landscape-level planning. Innovative uses of this and other emerging technologies have allowed conservationists to synthesize more effectively relevant field data (involving, for example, levels of species richness, the distribution of rare and endemic species, and the siting of protected areas).

At the ecosystem scale, Powell's call for greater attention to the native characteristics of geographic regions and his appreciation of the inherent need for social responsibility in devising ways to live with these characteristics remain essential more than a century later. Among the latest incarnations of these themes is ecosystem management, which seeks, among other goals, to overcome the boundaries between disciplines, agencies, interest groups, and political jurisdictions in the stewardship of lands, waters, and life-forms.[47] As an attempt to address the causes of environmental problems and not deal merely with symptoms, ecosystem management is still unproven and subject to wide interpretation. Still, it holds the potential to reweave, in more enduring patterns, the fabric of thought and life with respect to place.

We see responses at even larger scales. The most audacious of these is undoubtedly The Wildlands Project, a long-term, continental-scale endeavor that has taken emerging principles of conservation biology to ultimate lengths. The mission of The Wildlands Project is "to help protect and restore the ecological richness and native biodiversity of North America through the establishment of a connected system of reserves."[48] If the magnitude of the project seems incredible, this may itself be taken as a measure of the degree to which the grid has helped to transform the continent.

These and other experimental efforts are still ill defined. They are responding, after all, to unprecedented demands, using rapidly emerging ideas, data, and techniques. Yet, in them we hear echoes of the older hopes and dreams that the grid was intended to serve. For even as we inherit the grid, its flaws, its benefits, and its consequences, so do we inherit the aims that its Enlightenment authors sought to ensure in conferring it upon us: democracy, opportunity, an equitable share of wealth, a stake in the land, a home place. The difference is that we can and must see this legacy in a different, and larger, context.

So, HOW *DO* WE get around the bend in the road? How do we get from here to there? How do we fit ourselves realistically into what Snyder has called "the Big Watershed."[49] Nature has given

us ecological boundaries and systems that, all too late, we have come to appreciate. History has bestowed upon us political boundaries and systems that evolved before our understanding of the natural world revealed their limits. The natural and political systems operate at different scales of time and space. The pace of changes within and between them vary. Hence confusion and the sharp bend before us.

What if we cannot negotiate the turn? What sort of landscape will we pass on if we continue to follow past patterns of land use? Among other prospects: unsustainable patterns of resource use; repeated, intensified land-use conflicts at the local and national level; large, expensive, often ineffective resource management programs; a lengthening list of threatened species; inconsistent policies and shifting incentive structures; a greater degree of polarity in the landscape, with purely utilitarian ends served at one pole, and purely recreational or traditionally aesthetic ends served at the other, with less room anywhere for wild things and more integrated lives; and continued fragmentation of the body politic. The grid alone does not produce such trends, but they cannot be addressed apart from it.

Our work is to harmonize our natural and cultural legacies based on a realistic assessment of the situation. We require not a merely romantic rebellion against the aesthetics of the gridded landscape but well-grounded ways of dealing with the social, economic, aesthetic, and environmental costs that are now, because of the grid, inherent in the landscape. To negotiate the turn successfully, we will need to slow down, look around, and admit the world's nonlinearity and complexity.

We should not underestimate the task. There are major obstacles ahead: deeply ingrained land-use traditions, bolstered at every turn by economic and political incentives; extreme views of private property that have everything to say about rights and nothing to say about responsibilities; the drag of the already built; the fact that scientific information can never be complete enough to provide unerring predictions of long-term impacts; the constant challenge of crafting interdisciplinary solutions in a disciplinary culture; ethical systems that have only begun to extend our notions of community beyond the human circle; and the progressive loss of native knowledge and traditions.

A sobering prognosis. We are led on—involuntarily, by the push of history; compellingly, by the pull of posterity. We go forward out of necessity and responsibility. On the journey to become native to this place, each generation takes its turn and prepares a path for those who follow.

Acknowledgments

My colleagues in the Landscape Ecology and Culture seminar provided constant stimulus, information, and insight during the preparation of this essay. In particular, I would like to thank Deborah Karasov and Joan Nassauer for inviting me to participate and for introducing me to Hildegard Binder Johnson's *Order upon the Land*. This essay also benefited from the critical reading and comments of Eville Gorham of the University of Minnesota, Richard Knight of Colorado State University, and Gary Meffe of the Savannah River Ecology Laboratory.

Notes

1. G. K. Meffe, "Sustainable Development: Conservation Panacea or Politically Correct Ecocide? Presented at the 9th Annual Meeting of the Society for Conservation Biology, June 1995, Fort Collins, Colorado.

2. V. Scully, *Architecture: The Natural and the Manmade* (New York: St. Martin's, 1991), p. xi.

3. Scully, *Architecture: The Natural and the Manmade*, p. 2.

4. See, for example, M. Oelschlaeger, *The Idea of Wilderness: From Prehistory to the Age of Ecology* (New Haven: Yale University Press, 1991); J. Baird Callicott, "The Wilderness Idea Revisited: The Sustainable De-velopment Alternative," *The Environmental Professional* 13 (1991): 236–245; A. Gómez-Pompa and A. Kaus, "Taming the Wilderness Myth," *BioScience* 42, no. 4 (April 1992), 271–279; J. B. Callicott, "A Critique of and an Alternative to the Wilderness Idea, *Wild Earth* 4, no. 4 (winter 1994/95), 54–59; R. F. Noss, "Wilderness—Now More Than Ever," *Wild Earth* 4, no. 4 (winter 1994/95): 60–63; D. Foreman, "Wilderness Areas Are Vital: A Response to Callicott," *Wild Earth* 4, no. 4 (winter 1994/95), 64–68; J. Baird Callicott, "Deep Grammar," *Wild Earth* 5, no. 1 (spring 1995), 54–59; W. Cronon, "The Trouble with Wilderness: Or, Getting Back to the Wrong Nature," in *Uncommon Ground: Toward Reinventing Nature,* W. Cronon, ed. (New York and London: Norton, 1995), pp. 66–90. The winter 1996/97 issue of *Wild Earth* contains a series of responses to Cronon's original essay.

5. See D. B. Botkin, *Discordant Harmonies: A New Ecology for the Twenty-First Century* (New York and Oxford: Oxford University Press, 1990); S. T. A. Pickett, V. T. Parker, and P. L. Fiedler, "The New Paradigm in Ecology: Implications for Conservation Biology above the Species Level," in *Conservation Biology: The Theory and Practice of Nature Conservation, Preservation, and Management,* P. L. Fiedler and S. K. Jain, eds. (New York: Chapman and Hall, 1992), pp. 65–88; G. K. Meffe and C. R. Carroll, *Principles of Conservation Biology* (Sunderland, Mass.: Sinauer, 1994), pp. 16–18; W. S. Alverson, W. Kuhlmann, and D. M. Waller, *Wild Forests: Conservation Biology and Public Policy* (Washington, D.C., and Covelo, Calif.: Island Press, 1994), pp. 39–63; S. T. A. Pickett and R. S. Ostfeld, "The Shifting Paradigm in Ecology," in *A New Century for Natural Resources Management,* R. L. Knight and S. F. Bates, eds. (Washington, D.C. and Covelo, Calif.: Island Press, 1995), pp. 261–278; E. Gorham, "Human Impacts on Ecosystems and Landscapes," chapter 1, this volume.

6. H. B. Johnson, *Order upon the Land: The U.S. Rectangular Land Survey and the Upper Mississippi Country* (New York: Oxford University Press, 1976), p. i.

7. W. Jackson, *Becoming Native to This Place* (Lexington: University Press of Kentucky, 1994), pp. 17–18.

8. See W. H. Romme, "Creating Pseudo-Rural Landscapes in the Mountain West," chapter 8, this volume.

9. Johnson, *Order upon the Land*, p. 235.

10. G. Snyder, "The Etiquette of Freedom," in Max Oelschlaeger, ed., The Wilderness Condition: Essays on Environment and Civilization (San Francisco: Sierra Club Books, 1992), pp. 21–39; see p. 24.

11. A. Leopold, *A Sand County Almanac and Sketches Here and There* (New York and Oxford: Oxford University Press, 1949), pp. 200–201.

12. Snyder, "The Etiquette of Freedom," p. 38.

13. See H. W. Ottoson, ed., *Land Use Policy and Problems in the U.S.* (Lincoln: University of Nebraska Press, 1963); V. Carstensen, ed., *The Public Lands: Studies in the History of the Public Domain* (Madison: University of Wisconsin Press, 1968); M. J. Rohrbough, *The Land Office Business: The Settlement and Administration of American Public Lands, 1789–1837* (New York: Oxford University Press, 1968); D. W. Thompson, Men and Meridians: The History of Surveying and Mapping in Canada (Ottawa: Department of Mines and Technical Surveys, 1969); Johnson, *Order upon the Land*; W. Stegner, *Wolf Willow: A History, a Story, and a Memory of the Last Plains Frontier* (Lincoln and London: University of Nebraska Press, 1980), pp. 81–99.

14. Johnson, *Order upon the Land*, p. 30.

15. Quoted in Johnson, *Order upon the Land*, p. 39. For helpful discussions of Jefferson's views on land, nature, and democracy, see J. M. Brewster, "The Relevance of the Jeffersonian Dream Today," in Ottoson, *Land Use Policy and Problems in the U.S.*, pp. 86–136; C. Miller, *Jefferson and Nature: An Interpretation* (Baltimore: Johns Hopkins University Press, 1988); E. Hargrove, "Land Use Attitudes," ch. 2 in Foundations of Environmental Ethics (Englewood Cliffs, N.J.: Prentice-Hall, 1989); C. Merchant, ed., "Farm Ecology in the Early Republic," ch. 5 in *Major Problems in American Environmental History* (Lexington, Mass. and Toronto: Heath, 1993).

16. W. Stegner, *Beyond the Hundredth Meridian: John Wesley Powell and the Second Opening of the West* (New York: Penguin, 1992), p. 213. For a discussion of the "checkerboard" image in descriptions of the grid and its influence on land use, see Johnson, *Order upon the Land*, pp. 143–146.

17. J. Hildebrand, *Mapping the Farm: The Chronicle of a Family* (New York: Knopf, 1995), p. 16.

18. Johnson, *Order upon the Land*, p. 58.

19. C. Meine, *Aldo Leopold: His Life and Work* (Madison: University of Wisconsin Press, 1988), pp. 200–201, 224.

20. Johnson, *Order upon the Land*, p. 238.

21. R. K. Swihart and N. A. Slade, "Road Crossing in Sigmodon hispidus and Microtus ochrogaster," *Journal of Mammalogy* 65 (1984): 357–360. See also R. F. Noss and B. Csuti, "Habitat Fragmentation," in Meffe and Carroll, *Principles of Conservation Biology*, pp. 237–264; M. L. Hunter, *Fundamentals of Conservation Biology* (Cambridge: Blackwell Science, 1996), pp. 158–162.

22. R. P. Thiel, "Relationship between Road Densities and Wolf Habitat Suitability in Wisconsin," *American Midland Naturalist* 11 (1985): 404–407; L. D. Mech, S. H. Fritts, G. L. Radde, and W. J. Paul, "Wolf Distribution and Road Density in Minnesota," *Wildlife Society Bulletin* 16 (1988): pp. 85–87.

23. Originally reported in H. L. Whitaker, "Fox Squirrel Utilization of Osage Orange in Kansas," *Journal of Wildlife Management* 3 (1939): 117.

24. The most concerted example of the use of these images can be found in the anti-coffee-table book *Clearcut: The Tragedy of Industrial Forestry*, W. Devall, ed. (San Francisco: Sierra Club Books, 1994).

25. See R. F. Noss, E. T. LaRoe III, and J. M. Scott, *Endangered Ecosystems of the United States: A Preliminary Assessment of Loss and Degradation*, Biological Report 28 (Washington, D.C.: National Biological Service, U.S. Department of the Interior, 1995).

26. W. Cronon, *Nature's Metropolis: Chicago and the Great West* (New York and London: Norton, 1991), p. 102.

27. Recent treatments of these themes can be found in such diverse sources as Cronon, *Nature's Metropolis*; Jackson, *Becoming Native to This Place*; S. L. Yaffee, *The Wisdom of the Spotted Owl: Policy Lessons for a New Century* (Washington, D.C., and Covelo, Calif.: Island Press, 1994); Hildebrand, *Mapping the Farm*; and C. J. Herndl and S. C. Brown, eds., *Green Culture: Environmental Rhetoric in Contemporary America* (Madison: University of Wisconsin Press, 1996).

28. W. Stegner and R. Etulain, *Conversations with Wallace Stegner on Western History and Literature*, rev. ed. (Salt Lake City: University of Utah Press, 1990), p. 151.

29. On this point Carstensen writes: "Had a system of describing land by metes and bounds been employed, with the almost infinite possibility of odd-shaped parcels and hence overlapping and conflicting

claims, lawsuits and neighborhood feuds would have been one certain harvest of [the] vast movement of land-seekers on to new land." Carstensen, *The Public Lands*, p. xvi.

30. Johnson, *Order upon the Land*, p. 233.

31. Johnson, *Order upon the Land*, p. 219; Leopold, *A Sand County Almanac*, p. viii.

32. In a 1996 address at the University of Iowa titled "A Complex Weave: Changing Prairie Landscapes," environmental historian Donald Worster suggested that the hold of the grid has begun, in some sense, to weaken. On the one hand, nature had begun to "chew on the section lines," as floods, river meanders, revegetation, and wildlife have reclaimed certain abandoned areas. From another angle, the infrastructure of rails, paved roads, oil development, and other expressions of the ever-increasing corporatization of especially the midcontinent's prairie and plains regions has brought forth an emerging asymmetrical web overlain upon the grid. Worster's address provides a very useful socioeconomic and political take on questions that in this essay are asked from a more strictly biogeographical angle.

33. Carstensen, *The Public Lands*, p. xvi.

34. W. Stegner, *Beyond the Hundredth Meridian*, pp. 214, 227. The foundational document is J. W. Powell, *Report on the Lands of the Arid Region of the United States, with a More Detailed Account of the Lands of Utah*, first published in 1878 as 45th Congress, 2nd Session, H. R. Exec. Doc. 73; republished in 1983 by The Harvard Common Press, Boston.

35. Johnson, *Order upon the Land,* p. 200. Johnson, in discussing the difficulty in organizing effective soil conservation districts in the 1930s and 1940s, cites M. Harris, "Private Interests in Private Lands: Intra- and Inter-Private," in Ottoson, ed., *Land Use Policy and Problems in the U.S.* pp. 307–335: "[The] laws against waste [of land] have been ineffectual in cases of gradual deterioration. The whole conservation movement might have been unnecessary if the laws of waste had been more effective and had applied to owners as well as holders of lesser estates [e.g., tenants]. In society's efforts to establish the freest tenure, the pendulum probably swung too far toward complete freedom" (p. 329).

36. Johnson, *Order upon the Land*, p. 178.

37. Johnson, *Order upon the Land*, pp. 193–194.

38. A. Leopold, "Coon Valley: An Adventure in Cooperative Con-

servation," in S. L. Flader and J. B. Callicott, eds., *The River of the Mother of God and Other Essays by Aldo Leopold* (Madison: University of Wisconsin Press, 1991), pp. 218–223; see p. 219.

39. A. Leopold, *Game Management* (New York: Scribner's, 1933), pp. 129–132. For biological and historical overviews of the role of "edge effects," see Meffe and Carroll, Principles of Conservation Biology, pp. 254–256, 310.

40. Leopold, *A Sand County Almanac*, p. 204.

41. Johnson, *Order upon the Land*, p. 223.

42. I. McHarg, *Design with Nature* (Garden City, N.Y.: Doubleday Natural History Press, 1969).

43. See, for example, W. Hudson, ed., *Landscape Linkages and Biodiversity* (Washington, D.C., and Covelo, Calif.: Island Press, 1991); D. A. Saunders and R. J. Hobbs, *Nature Conservation 2: The Role of Corridors* (Minneapolis: University of Minnesota Press, 1991); D. S. Smith and P. C. Hellmund, *Ecology of Greenways: Design and Function of Linear Conservation Areas* (Minneapolis: University of Minnesota Press, 1993).

44. See J. B. Callicott, "The Land Aesthetic," *Environmental Review* 7 (winter 1983): 345–358; Curt Meine, "The Utility of Preservation and the Preservation of Utility: Leopold's Fine Line," in Oelschlaeger, ed., *The Wilderness Condition*, pp. 131–172; M. Eaton, "The Beauty That Requires Health," chapter 5, this volume; Joan Iverson Nassauer, "Cultural Sustainability: Aligning Aesthetics and Ecology," chapter 4, this volume.

45. K. Yeang, *Designing with Nature: The Ecological Basis for Architectural Design* (New York: McGraw-Hill, 1995), pp. 4–5.

46. See R. T. T. Forman and M. Godron, *Landscape Ecology* (New York: Wiley, 1986); R. T. T. Forman, "Designing Landscapes and Regions to Conserve Nature," in Meffe and Carroll, eds. *Principles of Conservation Biology*, pp. 292–293.

47. For a useful overview of ecosystem management, see R. E. Grumbine, "What Is Ecosystem Management?" *Conservation Biology* 8, no. 1 (1994): 27–38.

48. See "Mission Statement," *Wild Earth* 5, no. 4 (winter 1995–96); and "The Wildlands Project: Plotting a North American Wilderness Recovery Strategy," *Wild Earth* (special issue, 1993).

49. Snyder, "The Etiquette of Freedom," p. 38.

PART II
The Culture of Nature

4 | Cultural Sustainability: Aligning Aesthetics and Ecology

JOAN IVERSON NASSAUER

JOAN IVERSON NASSAUER is a landscape architect at the University of Michigan who specializes in the landscape ecology and design of settled landscapes. Formerly, she served on the faculty of the University of Minnesota. She is past United States chair of the International Society for Landscape Ecology. She has helped to build federal, state, and local government plans and designs to improve ecological health with aesthetic experience.

FROM THE AIR I can see the ecological patterns of my city. The enormous ribbons of the rivers and the intricate shapes of lakes and wetlands organize the landscape. Woodlands are embroidered into this connected pattern. From this vantage point, built artifacts diminish in importance. But when I am traveling around the Minneapolis–St. Paul metropolis, depending on the roads and buildings to tell me where I am, large-scale ecological systems are reduced to discrete places. They lose their continuity and no longer dominate my experience of the landscape.

To maintain these ecosystems for the future, the visible logic of rivers and woodlands seen from the air must be brought down to earth. The pattern obvious from the air must find an equivalent in cultural values visible on the ground. This translation is not immediate. What is apparent at the scale of $1' = 1,000'$ is not necessarily apparent at $1' = 1'$. Cultural equivalents are not simple unveilings of ecology; rather, new relationships between culture and ecological function must be defined. We should construct a kind of cultural necessity to underpin ecological health across the landscape, as if there were no other choice.

The cultural necessity that could make patterns for healthy landscapes recognizable exists ready-made. We are deeply attached to *beautiful* landscapes, and we have strong cultural conventions for how an *attractive* landscape should look. Landscapes that we describe as beautiful tend to conform to aesthetic conventions for the scenic, but they are relatively rare. Landscapes that we describe as attractive tend to conform to aesthetic conventions for the display of care, which can be exhibited in virtually any landscape. The display of care creates a cultural necessity about even the most ordinary places. Both the scenic aesthetic and the aesthetic of care are culturally ingrained and conceptually well developed. They are also resistant to change. Each creates a powerful cultural necessity for protecting and making landscapes.

The scenic landscape aesthetic is drawn from the eighteenth-century picturesque, in which the power of nature began to be seen as beautiful, as long as it was controlled. Rocky peaks, steep bluffs, crashing water, gnarled trees, and the ruins of ancient buildings began to be admired in the landscape. The picturesque was a cultural idea about how nature looks. It designated recognizable features of nature so that these features could be arranged for human enjoyment.

The picturesque has been so successful in becoming popular culture that scenic landscapes are often assumed to be ecologically healthy. But a scenic landscape aesthetic does not necessarily protect nature. It can be used to camouflage or distract us from actions that undermine ecological quality. While real ecosystems are dynamic, we try to protect scenic landscapes from changing. While some pristine ecosystems may exhibit the dramatic contrasts of the picturesque, some, like wetlands or deserts, do not tend to look conventionally scenic. At the same time, many landscapes that are far from pristine look scenic. The mining scar may look like a picturesque bluff to an unknowing eye; pesticide spilled in the scenic river may be entirely invisible. Where U.S. Forest Service policy has been aimed at meeting tourists' expectations, clear-cuts have been designed with curved, gradual edges that blend into the larger pattern of natural phenomena. Our strong cultural conventions for the way scenic landscapes should look has led to a contrived and frequently misleading nature.

Cultural conventions for the aesthetic of landscape care are even more omnipresent. Nearly all landscapes are judged and enjoyed according to the degree that they clearly exhibit care. In a wild landscape, care might be shown by the absence of trash or signs of human occupation. In most settled landscapes, care is shown by neatness. Cultivated fields are expected to have straight rows and no weeds. Farmers who allow weeds in their fields risk being seen as lazy or poor managers. A neat and tidy lawn is so expected that we have ordinances to force conformity upon those who do not take care of their lawns properly. People who do not mow their lawns are assumed to have problems that prevent them from doing the right thing. In his book *Second Nature*,[1] Michael Pollan recalled the social censure that befell his father when he failed to keep the lawn mowed in a tidy middle-class suburb.

The aesthetic of care is laden with good intentions and social meaning: stewardship, a work ethic, personal pride, contributing to community. But like many other ways that we improve our lives or our surroundings, landscape care can cause unintended and unexamined harm. We have begun to prevent the continued loss of habitats and species that were weeded out when immigrants from other continents settled North America and improved it. We have become leery of the damaging surprises that may await us after we have used herbicides to keep our yards, gardens, and fields looking neat and free of weeds. For some of us, lush green irrigated turf glowing from cities in dry prairie or desert regions has taken on an eerie shimmer.

To take advantage of the ready-made cultural necessities of scenic beauty and landscape care, we might ask how we can attach ecological health to these lawlike aesthetic conventions. Freezing nature to look scenic and making nature neat and tidy could create the antithesis of ecological health. But if we acknowledge that we live in a world dominated by humans, in which human perception of the landscape will ultimately affect how every landscape is used or protected, then we are led to find ways to use ready-made cultural necessities. Rather than focusing on the dire implications of some aesthetic features, we can critically analyze those features and selectively use them because we recognize the power of overall aesthetic experience. Landscapes that attract the admiring attention of human beings may be more likely to survive than landscapes that do not attract care or admiration.

Survival that depends on human attention might be called *cultural sustainability*. Landscapes that are ecologically sound, and that also evoke enjoyment and approval, are more likely to be sustained by appropriate human care over the long term. People will be less likely to redevelop, pave, mine, or "improve" landscapes that they recognize as attractive. In short, the health of the landscape requires that humans enjoy and take care of it.

Protecting Land: Ownership and Aesthetics

People take care of what they own. Land ownership can mean holding legal title to land. It also can have a broader meaning that extends to the land over which we feel a *sense* of ownership: our street, our neighborhood, our park, our school, or our town. If we notice how people take care of what they own, how they design, construct, and manage the landscape, we establish a starting place for creating new habits of care that promote greater landscape ecological health.

Looking down over Minneapolis–St. Paul, and the rings of suburbs and exurbs that are the home of 2.5 million people, nearly all the places that I see where ecological function is now protected are publicly owned land. Public ownership has great benefits. I know that the network of woodlands banding the Mississippi River and the Minneapolis chain of lakes is public park land (figure 1), and while land uses in the city may change over time, the park land is likely to stay intact. The public lands are relatively large parcels that contain diverse ecosystems, and

they can be managed by a unified set of principles for ecological health. Another benefit is the result of cultural expectations for the scenic aesthetic in parks and preserves. Indigenous ecosystems have often fit the scenic aesthetic sufficiently to survive on public lands.

Just over a century ago a visionary landscape architect, H. W. S. Cleveland, convinced skeptical city fathers that maintaining the great wooded gorge of the Mississippi blufflands and the wooded fringes of the cities' lakes was a worthy public investment. Seeing the value of protecting these natural features even before the city grew to surround them tested the vision of elected officials, but Cleveland persisted. A century later, all the residents of the metropolitan area use the great connected "Grand Round" of parks along the river and lakes, and they assume the parks to be their rightful civic inheritance. Their pride of ownership helps to assure the stewardship of the public parks.

Protruding from the northern edge of St. Paul, another network of wetlands, lakes, and planted and indigenous woodlands has a good chance of remaining intact because an early civic leader and entrepreneur envisioned that network and its watershed as the source of drinking water for the people of the city. Before Charles Gilfillan constructed a series of aqueducts that completed the flow of potable water from the Phalen Chain of Lakes and the Vadnais Chain of Lakes to the city of St. Paul (figure 1), the citizens all drank bottled water. About the same time Cleveland was at work convincing civic leaders to build parks connecting the rivers and lakes, Gilfillan sold the city water supply to a newly formed public water utility, and most of the immediate surroundings of the Vadnais Chain of Lakes also became public land. Public health, the protection of the water supply for 400,000 people in the city, assures the stewardship of these public lands.

At the top of the Vadnais watershed is the lake that serves as

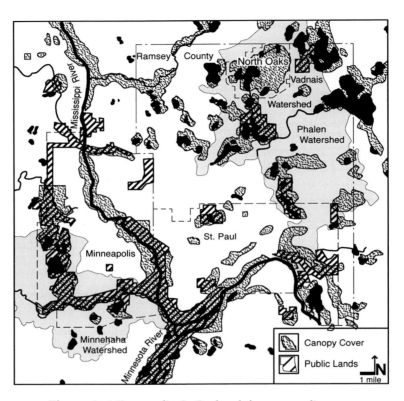

Figure 1. Minneapolis–St. Paul and the surrounding area.

one of the largest reservoirs for potable water for the city. Gilfillan sold eight square miles of land that drains into this lake to a railroad baron, James J. Hill. Hill's wealth allowed him and his heirs to manage their land with much the same aesthetic as the nineteenth-century English industrialists who wanted their estates to be picturesque. Hill experimented with raising bison, elk, and deer as well as prize beef cattle on North Oaks Farm (figure 1). Little of it was cultivated, and the oak woodlands and wetlands remained intact. In the 1950s, Hill's grandson began to develop the farm as an ideal ecological suburb. He spent the next 40 years engaged in a thoughtful and leisurely development process, advertising the suburb as a game refuge village. It was explicitly aimed to achieve the ecological function of habitat at the same time as it invited people to live within its picturesque landscapes. This ecological suburb has been private land since the nineteenth century, but its wealthy owners' love of nature and paternalistic values led this large tract of land to be developed within a unified scenic landscape aesthetic.

Today, Hill's village, the public-land system created by Gilfillan's water-supply system, and Cleveland's river park system contain the only remaining large remnants of indigenous habitats within wholly urbanized Ramsey County. They form the critical links in a connected system of woodlands, wetlands, and lakes. These are lands that have been owned in large parcels since before the city grew to surround them. They have been managed by single owners, in one case, a family that enjoyed great wealth and had an interest in the natural world, and in the other, by local government. Both large landowners, private and public, embraced a scenic aesthetic, and to the degree that indigenous ecosystems fit within that aesthetic, they were protected.

Ownership of large parcels of land allows ecosystems to remain connected at a *landscape scale*. However, most settled landscapes are not owned or managed in large parcels. As Curt Meine describes in chapter 3, the Public Land Survey and the success of Jefferson's ideal of democratic land ownership have tended to fragment ecological function at the same time as they have distributed land ownership among many small holders. In my city, the ecological framework created by Hill, Gilfillan, and Cleveland is an artifact of one set of historical circumstances. Today that era is over, and public-land acquisition has stumbled into a massive hole of public debt and popular reluctance. Large-scale ecological networks not yet in public ownership are vulnerable. The Vadnais and Phalen watersheds, which fed Gilfillan's public water supply, are now dominated by thousands of small city and suburban residential lots. Each lot has its owner, each owner takes care of his land as he sees fit. We must work at this democratic scale of ownership, the single lot or the single farm or ranch, to achieve ecological health beyond public lands and beyond the anomalies of privileged and enlightened land development. In the United States, where recent legal decisions have tended to narrowly interpret public interests in limiting private-

property rights, and where strong cultural traditions favor the rights of landowners to do what they deem most suitable on their land, overall ecological health depends on the aggregation of innumerable individual landowner's decisions.

Even if a different era allowed large public-land acquisitions, landscape ecology still would tell us that parks and reserves alone are insufficient to protect the ecological health of the metropolitan landscape. It would be a mistake for ecological health to depend solely on public lands, which are not always healthy and are not sufficiently large and connected to provide all the ecological functions we need. Beyond the edge of the park, and often within it, streets and lawns can pollute groundwater and aquifers. It would be a lost opportunity to ignore the ecological health of private lands, where components of some indigenous ecosystems are relatively healthy and where connections between other ecosystems can be formed. Woodlands and wetlands that span the boundaries of individual yards can provide habitat and protect some indigenous species. Air can be cleaned and climates moderated by the urban forest that is the product of countless trees planted.

The consequence of individual owners determining the management of many small parcels of land could be aggregation rather than fragmentation. To see the possibilities for aggregation, look at a subdivision unified by a blanket of turf (figure 2). Pause for a moment to contemplate this achievement. Inside the houses in this neighborhood live people who might have wildly different tastes in clothing or furniture. They might have dramatically different views about nature or environmental protection. Yet their front yards look almost the same. Cultural expectations for the appearance of front yards are so uniform, so well known, and so closely identified with the character of the inhabitant that we violate those expectations only at great social risk. Now imagine that blanket of turf replaced by cover that

Figure 2. This digital imaging simulation shows a suburban land-scape with conventional planting unified by turf.

Figure 3. This digital imaging simulation shows the same suburban landscape with front yards unified by gardens of native plants.

might exhibit greater ecological health (figure 3). Only if that new pattern were recognizable as meeting cultural expectations could it promote new possibilities for the appropriate appearance of landscapes.

The next generation of ecological-protection strategies must go beyond a sound tradition of land acquisition and also address individual management and development of private land. To be successful these new strategies should use the persuasive power of cultural expectations. The way people think their neighbors think the landscape should look is as important as their individual, more idiosyncratic tastes or knowledge. Andrew Jackson Downing was right in 1841 when he described the lawn as a democratic medium.[2] New paradigms for the appearance of landscapes must speak a widely understood and generally accepted aesthetic language. By first being palatable, landscape aesthetics

ultimately can go beyond the merely acceptable to evoke intelligent tending of the land so that aesthetic decisions can become intrinsically ecological decisions.

Intrinsic Properties of Landscapes: Scale and Change

An intrinsically ecological decision would contribute to landscape ecological health not as an addition to a standard development approach and not as an additional cost in a cost-benefit analysis of development choices. An intrinsically ecological decision would result in landscape patterns that build ecological health out of cultural necessity, because people expect the landscape to be that way. The possibilities for designing cultural necessity into ecological health are endless, and many ecological goals for such design are specifically described by William Romme in chapter 8 of this book and by others elsewhere.[3] Two intrinsic properties of landscapes that have been central to landscape ecology research—landscape scale and landscape change—are also central to how we can align aesthetics and ecology in the design of the landscape.

Landscape scale requires that our concept of landscape be large enough to accommodate flows of energy, materials, or species among heterogeneous ecosystems. For example, a wetland has little ecological value unless it is linked to other wetlands and to upland habitats as well. Landscape scale does not have a uniform meaning. Scale means size in proportion to some related measure. In landscape ecology, scale varies relative to the organism that is using a landscape. But landscape scale always refers to (1) a heterogeneous combination of ecosystems, which affect each other across space and time, and (2) a "middle" scale, within a hierarchy, of ecological processes that affects smaller-scale processes and is affected by larger-scale processes. Both the concepts of heterogeneity and hierarchy emphasize the connectedness of the landscape across space and time. Connectedness, then, is an essential property of the landscape scale.[4]

John Weins and Bruce Milne point out that at the scale of beetles, connectedness may be obstructed by a stone.[5] At the scale of human beings, connectedness refers to landscape structure that allows flows of water, nutrients, energy, or species that people have noticed and believe to have ecological value. The human perspective, even for such a fundamental concept as landscape scale, is ultimately cultural—it depends on what we notice and value. Because humans are the organism that manages landscapes, in practice, landscape scale often means the combination of ecosystems perceivable as management units to humans. With this definition in mind, landscape scale could mean a yard, a na-

tional park, or a watershed. In each case, the ecological functions of individual patches of lakes, streams, turf, fields, forests, or even pavement are connected to one another.

Achieving ecological function at a landscape scale is critical for all lands, but for the smaller parcels typical of privately owned land, making intrinsically ecological decisions at a landscape scale contradicts our cultural norm, which allows landowners to do what they deem suitable on their own property. People design the broad landscape matrix in small increments, a yard, a farm, a subdivision at a time. What unifies this landscape matrix is widely shared cultural expectations for what people want the landscape to look like. To affect ecological function over the broad landscape, whether on public lands or the matrix of private properties, landscape scale needs to be matched with cultural scale, overarching cultural expectations for the landscape. The way people see the landscape, what they prefer and what they believe to be the proper appearance of the landscape, profoundly influences the shape and location of each patch. We need to find ways to use widely shared cultural expectations to create a highly connected network of biodiverse ecosystems.

Landscape change refers to the results of flows from one ecosystem to another and to the growth and inevitable deaths of some individuals and communities and their replacement by others. In Ramsey County, because large parcels were held by a few owners, some critical connected ecosystems have been managed at a landscape scale. But even this ecological framework is vulnerable to the degree that it lacks resiliency to accommodate change. As the old trees die, as air and water quality changes, as climate changes, as browsing deer and tidying people remove the forest understory and dead trees, how will the old plants be replaced by new ones? Will the same wildlife be able to find habitat in the woodlands, wetlands, and grasslands of the twenty-first century as in the twentieth century? Most of the remaining biodiversity of Ramsey County has simply survived rather than reproduced itself during the past century of urban development. Passing the test of scale does not assure passing the test of time.

The scenic landscape aesthetic tends to obstruct the intrinsic property of change at a landscape scale. We try to protect scenic landscapes from changing. Martin Kreiger first wrote about the peculiar dilemmas posed by our cultural preference for preventing change in beautiful nature by posing the question, "Why not plastic trees?"[6] While plastic trees may seem absurd, Kreiger's question was drawn from a real proposal for the design of a Minneapolis street, and his example of shoring up Niagara Falls to meet the picturesque expectations of tourists was as real as the long-standing U.S. Forest Service policy to design clear-cuts to create a scenic image for the same audience.

Increasingly in our world dominated by humans, it is difficult to distinguish natural change from human-induced change. As Eville Gorham describes in chapter 1 of this book, industrial culture has changed landscapes at a rate that far exceeds previous natural history. These changes may be enormous and unanticipated, like the ozone hole, or small and intentional, like a patch of oak savanna cleared for a subdivision. In either case, such human-induced changes seem to be distinct from ecological changes: they occur faster and over larger areas, and they often may have undesirable ecological consequences. Where humans propose to change the landscape, the conservative drag of the scenic landscape aesthetic sometimes prevents damage; but without ecological knowledge, it also sometimes prevents ecological renewal.

The aesthetic of care incorporates change quite easily, if change appears to be mediated by human intention. A well-cared-for landscape is expected to change, but it is expected to exhibit the signs that well-intentioned people are watching over that change. We try to keep well-tended landscapes from "getting out of hand." We chafe against weeds taking over the field or shrubs growing over the windows. While we delight in seasonal change, we want the leaves to be raked. A forest fire allowed to burn would not exhibit care, except perhaps to the most knowledgeable fire fighter, who might see traces of thoughtful forest management in the moderation of the fire and in the appearance of the landscape after the fire. A forest timber cut could exhibit care—depending on how we expect good forestry to look. The aesthetic of care causes us to be watchful, if we know what to look for. If we know a well-cared-for woodland includes seedling canopy trees, we will look for them. If we know the oak woodland should not be diminished by fragmentation, we will look to see that the edge of the forest remains intact.

Scale and Aesthetics: Community Attention

An aesthetic that meets the approval of the neighbors may seem a peculiar place to start if our goal is to save the planet for human habitation. To most people aesthetics implies trivial decoration, and social conformity seems to contradict social change. But philosophers convincingly argue that aesthetics has a fundamental effect on how we see the world, and naturalists and ecologists who are interested in protecting the landscape have reached the same conclusion. Marcia Muelder Eaton's definition of aesthetic experience clarifies why aesthetics is fundamental, in part because it reflects cultural values: "aesthetic experience is marked by perception of and reflection upon intrinsic properties of objects and events that *a community considers worthy of sustained attention*" (emphasis mine).[7]

When applied to landscape ecology, properties that the community considers worthy of attention implies properties at a landscape scale, that is, properties that would be perceivable as people move throughout the landscape. The scenic aesthetic is perfectly suited to the landscape scale in that it explicitly values long distances (the beauty of distant horizons) and movement across the landscape (travel to enjoy a composed sequence of landscape views). Consequently, the scenic aesthetic has supported the protection of relatively large landscapes that are perceived as natural, like the large parks and public landscapes of Ramsey County, and within these landscapes it has allowed the protection of patches of some indigenous ecosystems. Ironically, the very qualities of distance and movement that fit the scenic aesthetic to the landscape scale make it inadequate to address the larger settled landscape, which is dominated by small parcels. The community values scenic places, and some people are lucky enough to live in them, but only the most wealthy might expect to *make* a scenic landscape in their own yard. In addition, the scenic aesthetic is fundamentally flawed by the premise that human presence should be hidden. The picturesque appearance of a landscape can distract us from asking questions about how humans have affected it.

The aesthetic of care affects landscapes more broadly than the scenic because it sets the aesthetic standard for even the most mundane places, including the small parcels that connect protected lands. Care implies that a person or community has ownership of a place—if not as personal property then as social identity. Fields of row crops in the Midwest, suburban lawns, and urban streets dotted with window boxes and planters all typify this aesthetic of care: neat, green, trimmed, straight, evenly mowed, painted and clean, and colorful flowers displayed. In all cases an ecological regime that depends on frequent human

tending tells all who pass by that someone is caring for the landscape. The place is perceived as the persona of its owner—whether the ownership is the caring of a community or a homeowner, whether the place is a park or a front yard. The place tells about the owner's pride, work ethic, or wealth. It tells about the owner's involvement in the future of that landscape.

The community values signs of care in the landscape, and these signs of care can prevent misuse of nature by showing traces of well-intentioned human action to maintain the landscape. We maintain landscapes to draw approving attention and to avoid the disapprobation of our community. A landscape that does not show signs of care may be perceived as abandoned and messy. A place that looks abandoned is vulnerable to development or misguided improvement: The prairie remnant becomes a superstore, the wetland becomes a neatly turfed pond. A place that looks messy is usually cleaned up so thoroughly that biodiversity is virtually eliminated. The new chief executive officer, who does not understand or appreciate the woodland restoration on the corporate headquarters site, replaces it with a conventional lawn. The happy owner of a building site in the country removes all the underbrush and weeds before installing a new landscape to equal the beauty of a new house.

Like the scenic aesthetic, care also can destroy ecological health while it satisfies community aesthetic values. The premise that human presence should be prominently displayed places no intrinsic value on nature. However, nature without clear human intention seems unoccupied and invites human presence, whatever its intention.

Both aesthetics, then, provide cultural rules for the landscape scale, but neither intrinsically supports large-scale ecological function. To support ecological function, the scenic aesthetic must be modified to reveal rather than obscure human effects.

The aesthetic of care must be modified to incorporate the apparent disorder of indigenous ecosystems within the reassuring visual framework of human presence.

Change and Aesthetics: Sustained Attention

Modifying the aesthetic of care may provide a key to attracting a community's sustained attention to ecological function. Eaton defines aesthetic experience as "perception of and reflection upon . . . (that which) the community considers worthy of sustained attention." Care of the landscape is a form of sustained attention that also invites the attention of others. When people notice landscapes, they are more likely to care about and take care of them. When people take care of landscapes or are flagrantly derelict in their care, people notice them.

Care is attentive to change. It means watching over something that changes. It means watching over a place and intervening in change to achieve a proper landscape. In this way, landscapes are more like children than works of art. They require tending, not making. They do not thrive under absolute control. Inevitably they change, and they change independently of those who enjoy and care for them. Regardless of good intentions, ignorant care can make a spoiled child, overindulged with too much of a good thing. Similarly, the signs of landscape care that we see in American neighborhoods and farms may show us spoiled landscapes, the products of superficial good intentions rather than a more profound understanding of what is ecologically good. Superficial appearances that belie ecological flaws leave us dissatisfied and uncertain. We know what we like, but we may learn that it is spoiled. We may come to see that neat landscapes of even, green lawns or straight, weed-free rows of crops have little biodiversity, little ecological structure, and require nutrients and pesticides from outside the ecosystem. Well-kept ponds seldom exhibit the ragged edges of biologically rich wetlands. Prairies seldom exhibit the riotous bloom that we recognize in a perennial garden. Care is beneficent, but a healthy landscape requires intelligent care.

The pleasure of aesthetic experience compels attention and action to sustain our pleasure. Attention to landscapes and sustained action to maintain their ecological function is what we need. In a world dominated by humans, we want landscapes that evoke our care over generations.

Proper Care and Evolving Aesthetic Expectations

Propriety drives much of our culture's extravagant attention to landscape care. We should enlist the powerful force of social approbation that drives homeowners out with lawn mowers on weekend afternoons to invest proper care with a broader, more authentic meaning. Care can be intelligent and strikingly apparent at the same time. If cues to propriety can be retained in the landscape, there may be room for greater ecological quality as well. Intelligent care would be knowledgeably attentive to ecological health. Vivid care would signify the existence of ecological health by unmistakable beauty or attractiveness.

Intelligent Care. Intelligent care depends in part on learning to recognize what is ecologically healthy. Eaton describes the aesthetic rewards of ecological knowledge in chapter 5. Because aesthetic satisfaction involves us more deeply in the landscape, we continue to learn more and grow more intelligent in how we tend the land.[8] Intelligent care also depends on knowing that we seldom know enough. It depends on *environmental humility*, a term Edward Relph coined to describe that we need to acknowledge the limitations of what we know and even what we *can* know when we change the environment. He suggested that "it is the responsibility for protecting and guarding environments as they are in themselves, and with neither domination nor subservience, that is the foundation of environmental humility."[9] Aldo Leopold's admonition that "to keep every cog and wheel is the first precaution of intelligent tinkering" suggests a first principle for exercising environmental humility.[10] As we confront the limitations of our ecological knowledge, we need to work conservatively in the landscape, saving every possible remnant of remaining indigenous ecosystems even if we cannot fully anticipate all of their potential values. Similarly, we are wise to extract what we can observe about indigenous ecosystems and imitate these observable properties when we construct and maintain the landscapes where we live.

A picture of environmental humility might look like a prairie in a garden in a prairie—all writ large on the landscape. At the broadest scale, environmental humility would require that tended places fit into a larger ecological scheme—avoiding the wet prairie or the driest prairie where a garden would not thrive. At a middle scale, the well-placed garden might look recognizably neat, an inviting place where we might expect to find the gardener. At a smaller scale, we might find a small patch of prairie in the garden, alongside the pumpkin patch and the rows of carrots. More than any other part of the picture, this little prairie symbolizes our environmental humility. It says that even where we think we know, we suspect we have more to learn about what the garden can produce. Intelligent care intentionally inserts valued properties of indigenous ecosystems into inhabited landscapes.

Vivid Care. Vivid care draws attention to the human presence in healthy landscapes in order to sustain ecological health over time. Emphasizing a benign human presence protects ecologically rich landscapes from less intelligent human control. A well-kept prairie park will not be mistaken for a weed patch. A carefully managed oak woodland is less likely to fall under a future subdivision. The more vivid the cues to human care in an ecologically rich landscape, the stronger the social claim to its ecological quality.

D. W. Gotshalk described the artist's work this way: to select, refine, and vivify what ordinarily is lost in the confused array of everyday experience.[11] Gotshalk's description suggests that designers should vivify ecological function if we want people to enjoy the health of the landscape. Designers' and artists' work to improve ecological quality may have its greatest effect where it selects valuable ecological functions and makes them vivid for human experience. In this way, small, special places can demonstrate the health that is required for a more authentic conception of care. Undoubtedly, artists' and designers' ecological visions for particular places move people to see all landscapes in a different way. Gotshalk's description also suggests that we can select, refine, and vivify the essential cues to care in the everyday landscape. Refined and concentrated, cues to care may be used sparingly to evoke public attention to ecologically rich landscapes over time and across space. Rather than dominating the landscape matrix, the well-kept landscape may evolve to include new forms of ecologically rich landscapes that clearly stake a social claim in their future.

We can align aesthetics and ecology by design. Bringing aesthetic expectations into play in a way that benefits landscape ecology requires designing strategies, landscapes, and policy with an awareness of what people enjoy and value in the appearance of the landscape now. A certain aesthetic conservatism about landscape change is not a bad thing when it prevents undesirable ecological consequences. But where the landscape should accommodate ecological change, how can landscape aesthetics evolve to make a place for dynamic ecological function?

People will sustain healthy landscapes if they enjoy them, and they will enjoy them when they know more about how to recognize ecological health. Eaton's central point in chapter 5 is that aesthetic experience of landscapes is increased by greater ecological knowledge. How do we achieve greater ecological knowledge? Environmental education is essential in all its forms. In the landscape, teachers can educate about the environment in places that are intended for education like school yards or nature centers. They can also teach about nature in a neighborhood, a farm, or a forest. In any setting, when people are directly involved in the landscape, for example, by constructing or planting or monitoring it, their sense of ownership may be greater and their attention to the place more sustained over time. Perhaps the most powerfully omnipresent form of environmental education is simply viewing the landscape. Looking at the landscape as we go about our everyday travels, we constantly judge what we see and learn from it. We should design landscapes and policies to intentionally use the appearance of the landscape to help people recognize ecological health.[12]

One way to do this is to design landscapes that protect or reveal ecological function. Analyzing and protecting ecological function has been part of the normal process of landscape architecture for more than a century. More recently, a new genre of art has aimed to reveal ecological function, and landscape architects have emphasized ecological revelation in their work as well. Each of these actions toward ecological function—to protect it or to reveal it—advances the evolution of new aesthetic conventions for the landscape. But as strategies, neither action is sufficient to evoke change at the scale of the landscape. Neither protection nor revelation necessarily involves people in maintaining ecological quality in the landscapes that are part of their everyday

experience, where artists or landscape architects have not designed every site. Art can speak to the condition of the larger landscape matrix, but it does not immediately transform it. Landscape-scale change beyond the edges of protected areas or art works must grow out of changed cultural expectations for the everyday landscape. Cultural expectations affect ecological health at the landscape scale—over the entire matrix.

Cultural expectations can change when familiar aesthetic conventions are used to frame the novel appearance of ecological function. Elsewhere I have described the juxtaposition of what we tend to see as "messy" ecosystems with orderly frames, cues to care in the landscape.[13] Cues to care include mowing, tidy fences and walks, bright flowers, and trimmed, straight edges—all used sparingly and placed strategically to frame ecosystems for sustained human attention. Along with the more large-scale features of the scenic aesthetic, cues to care can encompass ecosystems that bring greater biodiversity and more types of habitats into settled landscapes. They label the landscape as attractive in a way that is familiar and immediately apparent. Framing ecological change in recognizable aesthetic features allows us to use the cultural momentum of the present to benefit the ecological function of the future.

Aesthetic Expectations in the Service of Ecological Function: The Phalen Watershed

A new set of aesthetic expectations is emerging in the watershed surrounding the Phalen Chain of Lakes, which formed one arm of Gilfillan's public water supply system (figure 1). From the air, the watershed looks like other sectors of the city. It is covered largely by houses and yards, driveways and streets. Like much of the region, it encompasses hundreds of acres of connected oak woodland, once part of the indigenous oak savanna ecosystem. Happily, these beautiful trees fit easily into recognized cultural images for attractive yards. While their understory companions have been nearly eliminated and their means of regeneration is in doubt, for now the oak canopy exists as a dramatic wash across public and private land. However, the canopy has been severed where freeways and streets lay a placeless network of auto traffic over the landscape. Shopping centers, office parks, strip malls, schools, and churches establish nodes of human activity throughout the system. The Phalen watershed is also distinguished by its ecological spine, the chain of lakes, streams, and wetlands running down its center with their immediate perimeter protected as public land.

But I know that what I see from the air tells only part of the ecological story. Beneath the chain of lakes and the shaded neighborhoods is a complex network of storm sewers—all of which dump rainwater carrying the debris of suburban living into the lakes. The thin fringe of public land surrounding the lakes cannot protect them from the sediments, nutrients, and waste products that are expelled by the storm sewers. Both the quality of water entering the lakes and the biodiversity of the habitats that make up the network of Phalen watershed ecosystems are being addressed by vivid, intelligent care in new forms of urban landscapes. These new forms of care are encouraged by a watershed ecosystem-management plan that was developed by collaboration among six municipalities.[14]

At the mouth of the watershed, near where Gilfillan's pipe drained water from Lake Phalen, a five-acre wetland, apparent on nineteenth-century maps, helped to clean water before it flowed into the Mississippi River. In the 1960s a land developer tracing the route of a planned highway saw the wetland as a large un-occupied parcel of land in a densely settled neighborhood. It was purchased, the wetland was filled, and a shopping center and large parking lot were constructed in its place. The wetland soils and plants that had occupied this place soon made their presence known by the cracking foundations and wet basements of the shopping center buildings and the persistent large puddles in the crumbling asphalt of the parking lot. Today, people in the neighborhood envision a wetland park in place of the shopping center (figures 4 and 5). Soon the landscape will be constructed in a pattern that local people will recognize as a well-kept amenity they can be proud of and that the landscape ecologist will recognize as the replacement of a missing part of the ecological network. This double vision of cultural expectations for everyday landscapes and patterns for ecological function makes the wetland and its associated upland habitats sustainable as part of the community's image of the park.

Sloping south toward the wetland, a sunny, well-kept lawn will adjoin the apartment houses, where many children live. New businesses are planned along the street next to the lawn. From the shops and play area, people will look down on the lush wetland and a riparian woodland beyond. Brightly colored flowers indigenous to wet meadows will line the wetland in vivid bands. Before water runs into the wetland, pollutants from the lawn and the street will be filtered by the wet meadow and by neatly edged gardens of prairie plants pouring down the hill. All of these cues to care will frame the wetland and woodland. Ecological function will be more explicitly set forth in the storm-water-cleaning garden in the southeast corner of the park. Taking water directly from the storm sewer of the surrounding neighborhood, the garden will be a beautiful urban space that vividly demonstrates how storm water is cleaned before it enters the wetland. Finally, the wetland park will build connections to

Figure 4. The Phalen Shopping Center in St. Paul as it appears today.

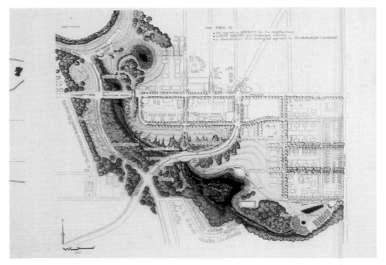

Figure 5. The design for the Phalen Wetland Park as it is envisioned for the current site of the shopping center includes a woodland corridor, filter strips of native prairie and wet meadow plants, and a storm-water cleaning garden.

landscapes at a larger scale. All along the busiest road in the park, a habitat corridor will connect the constructed ecosystems of the park with the larger migratory and daily foraging corridors of birds that have had to pass over the old parking lot. Cues to care in other parts of the park will encourage people to stay on the grassy slopes to observe wildlife rather than entering the woodland corridor.

Further north in the watershed, in a first-ring suburb, an imaginative city engineer questioned the fiscal cost and ecological benefit of retrofitting a subdivision established in the 1950s with a conventional storm-water system in the 1990s. He knew that a conventional system would only increase the direct flow of polluted water to the lakes and reduce local recharge of the aquifer. Beginning with an intensive interview process to understand what residents of the subdivision expected and enjoyed about the appearance of their yards, the city engineer has worked

with landscape architects to design a storm-water system that will infiltrate rainwater back into the ground rather than sending it down a gutter and into a pipe. This design increased the connectivity and biodiversity of the urban forest by constructing a wooded corridor down the abandoned alleyway. Open views to the fronts of the houses, ample (though reduced) front lawns, and new flower gardens (that infiltrate storm water) were designed as cues to care (figure 6). The modest homes and quiet street have become a model for other suburbs in the city.

Near the north end of the watershed, another suburb is constructing a new kind of urban ecology center. A wetland, which is being constructed on the site of an abandoned sod farm now in public ownership, has been designed to evoke a scenic aes-

Figure 6. The front yard of one house on the street that was retrofit to infiltrate storm water and increase biodiversity. New rainwater gardens have been designed to introduce people to native prairie and wetland plants and to improve ecological health.

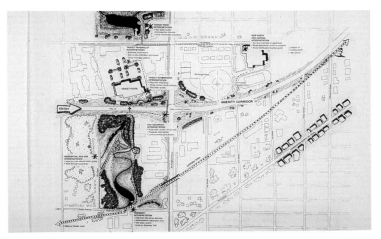

Figure 7. The new urban ecology center teaches students about the ecology of the surrounding city when they take the landscape ecology journey to and from the constructed wetland.

thetic, to look like a place where people can immerse themselves in nature. What is new about this urban ecology center is that it will show people in the community a nature that they themselves are actively constructing and monitoring over time. This is a conception of nature that requires intelligent care and makes it vivid, not a conception of nature that hides the effects of human tending. For the hundreds of children who will use it as part of their studies, the center will not only be an isolated place; it will also be experienced on a landscape scale, as part of an urban landscape ecology journey (figure 7). Walking from their school, they will follow a designed route that vividly displays the ecological effects of their school, a shopping center, and residential neighborhoods that are connected by water moving into and from the wetland. The journey will help people see the ecology center in its landscape-scale and cultural aesthetic contexts as well.

Conclusion

In the twenty-first century, landscape ecology must be supported by cultural sustainability. Landscapes that evoke the sustained attention of people—that compel aesthetic experience—are more likely to be ecologically maintained in a world dominated by humans. Waste places, where remnants of indigenous ecosystems survive unnoticed, will not be able to escape anthropocentric land management under pressures of population growth. We will no longer enjoy the unintended benefits of our own neglect. Public lands where parts of indigenous ecosystems remain will depend on increasingly active management to retain selected ecological functions in the face of disturbance regimes and atmospheric effects altered by culture. Selecting those ecological functions that will be supported by human action is itself a powerful expression of culture. The omnipresence of human disturbance demands that concern for ecological health extend beyond the boundaries of public lands to encompass the larger matrix of private land.

Enlisting human behavior to support ecological function requires cultural analysis. We must look beyond rational economics to aesthetic experience to understand why people maintain particular landscape patterns. People make and manage landscapes not only for what they produce but for how they look and how they are *supposed* to look. Policies and strategies, landscapes and technologies should be designed to align aesthetic expectations with ecological health.

If we align the aesthetic experiences that people already value with the ecological health they do not yet know how to recognize, we can build landscape ecological structure while we are building new cultural expectations for ecological health. We can open and correct the scenic aesthetic by engaging the aesthetic of care to show beneficent human intention. We can correct the aesthetic of care by aligning the complexity of healthy ecosystems with recognizable cues to human intention. A landscape is culturally sustainable if people pay attention to its quality. The pleasure of aesthetic attention can draw people to attend to the ecological quality of the landscape. The social significance of the well-kept landscape further compels people to attend to landscape care. We should use the pleasure of aesthetic experience and the social significance of care to build new aesthetic expectations that intrinsically rest upon ecological health.

Acknowledgments

The figures included in this essay are part of research projects conducted with the support of the USDA Forest Service Urban Forestry Project, the McKnight Foundation, and Minnesota legislature as approved by the Legislative Commission on Minnesota Resources. Their support was essential to this work. For assistance in creating the figures in this essay, I thank Andrew Caddock and Kevin McCardle (figure 1), Fred Rozumalski (figures 2 and 3), Ross Martin and Vera Westrum (figures 4 and 5), and Amy Bower (figures 6 and 7), all of whom assisted me in conducting research. For their leadership and collaboration in Phalen Watershed Projects, I am very grateful to: Sherri Buss, manager of the Phalen Watershed Project; Cliff Aichinger, director of the Rhamsey-Washington Metro Watershed District; Ken Haider, Maplewood City Engineer; and Karen Swenson, director of the Northeast Neighborhood Development Corporation.

Notes

1. M. Pollan, *Second Nature* (New York: Dell, 1991).

2. A. J. Downing, *A Treatise on the Theory and Practice of Landscape Gardening, Adapted to North America* (1841), reissued as *Landscape Gardening and Rural Architecture* (New York: Dover, 1991).

3. W. E. Dramstad, J. D. Olson, and R. T. T. Forman, *Landscape Ecology Principles in Landscape Architecture and Land-Use Planning* (Washington, D.C.: Island Press, 1996).

4. T. F. H. Allen and T. W. Hoekstra, *Toward a Unified Ecology* (New York: Columbia University Press, 1992).

5. J. A. Weins and B. T. Milne, "Scaling of Landscapes in Landscape Ecology, or, Landscape Ecology from a Beetle's Perspective," *Landscape Ecology* 2 (1989): 7–96.

6. M. Kreiger, "Why Not Plastic Trees?" *Science* 179 (1973): 446–455.

7. M. M. Eaton, *Aesthetics and the Good Life* (London: Farleigh Dickinson University Press, 1990).

8. J. I. Nassauer, "The Aesthetics of Horticulture: Neatness As a Form of Care," *HortScience* 23 (1988): 937–977.

9. E. Relph, *Rational Landscapes and Humanistic Geography* (London: Croom Helm, 1981).

10. A. Leopold, *A Sand County Almanac and Sketches Here and There* (New York: Oxford University Press, 1949).

11. D. W. Gotshalk, *Art and the Social Order* (Chicago: University of Chicago Press, 1947).

12. J. I. Nassauer, "The Appearance of Ecological Systems As a Matter of Policy," *Landscape Ecology* 6 (1992): 239–250.

13. J. I. Nassauer, "Messy Ecosystems, Orderly Frames," *Landscape Journal* 14 (1995): 161–170.

14. Phalen Chain of Lakes Comprehensive Watershed Management Project. *Phalen Chain of Lakes Watershed Comprehensive Natural Resources Plan.* (Maplewood, Minn.: Ramsey-Washington Metro Watershed District, 1994).

Recommended Reading

Andrews, M. 1989. *The Search for the Picturesque.* Stanford, Calif.: Stanford University Press.

Beardsley, J. 1984. *Earthworks and Beyond: Contemporary Art in the Landscape.* New York: Abbeville Press.

Costanza, R., B. G. Norton, and B. D. Haskell, eds., 1992. *Ecosystem Health: New Goals for Environmental Management.* Washington, D.C.: Island Press.

Crandell, G. 1993. *Nature Pictorialized: "The View" in Landscape History.* Baltimore: Johns Hopkins University Press.

Dwyer, J. F., H. W. Schroeder, and P. H. Gobster. 1991. "The Significance of Urban Trees and Forests: Toward a Deeper Understanding of Values." *Journal of Arboriculture* 17: 276–284.

Eaton, M. M. 1990. *Aesthetics and the Good Life.* London: Farleigh Dickinson University Press.

Eaton, M. M. 1990. "Responding to the Call for New Landscape Metaphors." *Landscape Journal* 9: 22–27.

Howett, C. 1987. "Systems, Signs, Sensibilities: Sources for a New Landscape Aesthetic." *Landscape Journal* 6: 1–12.

Hunt, J. D., and P. Willis. *The Genius of Place.* Cambridge, Mass.: MIT Press.

Jarchow, M. E. 1967. "Charles D. Gilfillan, Builder behind the Scenes." *Minnesota History* 40: 221–232.

Kaplan, S., and R. Kaplan. 1989. *The Experience of Nature.* New York: Cambridge University Press.

Kreiger, M. 1973. "Why Not Plastic Trees?" *Science* 179: 446–545.

Leopold, A. 1966. *A Sand County Almanac.* New York: Oxford University Press.

Minnesota Department of Natural Resources, County Biological Survey. 1995. *Habitats of Anoka and Ramsey Counties.* St. Paul: Minn. Dept. of Natural Resources.

Nadenicek, D. J. 1993. "Nature in the City: Horace Cleveland's Aesthetic." *Landscape and Urban Planning* 26: 5–16.

Nassauer, J. I. 1993. "Ecological Function and the Perception of Suburban Residential Landscapes." In Gobster, P. H., ed., *Managing Urban and High Use Recreation Settings,* General Technical Report, USDA Forest Service North Central Forest Experiment Station, St. Paul, Minn.

Nassauer, J. I., and R. Westmacott. 1987. "Progressiveness among Farmers as a Factor in Heterogeneity of Farmed Landscapes." In M. G. Turner, ed. *Landscape Heterogeneity and Disturbance,* New York: Springer-Verlag.

Neckar, L. 1995. "Fast-Tracking Landscape and Culture: Horace William Shaler Cleveland and the Garden in the Midwest" in *The Regional Garden in the United States.* Washington, D.C.: Dumbarton Oaks.

O'Neill, R. V., et al. 1986. *A Hierarchical Concept of Ecosystems.* Princeton, N.J.: Princeton University Press.

Pennypacker, E. 1992. "What Is Taste, and Why Should I Care?" *Proceedings of the Council of Educators in Landscape Architecture* 4: 63–74.

Robinson, S. K. 1991. *Inquiry into the Picturesque.* Chicago: University of Chicago Press.

Smardon, R. C. 1988. "Perception and Aesthetics of the Urban Environment: Review of the Role of Vegetation." *Landscape and Urban Planning* 15: 85–106.

Thompson, G. F., and F. R. Steiner. 1996. *Ecological Design and Planning.* New York: Wiley.

Wilson, J. B., and W. McG. King. 1995. "Human-mediated Vegetation Switches as Processes in Landscape Ecology." *Landscape Ecology* 10: 191–196.

5 | The Beauty That Requires Health

MARCIA MUELDER EATON

OVERLEAF

Top: Super Mall Entrance, Tacoma, Washington (May 1995).
Bottom: Prairie, near Warren, South Dakota (September 1995).

MARCIA MUELDER EATON is a philosopher who specializes in aesthetics and the philosophy of art. She has served as president of the American Society of Aesthetics and has been a visiting professor in England, Germany, Denmark, and the Netherlands. She is chair of the Department of Philosophy at the University of Minnesota.

Almost every Englishman, if asked what he means by "beauty," would begin to describe a landscape—perhaps a wood with bluebells and silver birches, perhaps a little harbour with red sails and whitewashed cottages; but at all events a landscape.

—Kenneth Clark, *Landscapes into Art*

W E CAN take as a given that aesthetic values play an important role in human experiences of landscapes. Almost every country has some legislation that has established national preservation zones, regulates waste, and so on. These laws often refer to what the U.S. Environmental Policy Act of 1969 calls "aesthetic amenities." In increasing numbers individuals spend weekends and vacations in places that they find beautiful. Residents of our ugliest cities treasure the presence of trees, squirrels, and birds in their everyday experiences.[1] Ecologists often report that what first led them to their specialty was an aesthetic response to nature. From being intrigued by beautiful butterfly designs to delighting in the smell of a forest interior, what drives people who study the environment is a profound concern for what Aldo Leopold called the "integrity, stability, and beauty of the biotic community."[2]

As a philosophical aesthetician, I have examined the nature and components of aesthetic experience—aesthetic objects, the people who create and respond to them, and the contexts in which this creating and responding takes place. Although my theories have sometimes addressed objects and events that occur naturally (sunsets or seashores, for example), my ideas about the nature of aesthetic experience have been derived largely from an investigation of discussions of works of art. My goal in this essay is to determine whether and to what degree this way of understanding what is special about aesthetic experience can be extended to the appreciation of nature. Increasingly in my work and in that of others, the contextual nature of aesthetic experience is being examined. How do social, economic, political, and cultural values affect making and responding to those things that one identifies as aesthetic? Such issues have special importance when one approaches the intersections between ecological and aesthetic problems. A theme of this book on culture and landscape ecology is that the environment cannot be managed or assessed in purely "objective" scientific terms; we must attend to how the ways that people appreciate nature influence nature per se. In this chapter I shall thus discuss the role of philosophical aesthetics in evaluating sustainable landscapes and ecosystems.

The Role of Knowledge in Aesthetic Appreciation of Landscapes

Aesthetic experience, I have argued, is marked by perception of and reflection upon intrinsic properties of objects and events that a community considers worthy of attention. I have also argued that anything that draws attention to intrinsic properties of objects and events can be described as "aesthetically relevant."[3] It is communities, not individuals acting in isolation, that determine what is worthy of attention and how aesthetic attention gets directed to objects and events. Again the role of culture in creating beautiful landscapes that are also healthy (and vice versa) must be emphasized. Can we produce landscapes that both repay repeated aesthetic attention and are ecologically viable?

The philosopher Allen Carlson has suggested a model of nature appreciation that is, in my opinion, the best so far presented if one's goal is to produce, protect, or preserve environments that are both beautiful and healthy. In a seminal essay in 1979, "Appreciation and the Natural Environment," Carlson asserted that we know fairly well how to go about appreciating paintings or piano performances, that is, what we should attend to and what we can disregard. In large part, he thinks, this is because these objects and events are human creations whose production we understand. But, he asks, what of those "unproduced" natural objects and events that we value?[4]

Carlson identifies two models for nature appreciation that he thinks have figured historically, both in theory and in practice,

in central ways: the nature-as-object model and the nature-as-scenery model. In the first, people interpret and evaluate parts of nature as if they were artworks. But, he says, this approach treats natural objects as if they were self-contained units and not as what they really are—parts of a larger organic whole. When we look at a rock as if it were a piece of sculpture, we see interesting shapes or pleasing light-reflecting planes, but we may miss seeing how these properties are related to the forces in the natural environment that shaped it. If aesthetic appreciation is of *nature*, the viewer must be aware of *natural* connections, and treating natural objects solely as artworks is inadequate to this task, Carlson argues. Many theorists share this view; some actually see danger in looking at natural objects as if they were art objects. Landscape architect John Tillman Lyle complains that for most people "shelter [is] separated from its environs and, in large terms, from the processes of global ecosystems and its heat balance. In the twentieth-century city, people . . . think of landscape as the frame around a picture . . . rather than as the source of life."[5] The result is that we become oblivious to and hence threaten the larger, nonartificial environment.

Similarly the scenery model, according to Carlson, distorts or leaves out what is special in nature. By emphasizing qualities that are related to prospect, such as coloration and overall design, nature is viewed as if it were a static unity. I shall say more later about ways in which this bias has distorted nature and acted against the production of sustainable landscapes.

What Carlson believes is necessary is a model of appreciation that emphasizes both *nature* and *environment* and allows for an involvement of all the senses but also of cognition. In Carlson's view, instead of a creative act guiding attention (as it does in our experience of a painting or of a piano performance), it is *knowledge of nature* that should guide our *aesthetic experience of nature*. "If to aesthetically appreciate art we have knowledge of artistic traditions and styles within those traditions," he writes, "to aesthetically appreciate nature we must have knowledge of the different environments of nature and of the systems and elements within those environments."[6] Appreciation based on knowledge is the only way to avoid aesthetic omissions and deceptions.

Like Leopold, Carlson also insists that sound aesthetic views will shape sound ethical views about how to manage environments:

> We do not aesthetically appreciate simply with our five senses, but rather with an important part of our whole emotional and psychological selves. Consequently, what and how we aesthetically appreciate cannot but play a role in the shaping of our emotional and psychological being. This in turn helps to determine what we think and do, and think it correct for ourselves and others to think and do. In short, our aesthetic appreciation is a significant factor in shaping and forming our ethical views.[7]

Carlson's outlook is precisely the sort needed not just for understanding at least many occasions of the appreciation of nature but also for establishing and maintaining sustainable landscapes.

There are, however, some possibly problematic consequences of Carlson's knowledge-based theory of nature appreciation. I want first to explain why I think his theory contributes to designing sustainable landscapes. I shall then raise some problems that I think philosophical aestheticians must deal with before Carlson's theory can help to solve specific problems in designing ecologically sound environments. I hope to show that attempts to achieve sustainability will only be successful if ecological sustainability and aesthetic sustainability are integrated—and this is how, I believe, philosophical aesthetics can be of use in designing and evaluating landscapes.

What counts as *sustainable* has, of course, been variously interpreted by ecologists.[8] A United Nations panel defined it as follows: "A sustainable condition for this planet is one in which there is stability for both social and physical systems, achieved through meeting the needs of the present without compromising the ability of future generations to meet their own needs."[9] Other authors in this volume interpret this concept with respect to specific cases.

I, and others, have claimed that aesthetic value is a matter of that which sustains attention. Great works of art repay prolonged and repeated perception and reflection. As Kenneth Clark puts it,

> I fancy that one cannot enjoy a pure aesthetic sensation . . . for longer than one can enjoy the smell of an orange, which in my case is less than two minutes; but one must look attentively at a great work of art for longer than that, and the value of historical criticism is that it keeps the attention fixed on the work while the senses have time to get a second wind.[10]

Aesthetically relevant information helps to enable sustained attention; indeed, it not only sustains but "regenerates" it. When one learns something that directs perception to or stimulates reflection on an aesthetic property of an object or event, one is drawn back to the object or event—and, in turn, the rich experience that results may lead one to seek for more information about the object. Knowledge redirects attention, which motivates a desire for more knowledge, which redirects attention, and so on and so on and so on. Thus is attention *sustained*. We protect artworks to which we want to give repeated attention—put them in museums, record and write scores for them, print or memorize them, for example. Through art education and criticism we provide the background necessary for delighting in intrinsic properties of objects and events. Aesthetic sustainability exists when cultures provide for repetition of aesthetic experiences over the long haul, as it were. Artworks engage a sustained aesthetic when they repeatedly support and invite aesthetic experiences.[11]

This is true for landscapes as well as for artworks. Building on the United Nations definition of *sustainability*, in aesthetics we require landscapes that repeatedly support and invite aesthetic experiences. Obviously environments, like artworks, must exist in order to be experienced; thus they must be *physically* sustained. But aesthetic sustainability goes beyond this. Institutions and practices must be in place that invite attention to intrinsic properties that yield aesthetic satisfaction once the culture has identified them as worthy of attention. Just as critics and educators help to sustain and regenerate attention to artworks by discussing them in a variety of ways that may direct attention to aesthetic properties, so ecologists provide information about ecosystems that may direct attention to aesthetic properties in the landscape. This is why Carlson's cognitive aesthetic model of nature appreciation is so powerful. Not only does it provide an explanation of why knowledge plays a key role in the enjoyment of nature, it suggests why his model *should* be the one that guides aesthetic education.

First, knowledge sharpens aesthetic experience (both of art and of nature). Furthermore, understanding a system enables one to perceive elements of the system and their relationships. Mushy, desultory responses become more vivid and focused. As the philosopher Ronald Hepburn has pointed out, perceptions can be attentive or inattentive, discriminating or undiscriminating, lively or lazy—just as thought can be.[12] Since thought and perception are components of aesthetic experience, sharper thought and perception make for sharper aesthetic experience.

Second, knowledge contributes to sustainability, for it not only sustains attention in the present, it also makes one more aware of what may or must be the case if attention is to be possible at all in the future. Even a modicum of ecological knowledge will force one who sees that a city park in an arid climate can only be maintained with enormous amounts of water to admit that it is unlikely that such a park will exist in the future. What is ecologically bad begins to be seen as aesthetically bad.

Carlson's knowledge-based theory of nature appreciation is not without problems, however. Many theorists agree with Immanuel Kant's insistence that aesthetic experiences, including those of nature, are purely subjective responses of pleasure or pain disconnected from intellectual or ethical concerns. According to this view, when one is enthralled with a landscape, one cares little about its biology or geology; indeed, one does not even care whether it is real.[13] Others regard imagination as the core of nature appreciation. The pleasure of a prospect, according to this view, derives from one's imaginative engagement with it.[14] Noel Carroll has worried that Carlson may have overintellectualized the human experience of nature at the expense of the importance of emotional engagement. Driving through the countryside would only truly involve appreciation of nature if one understood large-scale agricultural practices; responding positively, or at least profoundly, to a wildflower would necessitate not just knowing its name but also its evolutionary history. Carroll worries that this leaves out one important kind of nature appreciation—the ordinary experiences we all have had upon standing at the bottom of a raging waterfall or watching a bird in flight, when all we really know is that water is cascading or that some sort of bird is going somewhere. Carroll does not deny that there is always a cognitive element in emotional response. But "it is far from clear that all the emotions appropriately aroused in us by nature are rooted in cognition of the sort derived from natural history."[15] He does not think Carlson's arguments need to be completely abandoned, but he does think that we must also accept nonscientific arousal in nature as genuine aesthetic appreciation of nature. Stan Godlovitch further worries that Carlson does not leave room for the "mystery" that he thinks characterizes many of our experiences of nature.[16]

I certainly want to make room for the role of pleasure, imagination, emotion, and even mysteriousness in the experience of nature; as I said earlier, this sort of awe often accounts for individuals becoming interested in learning more about nature in the first place. Certainly we have all had "wow" experiences in the absence of any, or much, information about what we see or hear or smell or taste or feel; they are often among the most memorable experiences we have and contribute significantly to the meaning of life. Are expert experiences better than these?

I am reluctant to "rank" various ways of responding to nature. But even if it were possible to rank them, I see no point in, or necessity for, doing it in general. However, if we want to develop a basis for rational evaluation of a landscape's ecological sustainability, I am convinced that we must stress the cognitive. A patch of purple loosestrife, with its brilliant color, may cause a lot of pleasure. A fawn at a forest's edge may stimulate tender emotions, particularly in those of us who suffer from the "Bambi syndrome"—a tendency to sentimentalize this animal. A large expanse of closely clipped, deep-green grass may cause soothing flights of imagination. But all of these objects threaten certain biosystems, and only someone whose aesthetic response is based on knowledge will act in ways that are sustainable ecologically and, ultimately, aesthetically. Even a theorist such as Emily Brady, who favors an imaginative model of nature appreciation, finally agrees that one's imaginings must take into account the *integrity* of the object.[17] I do not see how the concept of integrity can be explained without relying on *knowledge* of the object and its relationships to other biota.

The Focus of Aesthetic Attention

What do we mean by *aesthetic* attention? Two definitions or characterizations that I have developed elsewhere might seem to conflict with Carlson's knowledge-based model of the appreciation of nature. Resolving the conflict, I believe, will advance us toward connecting ecology and aesthetics.

For precision's sake I include these formal definitions:

I. *F* is an aesthetic feature of an object or event *O* in a culture *C*, if and only if *F* is an intrinsic property of *O* and *F* is considered worthy of attention in *C*, that is, in *C* it is generally believed that attending to *F* (perceiving and/or reflecting upon *F*) will be rewarded.

II. *F* is an intrinsic property of *O* if and only if direct inspection of *O* is a necessary condition for verifying the claim that *O* is *F*, and, if someone knows the meaning of *F*, then (under normal conditions) direct inspection of *O* is a sufficient condition for verifying the claim that *O* is *F*.[18]

(The reader should be alerted to the fact that my use of *intrinsic* may differ from the ways other authors in this book and other philosophers use the term.) What my definitions boil down to is the fact that one has to see (or hear or smell or in some way directly perceive) something for oneself in order to have an aesthetic experience of the feature in question; and if one knows the meaning of the term referring to that feature, then this direct perception is all one needs to verify the presence or absence of that feature. (Typically direct perception involves just using one or more of the five senses; however, instruments such as microscopes or binoculars are also common in aesthetic experiences of nature.) An artistic example may help to make the definitions clearer. How a painting looks—its colors, its shapes, its composition—is what matters aesthetically; a painting's intrinsic properties account for aesthetic experiences of it, and in order to claim that one is having an aesthetic experience, one must look and see at least some of these intrinsic properties. Extrinsic properties are properties whose presence or absence cannot be settled simply by looking. I look at a painting and see how the shapes are balanced. If I know the meaning of balance, looking is both necessary and sufficient for an aesthetic experience of the balance. This is not true of "painted in 1717." Verification of this requires more than direct inspection of the work.

I do not think that extrinsic features necessarily get in the way of an aesthetic experience; indeed, they may direct attention to intrinsic features. Thus, knowing that a piece was written in 1717 may very well direct attention to features of the work that are indeed intrinsic to it and a focus of aesthetic experience—to the use of sonata form, for instance. (I shall say more about this sort of connection later.)

Here is the rub. Carlson (rightly, I claim) asserts that knowledge concerning the way in which natural systems operate is crucial for aesthetic appreciation of nature. Ecologists, as they come to understand the environment better, point to the kinds of information that one must have to understand how ecosystems work. William Romme refers to "inconspicuous but ecologically important plants" that contribute to the health of ecosystems (chapter 8). Many of the details of the ways in which individual landscapes work are not only inconspicuous, they are invisible. And if they cannot be perceived, how, given my two definitions above, can they be part of an aesthetic experience? Raging waterfalls, colorful sunsets, nicely shaped trees, or leaping deer pose no problem; all are intrinsic features of landscapes according to my definition and certainly are identified in many cultural traditions as worthy of attention. But other ecologically relevant features (what Carroll calls "natural history") are neither.

Here are some examples of the sort of "nonperceivable" facts that are increasingly commonplace within landscape ecology and that might seem aesthetically irrelevant if definitions I and II above are interpreted in a straightforward manner:

1. Wetlands are ecologically valuable because they provide a drainage system that removes certain toxins from runoff water before it reaches streams and rivers. This drainage is not directly perceivable. Is knowledge about it thus not part of aesthetic appreciation of wetlands?

2. Following disturbances such as high winds or fire, landscapes often appear quite devastated. But someone with knowledge in silviculture will know what succession of vegetation is likely to occur. The rest of us, unable to imagine what may follow, will concentrate on what is simply charred ruins; we may see a "burner" as a destroyer, not as an aesthetic hero. And even if I find the fire itself beautiful, how much will the thrill I get from watching it increase if I am told what the differences in undergrowth will likely be in the coming months or years?

3. A rare orchid, *Calypso bulbosa*, grows in some, but not all, mossy swamps dominated by old white cedar trees in the northern third of Wisconsin. Even experts are puzzled by the fact that cedar stands that appear identical do not support these orchids. They speculate that crucial information about the biosystem has eluded them.[19] Suppose one had the missing information; would one's aesthetic appreciation of the stands with or without calypso change? How much does just knowing the different names (a nonperceivable) of these flowers, commonly grouped as "lady slippers," yield in the way of *aesthetic* pleasure?

4. Beetles are incredibly numerous. There are 400,000 species of them, as compared to an estimated 8,000 species of mammals. They are also extraordinarily resistant to radiation and thus, as ecologist Eville Gorham puts it, are "waiting in the wings to take over center stage" should there be a nuclear holocaust.[20] Most people find beetles quite ugly and are actually glad for their general invisibility. Would knowing that they are around—just under

that log, for instance, and likely to be for a long time—enrich or diminish aesthetic appreciation?

5. Increasingly ecologists have become aware of what they call "edge effects." Landscapes consist of patches, each with its own biota, that interact with one another, particularly at the boundaries. Certain interior species flourish only when an appropriate distance from the edge is maintained. Harvesting trees via clear-cutting of patches has a disproportionate effect on these interior-loving organisms. If edges become overabundant, habitat for rare interior populations may lose out to species that are not threatened.[21] In the United States, departments of natural resources have typically had as their primary goal maintaining large populations of game animals and birds that frequent forest edges. One effect has been a decrease in the number of interior songbirds. Knowing this, if you see a deer or grouse at a forest's edge, should you have a negative aesthetic experience—or at least refrain from making a judgment until you know the status of the interior species?

6. A last example: Ecosystems managers typically rally for native species, knowing as they do that importing exotic species to an area can often have devastating intrusive results. Does that mean that one should feel aesthetic repulsion at the sight of a nonnative bird or tree? What about nonnative species that seem to fit right in, the way China pheasants have in the Midwest? Must I feel guilt when I respond positively to seeing one of them in the countryside?

All of these examples involve nonperceivables—properties that cannot be immediately seen (or heard or smelled or tasted or felt). In general, it is very difficult to say what ecological health *looks like*, as Joan Nassauer discusses in this volume (see chapter 4) and elsewhere.[22] Many of the examples above involve plan-

ning or thinking in terms of scales (both spatial and temporal) that go far beyond human experience, even as imagined. Aesthetic experience, as I have characterized it, is immediate—focused on what is present in the moment. So how can one explain how knowledge concerning the nonperceivables that determine ecological health is important, perhaps even necessary, for aesthetic appreciation of nature?

The explanation is twofold, with the second (the topic of the next section) being a specific case of the first general point. First, knowledge of certain nonperceivables is generally relevant to (and hence even a part of) aesthetic experience in just the way that certain extrinsic features of objects or events are relevant to experiences of intrinsic features of those objects or events. Elsewhere I have defined *aesthetic relevance* very simply as follows: "A statement (or gesture) is aesthetically relevant if and only if it draws attention (perception, reflection) to an aesthetic feature of an object or event."[23] Strictly speaking, an aesthetic property is intrinsic; broadly speaking (by reference to what draws attention to an intrinsic property) anything aesthetically relevant can be construed as an aesthetic property. Does it matter that a painting is located in a particular museum? Only when we know how knowledge of this is or is not causally related to what is actually perceived or reflected upon can this question be answered. An extrinsic fact about a piece of music—being written in 1717, for instance—will be aesthetically relevant just in case knowing this fact causes the listener to attend to an intrinsic property of the music, its particular structure, for instance. Knowing that a painting was made in Italy in 1540 will cause someone who is "in the know" to experience in a special way the glow around the head of a man who is attached to two pieces of wood nailed together in a T-shape. When one has an aesthetic experience, there are always intrinsic properties of the object of the experience that one can claim to be attending to and that one believes are at least a partial cause of the experience. But both the attention to the intrinsic properties and the directing of attention can themselves be caused by awareness of properties not intrinsic to the object.

Just as works of art must often be "read"—with extrinsic information determining the reading that results—so landscapes will be read in terms of the knowledge one brings to the experiences of them. Even intrinsic properties (such as the number of hidden beetles or the presence or absence of microorganisms affecting a species of orchid) may not be directly perceivable without action that would seem extraordinary when viewing works of art—digging up the soil or using a microscope. But the knowledge that a microorganism is present, or that drainage is taking place, or that too many deer may result in too few songbirds may very well cause a viewer to perceive genuinely intrinsic properties that would otherwise be overlooked. Just learning the *names* of wildflowers (surely an extrinsic property) does sometimes make it more likely that we will see the flowers. As one learns more about the invisible things that make particular ecosystems healthy, landscapes begin to *look* more or less healthy. As aestheticians I think we should concentrate more effort on determining the extent to which looking healthy and looking good or beautiful are related, and give more attention to specific ways in which knowledge influences particular aesthetic experiences. Thus, I want to suggest a second, more specific way of understanding how ecological knowledge directs attention to aesthetic properties and vice versa.

Categories of Aesthetic and Ecological Attention

In a 1992 essay, "The Appearance of Ecological Systems As a Matter of Policy," Nassauer insists that reliance on what is typically considered the picturesque in landscape design will not protect ecosystems. Designers must use "social signs" to indicate ecological function. "The general principle that we can use to guide design and policy is to label ecological function with socially recognized signs of human intentions for the landscape, setting expected characteristics of landscape beauty and care side by side with characteristics of ecological health."[24] The development of *specific* principles, I believe, challenges philosophical aestheticians to explain more fully what is involved in aesthetic landscape preferences and how it might relate to ecological sustainability. Thus, what I would like to attempt here is an extension and elaboration of Nassauer's general principle that is related to contemporary cognitive models of nature appreciation of the sort that Carlson has presented. (Philosophers will also see essential connections in what follows to Kendall Walton's "categories of art" and Arnold Berleant's "aesthetics of engagement."[25])

Some of the factual examples I gave earlier deal with matters of scale where it is more difficult to see a direct causal connection between the nonperceivable and the directly perceived. In landscape ecology and conservation biology, categories of scale are emerging as primary factors. As one research team puts it, "No issues attract as much attention within conservation biology as those connected with geographic scale and distribution: How large should reserves intended to maintain diversity be? How should they be arranged relative to each other? Should they be connected via corridors? Do species common within old growth require areas of some minimum size?"[26] Due attention to scale can produce the "problem of nonperceivables," which I raised earlier. When stretches of time and space become too big, human beings can no longer "see" them—and hence it is hard to conceive of how aesthetic experience at such scale is possible. This problem was recognized early by Aristotle, who pointed out that things too big or too small cannot be beautiful because they cannot be held in the memory. Therefore, he insisted, the action of a play must cover just the amount of time that a human being can take in. More recently Lyle has acknowledged that the holistic treatment of landscape rarely works because "it is so difficult to see . . . a vast landscape as a whole."[27]

To some extent the problem of nonperceivability at large or small scales is handled by the general method I suggested earlier, whereby extrinsic information directs attention to intrinsic properties. But the scale factor in ecology also has important connections of a different kind to the aesthetic appreciation of nature. Ecologists must pay attention not only to different scales but to different types or categories of landscapes. Obviously, what is studied in a desert will not be studied in an ocean. An increased awareness and understanding of the primary role of categories of scale and landscape type in ecology has suggested to me that philosophical aestheticians should pay closer attention to the role of scale and landscape categories. Just as ecologists try to avoid making "category mistakes" of scale or type, so aestheticians should try to avoid analogous mistakes.

In discussions of works of art we are accustomed to the fact that certain features are category-specific. Properties possessed by a measure of music will not typically be possessed by the work as a whole. What characterizes a line of a poem (having 22 syllables, for instance) will not typically characterize a stanza.[28] Observations "upscale" affect observations "downscale." Furthermore, one must know the type of work one is dealing with. "It's an epic" will direct attention to couplets or plot development in a way that "it's a sonnet" will not—since sonnets have neither couplets nor plots.

Category mistakes have consequences for the experiences of artworks. Someone who mistakes a satire for a serious political essay, to cite another example, will miss or misinterpret many important intrinsic properties. Similarly, landscape-aesthetic-scale category mistakes have consequences for the appreciation of na-

ture. Before I describe some specific landscape-aesthetic categories, I want to mention some of the mistakes (many of these have been acknowledged by landscape architects) that my proposal is intended to help avoid.

One of the most serious criticisms that have been leveled against conventional design practices is that designers have too often acted as "beauticians," that is, as if their task were to "prettify" by covering up, not really altering, underlying flaws. (Several of Chris Faust's photographs in this volume show this.) This criticism is not just a recent complaint. At the turn of this century in the Midwest, such landscape architects as Jens Jensen argued that Beaux Arts formalism or romantically picturesque standards that had a grip on city planning should give way to more regionally appropriate styles. Thus, the Prairie School called for greater use of indigenous species and materials to express the spirit of the midwestern United States. But the use of particular design principles may not be a mistake simply because of regional inappropriateness. It may result from what others have described as landscape architects' undue emphasis on "scenery." Clearly agreeing with Carlson, Paul Hellmund writes, "[O]ne of the traditional concerns of landscape architects has been preserving or enhancing views. But, narrowly pursuing visual goals by trying to capture or re-create a static image can have tremendous costs, both financial . . . and ecological."[29] Hellmund is worried, for example, that trying to offer motorists beautiful vistas may threaten wildlife migration corridors. I would also like to suggest that there may be *aesthetic* costs when landscape architects treat all landscapes as if they were located within a single landscape-aesthetic category.

Another mistake is a tendency to leave human beings out of "nature." *Natural* is, I believe, a term whose meaning changes when there is a shift in aesthetic scale. What is natural on a farm or in a city will not be natural in a desert or forest. J. B. Jackson has criticized the ways in which undisturbed, conventionally photogenic landscapes have been taken as the sole standard of ecological and aesthetic integrity.[30] He has also discussed Edgar Anderson's work on the effect of human beings on plants, not all of which has been deleterious. Sunflowers, for instance, which grow only in poor soil where grass does not overtake them, thrive in areas where humans have depleted nutrients. This provides an example of "how man has not only destroyed ecosystems but also devised *new* ones."[31] Jackson's most famous nonconformist defense is of mobile homes—a human artifact that may be as natural in the landscape as the beaver dam:

> Indeed, it almost seems as if those shortcomings which critics never tire of mentioning—the lack of individuality, the functional incompleteness, the dependence on outside services and amenities, and even the lack of such traditional architectural qualities as firmness, commodity, and delight—all are what make the trailer useful and attractive to many of its occupants.[32]

But even those who are not generally put off by trailer courts will not relish them in a wilderness. What counts as "natural" depends on the category within which one is operating.

Another category-relative term is *stewardship*. What counts as care for the land or sound management practice in a forest does not translate directly into care at the urban level. (I will say more about this when I discuss specific landscape-aesthetic categories.) *Biodiversity* is another ambiguous term. One often comes across the following sort of admonition: "We want to conserve all cultural approaches that are compatible with conserving biodiversity."[33] Reed Noss and Allen Cooperrider write, "[A]reas set aside to fulfill recreational or esthetic objectives do not necessarily meet biodiversity conservation goals."[34] But is the converse true? Too often the unexamined assumption is that biodiverse environments will automatically meet aesthetic goals.

What I hope attention to landscape-aesthetic categories can do is to undermine the often too glibly held attitude that we all know and agree about what in nature is beautiful. Jackson and others have made us wonder about mobile homes and fast-food restaurants. Leopold urged us to think not about "building roads into lovely country, but of building receptivity into the still unlovely mind."[35] But are all roads into lovely places ugly? Don't some of Faust's photos show otherwise? In his report of discussions with David Brower, an early leader of Friends of the Earth, John McPhee describes how Brower's early love of trains affected his aesthetic sensitivities: "A railroad over the Sierra is all-right. It was there. An interstate highway is an assault on the terrain."[36] Lyle wonders why Dutch windmills are so lovely and powerlines are not.[37] Are trailer courts always ugly? Again, one can see in Faust's photos that agreement about such questions is not universal.

Hepburn has urged, "If we wish to attach very high value to the appreciation of natural beauty, we must be able to show that more is involved in such appreciation than the pleasant, unfocused enjoyment of a picnic place, or a fleeting and distanced impression of countryside through a touring-coach window, or obligatory visits to standard viewpoints."[38] I believe that one component of progress in understanding more about such appreciation and hence of avoiding some of the mistakes described earlier is a greater awareness of environmental aesthetic categories and aesthetic scales.

There are various ways of thinking about scale, of course. To ecologists and geographers, scale is a quantitative concept defined in terms of sheer numbers of organisms or patch acreage or mapping grain. Just as the set of intrinsic properties valued in a sonnet is not identical with the set of intrinsic properties valued in an epic (these artworks have different "scales"), so the set of intrinsic properties valued in a bonsai garden is not identical to the set of intrinsic properties valued in a vista from a mountaintop or airplane. Due attention to a rough continuum ranging from the microscopic to the macroscopic is essential. Awareness that one is judging a small, medium, large, or very large area is required if one is to avoid category mistakes.

Although size is relevant, aesthetic evaluation obviously goes beyond quantification. Another important, more traditionally entrenched aesthetic category is the perception of *the purpose(s) behind the particular manipulation of a medium*.[39] Attention to purpose will be as important in assessing nature cognitively as it is in assessing artworks. Some landscape units are what they are almost completely as a result of an individual's or group's aesthetic intentions; in others, intentional design is a lesser factor in the way they are. At each scale the intention of the designer affects the aesthetic properties meant to be a focus of attention. Designing sustainable landscapes requires relating the geographers' and ecologists' attention to scale and biota type that is so important to their work with the aestheticians' attention to category and manipulation of medium in an attempt to draw attention to intrinsic properties that reward perception and reflection.

Here are examples of categories that differ considerably from one another with respect to the extent to which their intrinsic properties are what they are as a direct result of the particular purposes of human manipulation and intervention:

1. Landscape art

2. Parks and gardens

3. Managed urban/suburban landscapes

4. Managed rural landscapes (primarily farms but also mines or other "worked" nonurban areas)

5. Relatively pristine managed landscapes

6. Relatively pristine unmanaged landscapes

Specific examples of each category will be discussed shortly. At the first level we have discrete artifacts (objects or events) that have landscape elements as core components. At the final level we have landscapes in which human manipulation drops out—though I describe them as only "relatively" pristine because such human effects as acid rain influence even the wildest environments. In between, and even within a particular element, a continuum of intent and possibility for control exists. Individual artists often have a greater control over what they produce and a firmer image of what they want to produce than urban designers, farmers, or wilderness managers. But we need to bear in mind that "reading" intentionality into a landscape will be greatly influenced by cultural factors. For example, many people see a garden as more intentionally determined than a farm, though in fact the former may be more a matter of chance.

Each category has its own history—both natural and cultural; and these histories have a tremendous influence on the properties that are considered relevant to an aesthetic evaluation of the entities within these elements. Martin Warnke has described the ways in which political values can be read off of landscapes;[40] for example, roads converge at castles, churches, and city squares, and the size of fields reflects equal or unequal distribution of wealth. Nonaesthetic values affect one's preferences. Do you see a castle or church as a positive sign of stability or a negative sign of oppression? Curt Meine describes in this volume (chapter 3) how the sociopolitical grid permeates the design and perception of many American landscapes. Sociopolitical values affect, and are in turn affected by, aesthetic values.

This interdependence is also true of aesthetic and ecological values—or at least they should be, if we hope to have sustainable landscapes and hence sustainable landscape aesthetics. For every site or design project, an aesthetic as well as ecological inventory must be made. Other writers have proposed inventories, of course, but too often they have been formulaic; that is, they have assumed that one can simply apply a list of a priori properties like "vividness" and "uniqueness." But categories are culture-bound; descriptions of sites will vary to a greater or lesser extent from culture to culture, both temporally and spatially. For example, the presence of red barns in a rural setting is not universally valued. Just as one cannot expect all ecological features to be found at every site (the presence of a particular microorganism, for instance), so aesthetic categories and the properties relevant therein can only be determined after a site has been fully studied. Categories used elsewhere may provide guidelines but should never be simply reapplied without being "translated" for each new project. Even when one is deeply fluent in a culture and tremendously knowledgeable about the ecosystems in which one is working, one must constantly remind oneself that disagreement is possible. Individuals who share a culture often disagree and have inconsistent goals (as Judith A. Martin and Sam Bass Warner Jr. show in chapter 6). Scientists also disagree, of course. Eville Gorham's watchwords "If you don't know, go slow" should provide guidance in environmental aesthetics as well as in ecology. The best assessments will be those produced through holistic, interdisciplinary work—a theme that unifies all of the essays in this volume.

Some examples will be useful, perhaps; but these can only be interpreted as prototypes, since actual analysis must be site-specific. Even prototypes are local—for what counts generally as beautiful or healthy in one sociogeographical locale may not apply in others. In the upper Midwest of the United States, what people tend to like in medium-sized urban parks is serenity, clean water flowing in fountains, a variety of plants and flowers arranged in recognizable patterns, careful maintenance (often expressed as "neatness"), and wildlife that is clean and friendly; and what they tend to dislike is messiness, stagnant or dirty water, and

"vermin."[41] I have put *vermin* in scare quotes, for which animals are classified as such will differ from site to site. Rats, for example, are acceptable—even enjoyed—in relatively pristine landscapes. In large, relatively pristine unmanaged landscapes, people want vast outlooks and majestic, sublime scenery and are irritated if there are too many other people around or if trails appear overmaintained. They even like "messiness" here, though of course they will not typically use that word to describe what they see and admire.

Serious mistakes will occur if one ignores the fact that values are specific to a particular location. As Nassauer has pointed out, what counts as "messy" at the scale of gardens will not count as messy in a forest.[42] The presence of windmills may enhance a landscape at one point and diminish it at another scale or at a different level of manipulation. Adding a windmill will probably not enhance the beauty of a relatively pristine vista or a postmodern city center. The fact that people treasure human-built structures along the Rhine River but not on some stretches of the Colorado River is not inconsistent when one realizes that different kinds of sites are involved. The Rhine is much more urban than it is pristine. In aesthetics as in ecology, we must first be clear about the locale and the relevant positive and negative features if we are to avoid inappropriate or misguided assessments and designs.

Earlier I referred to the fact that categories have a history. I want to provide more detail about some examples in order to show the importance of reminding oneself continually about the appropriateness of the features one attends to.

As with all art, twentieth-century landscape art has changed dramatically from what may still be the vernacular stereotype of landscape art—a nineteenth-century Hudson Valley representation, for instance. Viewers must thus attune themselves to category shifts while remaining conscious of the artistic traditions in which artists work. In Mel Chin's *Spirit*, a barrel (symbol of commerce and/or the effects of alcohol abuse) precariously balances on a rope made of samples of vanishing indigenous prairie grasses. It derives its power not from the viewer's admiration of the picturesque but from the awareness of the forceful way in which Chin has symbolized the impact of European immigrants on the American prairie. Nonetheless, it still depends on the viewer's close attention to many intrinsic properties (shape, proportion, balance) resulting from as meticulous a manipulation of the medium as that found in nineteenth-century landscape paintings.

Other landscape works of Chin seem to me less clearly located in the category of landscape art. In *Revival Fields*, Chin's interest in chemical pollution led to his collaboration in 1990 with a soil scientist, Dr. Rufus Chaney. Though Chin did use some conventional design principles—circular plantings within a square, for instance—the main goal of this project was experimentation with "hyperaccumulators": plants that absorb large amounts of minerals and metals and thus act as toxic sponges to restore the soil in which they grow.[43] Chin and Chaney's field was not found in a museum but in a landfill. It no longer exists, and even when it did it was very difficult to get to and hence to perceive. Enabling attention to intrinsic design properties was simply not the primary intention. It is difficult to do an aesthetic evaluation of such "works" when there is uncertainty about the category into which they fit; the ability to provide aesthetically appropriate descriptions is lacking. In some ways, Chin's work is rural, for the toxic metals absorbed in the plants were meant to be "harvested" or "mined." Perhaps another category needs to be created. (This has, after all, often happened in the history of art.) Or one object may need to be evaluated according to different categories. For example, the environmental artist Lynne Hull's work *Raptor Roost* provides a roost for birds that will not electrocute them, and she does "hydroglyphs"—drawings in desert stones that provide water storage for animals. The shape of the roost or the delicacy of the drawing is aesthetically pleasing in the category of small or medium landscape art; the fact that habitat is sustained and often present will be characteristic of aesthetic pleasure within the category of larger parks or relatively pristine landscapes.[44]

Many works of landscape art move upscale or cross categories into the realm of parks and gardens and vice versa. Indeed, Mara Miller titles her very interesting book on gardens *The Garden As Art*. She defines a garden as "any purposeful arrangement of natural objects (such as sand, water, plants, rocks, etc.) with exposure to the sky or open air, in which the form is not fully accounted for by purely practical considerations such as convenience."[45] This definition also covers parks. Both are marked by what she calls an "excess of form"—and this is what connects gardens to artworks. Biology and culture, she argues, intersect. Biology is "categorized" via culture.[46] Gardens and parks are often designed with wildlife habitat in mind, but the territory or corridor provided therein differs significantly from that which guides designers at the level, for example, of managed wilderness. (In this sense, "national parks" are not *parks* at all, a fact that both aestheticians and ecologists should remember.) Ornamentality, such as that provided via topiary, for instance, is quite valuable in city gardens and parks; it can easily become excessive in residential lawns and would be jarring or absurd in a relatively pristine landscape.

Urban landscapes are, of course, very mixed and perhaps can only be fully comprehended as such. Parks must coexist with landfills. (Indeed some landfills have been turned into golf courses.) Concrete jungles provide habitat for raptors. Within the same residential lot one finds native and exotic species. One simply cannot plan rationally for anything except a multifunctional domain. Though trees within cities certainly provide ornamentation and some wildlife corridor, it is unreasonable to expect them in the vast numbers that will result in majestic forests. Safety will contribute positively to aesthetic experiences of cities and the open spaces therein; this is not usually managed for in the same way in landscape artworks or pristine landscapes. Rutherford Platt's history of urban open-space paradigms shows how factors relating to aesthetic value have changed in North America over the past two centuries.[47] He identifies eight paradigms that characterize nonnative settlements. They have overlapped but are roughly chronological: a civic/agrarian colonial commons, picturesque parks, areas providing public health, cities beautiful with their monumented plazas, garden cities with greenbelts separating zones, preserved ecological sites bordering cities, recreational areas, and restored or preserved ecological sites within cities. None should be given automatic priority in urban planning; both vegetable patches and preserved wetlands clearly provide citizens with aesthetic opportunities. But it is crucial for city planners to keep these straight. A single park zoned for both gardening and wetland would fail in achieving much success for either—unless it is designed to distinguish clearly and label inherently each category.

Of course, neither wetlands nor gardens are by any means the most typical urban landscape in an age in which most open space in cities (at least in the United States) is devoted to parking lots and human corridors. Martin and Warner discuss the conflicting policies and values that create tensions in city planning (see chapter 6). As the fact that people value both wide and narrow streets shows, people like different things depending on the context. Applying values from other categories must be done carefully and consciously. At the same time, undue observance of conventional or vernacular values (e.g., insisting that all city lawns be a uniform height, green, and edged with sidewalks and

curbs) has also caused a great deal of environmental harm. Martin and Warner suggest ways in which awareness and open discussion of conflicting interests can have positive results. Recognition of ways in which particular means and particular ends are related (or conflicting) supports the category-bound cognitive model of landscape appreciation that I am advocating.

Nassauer's research on the aesthetic preferences of rural dwellers is very telling here.[48] Farmers tend to aesthetically appreciate landscapes that signal stewardship. *Stewardship* is not itself a sufficiently specific concept; caring both by fertilizing and refusing to fertilize are signs of stewardship to different persons. What is category-specific is the sort of care and control that is ecologically sound in specific biosystems. The fact that a city or rural resident exerts a great deal of effort in the creation of a particular landscape does not in itself guarantee health. Signs of pollution are not always obvious; effects of fertilizers, irrigation, or overgrazing are not immediately nor easily perceived, particularly by viewers whose only experiences of farms are those had speeding through or above the countryside. Rural dwellers themselves are often oblivious to the fact that what pleases them visually may hide or cover unsound ecological practices. Contour planting—a component of many farms still found lovely by many farmers—is usually accompanied by the unsustainable use of chemical fertilizers and weed-killers. One problem for designers and philosophers is developing a "language" that will communicate ecological health within this category. Experimental farming techniques will not be seen as beautiful until the ecologically valuable properties of this landscape type are more readily recognized.

The term *nature* for most people typically connotes relatively pristine landscapes. Vastness, majesty, presence of a wide variety of plants and wildlife, vistas viewed from elevated outlooks—in general "the scenic" is what people like. Even in areas that one knows are highly managed, one generally prefers as little trace of that management as possible. Some things, for example, clearly marked trails, will be acceptable within managed, but not within unmanaged, relatively pristine landscapes. There have been several excellent studies of the ways in which human perceptions and assessments of wilderness have changed across the centuries and of how they differ geographically and culturally.[49] These changes can be read, for example, in tourism trends. There has been less study of what is valued in "nature" in rural or urban environments. Ecologists—largely for aesthetic reasons, I think—have tended to concentrate on relatively pristine landscapes and too often have assumed that what is beautiful there must be what is beautiful everywhere else. City "beautification" has too often taken the form of planting along corridors whose concreted soil produces unlovely, usually soon dead trees. Nassauer describes ways in which paradigms of "scenic beauty" have often widened the gap between vernacular conceptions of beauty and ecological conceptions of health (see chapter 4).

Most people assert that the presence of human structures in pristine landscapes, especially unmanaged ones, is a negative factor. But further investigation of this reinforces the claim that specificity of category is a crucial factor of aesthetic appreciation of nature.[50] Most people admit that not every human structure in a relatively pristine landscape is distracting; coming across a log cabin is not upsetting in the way that coming across a fast-food chain restaurant would be—indeed, the cabin might heighten an already positive experience. What is the difference? The answer lies in fuller awareness of how what is "natural" is category-specific. Since human beings are part of nature, signs of action that are "native" are not jarring. Fast-food restaurants are landmarks that we expect and are therefore appropriate to, and even admired by, some at some urban scales—those urban patches where the population of meat-eating, economically able bipeds has at-

tained a certain level. Abandoned shacks in urban areas are eyesores. The occasional abandoned hut—but not a busy Pizza Hut—will be fine in relatively pristine landscapes. Thus, the term *presence of human structures* is in itself too vague to explain positive or negative aesthetic response. Attention to scale and to degree of manipulation is essential to making this term precise enough to guide planning.

Relating Aesthetics and Ecology

I have talked about the mistakes that can be made if one fails to attend to category specificity in the aesthetic appreciation of nature. But how else might such attention be positively useful? If landscapes architects are to take advantage of aesthetic values as they design ecologically sound landscapes, then they must make the aesthetic properties accessible. Ecologically sustainable landscapes will only be possible if due attention is given to the cultural values that determine people's choices and actions. I suggested earlier that a general strategy for drawing attention to aesthetic properties consists of showing viewers how nonperceivables or factors in themselves not aesthetically valued are connected to the perceivable intrinsic properties that members of a community consider worthy of attention and reflection. I would now like to suggest another way in which designers might exploit aesthetic values, one that utilizes aesthetic and ecological categories and one that underscores the relation between aesthetics and ecology.

In general *showing* consists of using gestures or signs that point to something and draw a viewer's attention. There are, of course, many theories of signifying, and discussing them is beyond the scope of this essay. Briefly, a sign can be "natural" (e.g., a sign is related causally to its referent: smoke signifies fire) or "conventional" (e.g., a word in a spoken language stands for something:

cup signifies something from which one drinks). Design must use both kinds of signs. By having a certain kind of tree pointed out, one may look more closely to see if (or at least value the possibility that) a particular kind of orchid may be present, for some trees are natural signs of some varieties of orchids to people who have adequate knowledge of the biosystem in which they occur together. Nassauer's research is again helpful here, for she has proved that simply putting up a placard (a "conventional" sign) that says that an area is being cared for via certain conservation practices enhances the aesthetic value of the area for most viewers.[51] In this volume (chapter 4) she details some ways in which a "double vision" is being created in an area of St. Paul, Minnesota, so that people see both ecological and aesthetic health. Beautiful trees that play a central role in a savanna ecosystem are readily valued for their beauty. Indigenous prairie plants are neatly trimmed, thereby giving cues that frame both ecological awareness and aesthetic pleasure. Signs that simply help us know where we are in a system (for instance, "You have just crossed the Continental Divide") may also enhance aesthetic experience.

In each aesthetic category there are properties valued by members of a community: carefully laid out patches, vistas, winding roads, monuments, clearly marked trails, colorful forbs, bright lights. I want to suggest that these clear indicators may be borrowed and used in a variety of environments to signify that attention to aesthetic values has been given by designers. Not every property is a clear indicator, of course. Silence may be a positive indicator of a serene garden but not of an exciting city; it may even be a negative indicator in a forest where one had hoped to hear songbirds. Nor will all indicators cross categories. A mass of lights will not be appropriately borrowed from the city as a sign of aesthetic attentiveness in a rural or pristine landscape. A chaotic jumble of species valued at the relatively pristine level may not translate automatically to city parks. But

clearly marked (i.e., "socially signed," to use Nassauer's phrase), a chaotic patch in a city's open space may come to have aesthetic value for residents if they read it as a sign of an attempt at achieving biodiversity within urban boundaries. Formal properties such as balance, color, or shape (valued at rather small scales, for example, in residential yards) become signs of due attention to aesthetic amenities at larger scales, even in relatively pristine landscapes. Whether the signs actually work, of course, depends on the knowledge of the "reader." Park boards that opt for less mowing will only be reelected if the public sees too much mown turf as a sign of an unhealthy ecosystem. A wetland initially read as a dirty swamp may be read as a park if there are boardwalks or species markers.

Artists are in the business of providing communities with new metaphors that challenge and hence broaden our comprehension of the world.[52] I suggest that landscape designers can do the same thing, and that one way of providing new vision is by crossing categories. Once aesthetic and ecological studies have been produced that take careful account of the categories specific to a site, one is in a position to ask whether properties valued at other sites can fruitfully be borrowed and used. Like artists who expand languages by describing or portraying one thing as another (a petroglyph as water source), landscape architects may be able to expand their vocabularies and those of their patrons by borrowing clear signs from other categories. Of course, this will be successful only if we have a clearer understanding of the specific properties valued at each specific site and of what the clear indicators are. The "messy" may be incorporated at smaller scales, but successful incorporation will demand deep attention to aesthetic values at the location of the particular design project.[53]

There are dangers in borrowing. Signs can be confusing, even deceptive—as when a company announces that it is employing environmentally friendly safeguards when it is not. We often have trouble knowing where we are. How many of us know the watershed or soil chemistry of our residence, for example? Honest, clear use of signs may help to alleviate the dissonance that characterizes so much of the contemporary human condition, especially when they inform us not just about the names of things but about the workings of an ecosystem as well. Details of a system that promotes category crossing for aesthetic purposes remain to be worked out. It is an area in which ecologists, landscape architects, and philosophical aestheticians may work fruitfully together in the effort to design ecologically sustainable landscapes that succeed culturally. One theme of this book is the necessity of such interdisciplinary effort, as I have urged earlier. Philosophical aestheticians need to know more about ecology and vernacular values than they often do. But ecologists and social scientists also often act in ignorance of what the "aesthetic richness" they often refer to really involves. Philosophers can help to sharpen awareness of the complex issues that underlie an often too simplistic notion of what constitutes aesthetic value and the unexamined assumption that ecological and aesthetic value always go hand in hand.

Ideally we want landscapes that show which aesthetically valuable properties and which ecologically sound properties come together, and a human population that recognizes this. We want educated people who do not destroy what they value as they seek it out—for instance, do not build houses in critical habitat for elk (see Romme, chapter 8, this volume). We aim for a public that does not, as Nassauer puts it, mistake a well-kept prairie park for a weed patch. Human-dominated landscapes can be very beautiful. Although we must fully recognize that neither aesthetics nor ecology can be *reduced* to the other, there are examples of connections that can be used to show that an aesthetic-ecological "fit" exists. Hedgerows that maintain diversity will be perceived as creating pleasing contoured patterns. Colorful native flowers will be read as an indication of soil unpoisoned by harsh chemicals. An adequate canopy will signify the presence of songbirds. Too rapid runoff of rainwater will go hand in hand with the perception of concrete curbs as ugly. Aesthetic and ecological soundness will be perceived simultaneously. The upshot will be, I hope, that health and beauty begin to come together. If this happens, then both aesthetic and ecological sustainability may result.

Acknowledgments

For many of the ideas in this essay, I am deeply indebted to the faculty and graduate students who participated in the seminars that led to the publication of this book.

Notes

1. C. H. Nilon, "Urban Wildlife Management in 2020," in *2020 Vision: Meeting the Fish and Wildlife Conservation Challenges of the 21st Century*, T. J. Peterle, ed., proceedings of a symposium held at the 53rd Midwest Fish and Wildlife Conference, Des Moines, Iowa, December 3, 1991, p. 61.

2. A. Leopold, "The Land Ethic," in *Sand County Almanac* (London: Oxford University Press, 1996), p. 61.

3. M. M. Eaton, "Where's the Spear? The Nature of Aesthetic Relevance," *British Journal of Aesthetics*, (January 1992): 1–12.

4. A. Carlson, "Appreciation and the Natural Environment," *Journal of Aesthetics and Art Criticism*, (spring 1979): 267–276. I have a minor quibble with Carlson's view that nature is "unproduced." If scientists and designers are right about the extent of human dominance in the global landscape, then perhaps nature is less unproduced than Carlson believes. Certainly many environments that people describe as "natural" are highly designed and managed. Indeed, many ecologists and

landscape architects have recently drawn attention to the extent to which people are made to think or feel as if they are "out in nature" when in fact they are in highly artificial, even deceptive landscapes. A related confusion comes from widespread attitudes that exclude human beings from *nature*. Too often the very individuals who urge a renewed sense of the human being's connectedness with other organisms also talk as if people are enemies of nature. Some theorists have stopped using the term; where I want to make it clear that I am including the role of humans in landscapes or ecosystems, I shall refer to more or less "pristine" landscapes. This difference aside, I believe that Carlson's question—do we appreciate nature the way we appreciate art?—is an extremely important one, as is the answer he gives.

5. J. T. Lyle, *Regenerative Design for Sustainable Development* (New York: Wiley, 1994), p. 99.

6. Carlson, "Appreciation and the Natural Environment," p. 273.

7. A. Carlson, "Nature, Aesthetic Judgment, and Objectivity," *Journal of Aesthetics and Art Criticism* (fall 1981): 24. Carlson and A. Berleant have engaged in a debate about the nature of aesthetics and the extent to which objects with the special status of artworks regarded in a special way are the central focus of aesthetic experience. Berleant has called for an "aesthetics of engagement" in which one's whole being is relevant. In this passage of Carlson's I think the debate between him and Berleant fades, insofar as it is nature rather than art that they are interested in. An exchange between the two theorists is found in *Journal of Aesthetics and Art Criticism* 52 (spring 1994): 237–241.

8. Some theorists worry about sustainable development—a term that some other theorists consider an oxymoron. Stability, richness, productivity, and diversity of species and function are all relevant, but some of these factors play a more central role in some theories than in others. For a discussion of sustainability, see, for example, J. T. Lyle, *Design for Human Ecosystems: Landscape, Land Use, and Natural Resources* (New York: Van Nostrand Reinhold, 1985).

9. Quoted in R. T. T. Forman "Ecologically Sustainable Landscapes: The Role of Spatial Configuration," in *Changing Landscapes: An Ecological Perspective*, I. S. Zonneveld and R. T. T Forman, eds. (New York: Springer-Verlag, 1990), p. 262. Although sustainability has become an increasing problem for the globe in the twentieth century ours is not the first degenerative civilization. For example, C. Pointing provides a fascinating account of the degradation of Easter Island and other pretechnological cultures in *A Green History of the World* (New York: St. Martin's, 1991).

10. K. Clark, *Looking at Pictures* (London: John Murray, 1960), p. 16.

11. I discuss the notion of aesthetic sustainability more fully in "A Sustainable Definition of 'Art,'" forthcoming in *Theories of Art*, N. Carroll, ed. (University of Wisconsin Press)

12. R. Hepburn, "Trivial and Serious in Aesthetic Appreciation of Nature," in *Landscapes, Natural Beauty and the Arts*, S. Keman and I. Gaskill, eds. (Cambridge: Cambridge University Press, 1993), p. 68.

13. For more on the approach, see I. Kant, *Critique of Judgment*, 1790.

14. E. Brady, "Imagination, Aesthetic Experience, and Nature," forthcoming.

15. N. Carroll, "On Being Moved by Nature: Between Religion and Natural History," in *Arguing About Art*, A. Neill and A. Ridley, eds. (New York: McGraw-Hill, 1995), p. 140.

16. S. Godlovitch, "Icebreakers: Environmentalism and Natural Aesthetics," *Journal of Applied Philosophy* 11, 1994. Carlson has responded to the criticism of Carroll and Godlovitch in "Nature, Aesthetic Appreciation of Knowledge," *Journal of Aesthetics and Art Criticism* 53, no. 4 (fall 1995): 393–400.

17. Brady, "Imagination, Aesthetic Experience, and Nature."

18. These definitions are discussed in detail in M. M. Eaton, *Aesthetics and the Good Life* (Cranbury, N.J.: Associated University Press, 1989). Aesthetic attention is discussed in my "Where's the Spear?"

19. W. S. Alverson, W. Kuhlmann, and D. M. Waller, *Wild Forests: Conservation Biology and Public Policy* (Washington, D.C.: Island Press, 1994), p. 27.

20. E. Gorham, "An Ecologist's Guide to the Problems of the 21st Century," *The American Biology Teacher* 53, no. 8 (November/December 1990): 4.

21. R. F. Noss and B. Csuti, "Habitat Formation," in *Principles of Conservation Biology*, G. K. Meffe and C. R. Carrol, eds. (Sunderland, Mass.: Sinauer, 1993).

22. J. Nassauer, "The Appearance of Ecological Systems as a Matter of Policy," *Landscape Ecology* 6, no. 4 (1992): 239–250.

23. Eaton, "Where's the Spear?" pp. 1–12.

24. Nassauer, "The Appearance of Ecological Systems As a Matter of Policy," p. 248.

25. K. Walton, "Categories of Art," *Philosophical Review*, LXXIX (1970): 334–367; A. Berleant, *The Aesthetics of Environment* (Philadelphia: Temple University Press, 1992).

26. Alverson, Kuhlmann, and Waller, *Wild Forests,* p. 75. Fascinating "perceivable facts" have been uncovered by attending to less-visible holistic connections between fragmentation, edge increase, corridor interruption, and so on. For example, red-headed woodpeckers seem not to be sensitive to forest area, whereas pileated woodpeckers are never found breeding in forests of less than 100 hectares. And it is not only spatial scale that demands attention. One must also attend to temporal scale. What will a particular seashore look like in 100 or 1,000 years if certain practices are carried out now? Is it true, as Clive Ponting says (*A Green History of the World*, p. 23), that an uncultivated patch in many parts of England would revert to oak and ash forest in 150 years? For an interesting discussion of geological effects on the landscape and on human history, see H. R. Muelder and D. M. Delo, *Years of This Land: A Geographical History of the United States* (New York: D. Appleton-Century Company, 1943); and L. C. K. Shane and E. Cushing, *Quaternary Landscapes* (Minneapolis: University of Minnesota Press, 1991).

27. Lyle, *Design for Human Ecosystems*, p. 77.

28. Kendall Walton's influential work "Categories of Art" is relevant again here. He argues that one must know the appropriate category, for example, epic or sonnet, in order fully and correctly to experience a work. Although his theory of the category determinedness of experiences of artworks explicitly addresses artworks as wholes, what he says can easily be extended to parts, for there will be subcategories that relate to parts of epics or parts of symphonies and that thus distinguish types of epics or symphonies. Carlson discusses categories in nature that are analogous to Walton's categories of art in "Nature, Aesthetic Judgment, and Objectivity." In what follows, I attempt to give a fuller account of this possibility.

29. P. C. Hellmund, "A Model for Ecological Greenway Design," in *Ecology of Greenways*, D. S. Smith and P. C. Hellmund, eds. (Minneapolis: University of Minnesota Press, 1993), p. 123.

30. J. B. Jackson, *A Sense of Place, A Sense of Time* (New Haven, Conn.: Yale University Press, 1994), p. 102.

31. Ibid., p. 195.

32. Ibid., p. 62.

33. R. F. Noss and A. Y. Cooperrider, *Saving Nature's Legacy* (Washington, D.C.: Island Press, 1994), p. 14.

34. Ibid. p. 22.

35. Quoted in ibid., p. 22.

36. J. McPhee, *Encounters with the Archdruid* (New York: Farrar, Straus, & Giroux, 1971), p. 29.

37. Lyle, *Design for Human Ecosystems*, p. 76.

38. Hepburn, "Trivial and Serious in Aesthetic Appreciation of Nature," p. 65.

39. In philosophical aesthetics a debate rages about the extent to which knowledge of an artist's intentions is required for an adequate interpretation and/or evaluation of his or her work. I am a "friend" of the intentionalists. The reader should be alerted to the fact that some philosophical aestheticians might not put as much emphasis on purpose in landscape aesthetics as I do.

40. M. Warnke, *The Political Landscape* (Cambridge, Mass.: Harvard University Press, 1995).

41. For a discussions of these preferences, see T. R. Herzog, "A Cognitive Analysis of Preference for Urban Nature," *Journal of Environmental Psychology* 9 (1989): 27–43; and R. Kaplan, "The Role of Nature in the Urban Context," in *Behavior and the Natural Environment*, I. Altman and J. F. Wohlwill, eds. (New York: Plenum, 1983).

42. J. Nassauer, "Messy Ecosystems, Orderly Frames," *Landscape Journal* 14 (1995): 161–170.

43. Chin is not the only artist who has engaged in such practices. In 1983, for example, Joseph Beuys planned the "Spufeld Altenwalder Project" for Hamburg. Trees and shrubs were planted that would help to bind toxic substances in the soil and groundwater. Other artists such as Alan Sonfist have created earthworks that challenge categories.

44. The catalog for an exhibit of Hull's work, "Visions of America: Landscapes as Metaphor in the Late Twentieth Century," shown at the Denver Art Museum and the Columbus Museum of Art, provides an excellent sample of contemporary landscape artworks and discussions of them by prominent critics (New York: Abrams, 1994).

45. M. Miller, *The Garden As Art* (Albany: SUNY Press, 1993), p. 15.

46. Ibid. p. 54.

47. R. H. Platt, "From Commons to Commons: Evolving Concepts of Open Space in North American Cities," in *The Ecological City: Preserving and Restoring Urban Biodiversity*, R. H. Platt, R. A. Rowntree, and P. C. Muick, eds. (Amherst: University of Massachusetts Press, 1994).

48. J. Nassauer, "Aesthetic Objectives for Agricultural Policy," *Journal of Soil and Water Conservation*, 44, no. 4, (1989); and "Landscape Care: Perceptions of Local People in Landscape Ecology and Sustainable Development," *Landscape and Land Use Planning* 8, American Society of Landscape Architects, Washington, D.C., 1988.

49. See, for example, J. R. Stilgoe, *Common Landscapes of America, 1580–1845* (New Haven, Conn.: Yale University Press, 1982); and M. H. Segall, "Visual Art: Some Prospects in Cross-Cultural Psychology," in *Beyond Aesthetics*, D. R. Brotherwell, ed. (London: Thames & Hudson, 1976).

50. See, for example, J. F. Wohlwill and G. Harris, "Response to Congruity or Contrast for Man-Made Features in Natural Recreation Settings," *Leisure Sciences* 3 (1994): 349–365.

51. Nassauer, "The Appearance of Ecological Systems as a Matter of Policy," pp. 239–250.

52. N. Goodman's theory of metaphor is helpful here. See his *Languages of Art* (New York: Bobbs-Merrill, 1968).

53. For a study of how much "messiness" suburban dwellers allow in their yards, see J. Nassauer, "Ecological Function and the Perception of Suburban Residential Landscapes," in *Managing Urban and High-Use Recreation Settings*, P. H. Gobster, ed. (St. Paul, Minn.: USDA Forest Service North Central Experiment Station, 1993), pp. 55–60.

Recommended Reading

Eaton, M. M. 1988. *Basic Issues in Aesthetics*. Belmont, Calif.: Wadsworth, 1988.

Kemal, S., and I. Gaskell 1993. *Landscape, Natural Beauty, and the Arts*. Cambridge: Cambridge University Press.

Neill, A., and A. Ridley, eds. 1995. *Arguing about Art: Contemporary Philosophical Debates*. New York: McGraw-Hill.

PART III
Landscape Ecology in Place

6 Urban Conservation: Sociable, Green, and Affordable

JUDITH A. MARTIN AND SAM BASS WARNER JR.

Judith A. Martin is a geographer who has directed the Urban Studies Program at the University of Minnesota since 1979. She has taught geography and American studies at universities in London, Amsterdam, and Munich. For the past six years, she has been a member of the Minneapolis City Planning Commission.

Sam Bass Warner Jr. is an urban historian and visiting professor at the Department of Urban Studies and Planning, Massachusetts Institute of Technology. His recent research concerns the problems of merging urban history with the environmental history of American metropolitan regions.

OVERLEAF

Top: Backyard at a Model Home, Chanhassen, Minnesota (April 1991).

Bottom: Centennial Lakes, Edina, Minnesota (October 1996).

THE MYRIAD WAYS in which we Americans arrange our spatial lives influences more than we might think. Today three-quarters of the American population (193,000,000 people) live in metropolitan settings, comprising 16 percent of the land area of the United States.[1] Thus, our metropolitan ways of life can either advance or hold back regional and national goals for a sustainable world. Whether we are isolated one from another; whether people walk or drive to errands and work; whether our homes, stores, workplaces, and social interactions are near or far; whether our communities make use of many natural systems or rely primarily on engineering solutions—all of these choices affect the well-being of all citizens and the richness of our natural environments.

Until recently, ecology has not attended to the institutions and habits of urban life, often dismissing these settings as degraded environments. Ecologists have worked hard to understand the natural processes of the lands beyond the metropolitan fringe, where processes uncontaminated by continual human intervention and maintenance could be observed. With most of the population of America (and of most other developed countries) living in cities, suburbs, and developing edge landscapes, it is appropriate that landscape ecologists are now turning their attention to issues of the design and management of urban and suburban areas.[2] The social and cultural aspects of metropolitan landscapes have desperately needed admission to these discussions.

For ordinary citizens without ecological leanings or training, residential settings and choices are rooted in profoundly social and cultural values. These values cause Americans to view the vast tracts of suburbs as wholesome and green, and to see urban landscapes as decidedly less desirable, although ecologists might dismiss all of these settings as having marginal value for biodiversity and habitat. All communities and neighborhoods, whether new or old, come already infused with regulations established by municipal laws and banking standards. These, in turn, incorporate widely accepted ideas about fashion, class, and personal expectations to create an ever-escalating regulatory climate. We use zoning, for example, to decide who will live where based on such things as lot size, or to limit the number of unrelated persons who live in a single dwelling. For the most part, landscape ecology is not present in this world of regulation, planning, financing, and building.

In contrast, the professionals directly concerned with city building—architects, landscape architects, and developers—began some years ago to consider ways to improve metropolitan environments through alternative building methods. Their perspectives necessarily embraced both human social needs and the improvement of urban natural systems.

These builder-critics directed their attention toward two targets: urban sprawl and the increasingly obsolete older cities and suburbs. The first target was metropolitan fringe sprawl, the bit-by-bit building of new houses and commercial properties in a patchwork beyond the edge of settlement and services. This development pattern ate up land without regard to a region's needs to manage its air and water, without considering the need to preserve natural systems, and without attention to transportation improvements.[3] Such development choices also created bits and pieces of settlement without unified shopping, visiting, or commuting pathways for the new residents. More often than not, the results were residential options disconnected from the possibility of creating vibrant local communities. Second, the effects of fringe sprawl left many older cities and suburbs with vacated industrial and commercial land, rat-run traffic on unmaintained streets, and residential areas that required substantial new investment to meet modern expectations.

The builder-critics in time moved toward a response to these problems. We now recognize this as the beginnings of "New Urbanism," a movement that calls for increasing the density of housing units per acre both at the new fringes and in pockets throughout the metropolis. New Urbanism also calls for clustering of new development, so that residents might be served by public transportation, and for an alternative management of old suburban and city streets to make them safer and more useful to their immediate neighbors. These proposals also incorporate the careful planning of open land and attention to the preservation of natural systems. Although the details of New Urbanism projects differ from metropolis to metropolis and from site to site, they have in common their call for higher densities, new traffic patterns, and new methods of land management.[4]

As a package of ideas, this criticism and these proposals seem very compatible with landscape ecologists' goals. Species preservation and the assembly of channels of open land to preserve the ecosystems of each American region can be accomplished within the frameworks of New Urbanist development. At the same time, both landscape ecologists' agendas and New Urbanist development approaches run quite contrary to the commonplace patterns of housing development that have prevailed in the United States for the past century. American home buyers value their private green spaces and also seem committed to devoting as much space as possible to streets and highways. The apparent conflict between development proposals that have ecological merit and the values and habits of established residential practice seem well worth exploration.

Accordingly, in August 1995, we convened a group of experienced builders, municipal officials, and landscape professionals to discuss the possibilities and barriers to these new development ideas.[5] Our discussion focused on the following questions:

• Is higher density possible or desirable, and what should it look like?

• What patterns of development are merely a matter of current fashion, and what adjustments are actually doable?

• What regulations, ecological or otherwise, can or cannot be altered or instituted?

• What is the role of the municipality in encouraging or discouraging new types of development? What could or should be done differently?

It is not surprising that the developers and municipal officials we talked with had good and strong ideas about these issues. They had thought about changing demographics, about the role of cars in the environment, and about barriers to higher-density development. We have organized our discussion of their responses under the following broad categories: density, the automobile and its effects on development, the question of community, public attitudes and shared opportunities, the New Urbanism and landscape ecology, the problem of politics, and opportunities for convergence between development and ecology.

Density

Evaluating human settlements by their density—that is, counting persons per acre—is a basic measure common to developers, planners, and landscape ecologists. Indeed, determining density is perhaps the premier decision that developers make when considering the possibilities for building on any property. Municipal zoning and subdivision regulations to which developers must conform are cast in terms of dwelling units per acre, and many other regulations for parking spaces, street widths, water supply, and waste management depend on the density of settlement.

Accordingly, whether implied or specifically stated, this universal measure informed most of the topics taken up in our discussions. For instance, the basic configuration of the population of Minnesota holds tremendous import for both urban design and landscape ecology. The state has a land area of 79,617 square miles; the Twin Cities of Minneapolis–St. Paul Metropolitan Statistical Area (MSA) had a land area of 5,051 square miles in 1990. The state's population in 1990 was 4,375,000; the population of the Metropolitan Statistical Area was 2,464,000. It is of the utmost significance that 56 percent of Minnesota's population lives in the metropolitan area at a density of 0.76 persons per acre, while the nonmetropolitan population is settled on the land at one-twentieth the density, or 0.04 persons per acre.[6] Thus, the concentration of half the state's population in the Twin Cities metropolitan area creates the long-term possibility elsewhere in the state for the large meadow, forest, wetland, and lake preserves and the major watershed restoration that landscape ecologists say are necessary for successful species preservation and resource management.

What possibilities for landscape ecology, then, does the metropolitan portion of the state offer? Some of our developer and planner informants had previously attended workshops on environmental management where they were told that only very large parcels of land could be useful for environmental restoration and species preservation. To no one's surprise, they came away from these sessions with the impression that land within the metropolitan region should simply be written off as already built upon and too engineered to be of environmental concern. Their impression is, in fact, reinforced by the focus of most of the current landscape ecology literature.[7]

One of the goals of the focus-group discussions was to question this attitude that ignores the human and nonhuman natural systems of the metropolis. Even the grossest density measures record the presence of a rich variety of metropolitan environments. For example, the city of Minneapolis is currently settled at a density of about 1 person per acre. Nearby Bloomington, by contrast, has been built up since the 1950s at a density that is one-third that level (0.34 persons per acre). And there are sub-urbs even further out with lower levels of overall density.

In developers' and planners' terms, density raised issues of building single-family detached houses, duplexes, town houses, and apartments. It also raised issues ranging from the refurbish-ing and rebuilding of older sections of the metropolitan area to concerns for local community relations and governance to the alteration of automobile traffic patterns. In the ensuing discus-sion many of these topics, in turn, were of central concern to the goals of landscape ecology.

The Automobile

The automobile proved to be the subject about which the de-velopers and planners were most knowledgeable and imagina-tive, and the subject on which the literature of landscape ecology sheds the least light. Because metropolitan development over the past seven decades has been largely driven by the convenience af-forded by cars, accommodating these demands is all too familiar in the world of planning. For our informants, as for the lived ex-perience of most Americans, the automobile dominates the en-vironment of the metropolis; the highway, road, and street net-works control the organization of metropolitan areas. All else must accommodate itself to the car, save the steepest ravine and the boggiest wetlands. If a development fits the auto network ap-propriately, all the other utilities—electricity, gas, telephone, cable, fiber-optic, water, and sewerage—can be tailored to fit.

It is the auto network that is currently facilitating the fashion of very low-density fringe developments of five- to ten-acre house lots. And it is this same network that sets the standards that developers and planners must meet when building within the suburbs, or when rebuilding in the center city or in the old first-ring suburbs. In their experience, the demands of accommodat-ing the use of automobiles have been growing ever more insis-

tent over the past 40 years. Year after year old streets have been widened, parking garages and parking lots added, road lanes made wider and multiplied. Even little-used residential streets that are all-weather unpaved surfaces have been required to be-come paved and sized to carry 8-ton trucks at 30 miles per hour and to have turning radii for the largest moving vans and the most extensive fire apparatus. The goal of this building and re-building was understood to be the creation of a metropolitan traffic system of continuous flow, a network where no one need stop for other traffic.

One developer, a man of many years' experience, predicted the future of this system over the next 30 years. Because he foresees that neither the federal nor the state government will be willing to invest large sums in new freeways, he guesses that the existing system will remain almost as it is now for the next generation. He expects, therefore, that the continuing spread of the me-tropolis, through the dispersal of houses and the scattering of job sites and of retail locations will multiply the number and lengthen the distance of metropolitan drivers' trips. Conse-quently congestion, especially at the outer edges where the sys-tem is most spread out, will increase, and commuting and errand times will stretch out. This congestion, the developer guesses, will foster a demand for high-density settlements throughout the region so that households will be able to choose to locate near their jobs or errand clusters.

This comprehensive analysis of the metropolitan automobile network by the developers and planners also fostered keen crit-icisms of current development practices and called forth a range of alternatives to present building fashions and federal, state, and municipal regulations.

First of all, our informants see much of the street widening and paving as excessive. In new suburbs, streets cover land that might instead have been given over to houses, yards, or commu-nity open space. These same excessive street demands consume badly needed capital that could otherwise be better spent either on housing or the nearby landscape.

Here the developers' and planners' concerns overlap with those of landscape ecologists interested in water management. Both groups want to reduce the area of impervious surface within metropolitan watersheds, while ecologists also wish to free up green space for storm-water retention, runoff purification, and wildlife corridors. At present, depending on the site, the roads, and parking designs, a single-family housing development can roof and pave anywhere from 25 to 60 percent of a subdivision's land surface. Yet this combined effect of roof, parking, and street is not now subject to unified guidelines. Instead the roof is disciplined by municipal zoning, and the streets are the subject of traffic-engineering standards and of curb and drain regulations.[8]

These street fashions and regulations, in turn, have very strong impacts on the socioeconomic patterns of the metropolis. The costs of excessive paving and of conventional storm sewers make it impossible for developers to construct new unsubsidized housing for residents with moderate or low incomes. Other informants added their objections to these regulatory burdens to their concerns for the reconditioning of the center city and of old first-ring suburbs. The idea is that older neighborhoods could be modernized to meet current consumer demands for lesser traffic impacts if streets could be narrowed, if tuck-in parking spaces could be provided, or if related traffic-calming measures such as rotaries and speed bumps could be instituted. The current commonplace regulations that require wide paved streets, and that simultaneously forbid on-street parking, were uniformly viewed as particularly wasteful and foolish.

Finally, several of the developers expressed concern about the effects of the auto-dependent metropolis on human communities. One developer stressed how isolating the private experience of the motorist is in comparison to walking on sidewalks, taking public transportation, or even bicycling. He would like to see some of the current gasoline revenues be directed toward the improvement of other modes of transportation so that the general taxpayers' subsidies of the automobile network could be diminished.

Community

"What we have is what we are, and what we are is what we have."[9] More effectively than anything we might say, this sentiment sums up the feelings of developers about the potential for the much discussed concept of "community." Here, we and they take community to mean a set of ideas about the ways in which people relate to one another and the spaces in which they do this. Traditionally such concerns have not been central to most ecologists, but the issue of community management clearly is significant for developers, New Urbanists, and municipal officials, and it is now beginning to surface in landscape ecology as well.

Within our discussion there was a tension in views about community possibilities. These vacillated between support for notions of neighborly relationships (well beyond what they believed many people want) and a recognition of the limits of attempting to force people to associate. In a highly mobile and consumer-oriented society, where houses are just another commodity, coming together around shared values is clearly a challenge.

Several participants pointed out the problems inherent in trying to build community along with building houses. Among the biggest hurdles is the overwhelming role played by individual self-interest and the desire for privacy among home buyers. There was a general sense of despair about trying to get people to come together in an age when most everyone is fearful and distrusting of strangers, and in which there is a growing market for security systems and a growing interest in gated developments. What home buyers are thought to want, in order of priority, is privacy, convenience, identity, comfort, and romance (where romance is equated with open space). Participants noted that even in higher-income projects, people are now willing to sacrifice identity (e.g., all town homes are to be the same color so no one stands out) to achieve a sense of privacy. People seem to want "rural" settings and a sense of isolation but also want to be closer to the center of the metropolitan area, so dead-end streets are increasingly popular.

A developer who has built a lot of multifamily housing offered an example of the challenges that exist in trying to provide opportunities for community. The proposed project was on a bluff-side suburban location. He proposed to donate 27 acres of bluff from a 47-acre site to the municipality for open space, only to discover that the bluff area represented a *threat* to adjacent householders because of the potential public access it could provide. On the other hand, the same developer touted the potential value of home-owner associations, which he creates through covenants on the land, despite the recognition that such legal tools can become very contested. These associations have the power to tax each home and to enforce the common rules. Another developer sees local resident cooperation and community governance as the best hope for neighborhood maintenance and improvement.

Public Attitudes and Shared Opportunities

For developers and planners the metropolitan landscape is much more the product of culture than of nature. They must cooperate to build settlements that sell and rent; thus, the values, habits, and outlook of their customers and of governmental officials are always uppermost in their minds. The cultural remnants of the past are also their raw material—abandoned farms and woodlots,

empty rail yards, and vacant and used-up parcels of all kinds. For example, a successful recent Twin Cities high-density development, Centennial Lakes in Edina, a cluster project designed for 40 people net density per acre, was built upon the remains of an old worked-out gravel pit. In our metropolitan areas, these opportunities for refashioning landscape remnants abound, though they are often the subject of political debate.

The developers and planners feel that current public attitudes threaten some of their best landscape work. During the prosperous 1970s, fashions in new suburban housing called for large patches of community green space. Developers responded by constructing miniparks; they laid out pathways around wetlands and established jogging and bicycling trails. This practice of clustering the house lots and setting out common community lands might well have been adapted to the hydrologic and wildlife goals of landscape ecology had the fashion persisted. The developers themselves take pride in these designs, something they thought fitted the new residents to the inherited landform.

Now such layouts are threatened by the new fearfulness of suburban home buyers and renters. Such common spaces used to be pluses for the salespeople, now they are minuses. The public now imagines human predators everywhere. One developer noted that people phone the police when a strange car shows up in their cul de sac. Moreover, the wildlife that suburban and exurban green spaces attract—geese, deer, and raccoons—are now perceived as nuisances, not as ornaments to suburban nature. As yet the public seems to have no awareness that these heavy concentrations of a few species are signs of decreasing biodiversity.

Developers and planners also stressed the shortcomings of the present political system. Complex projects for mixed uses and mixed housing types that might create pleasant high-density living require four or five years to bring to completion. They usually also require a good deal of cooperation and flexibility on the part of municipal regulators. But mayors and city councils are fixed upon the short term and are often the victims of explosions of single-issue campaigns (such as pro- or antidevelopment outbursts). Such local politics punishes governmental risk taking and makes it difficult, if not impossible, for any developer to plan, finance, and build a novel or complex project. For the moment, the public and their politicians seem uninterested in changed ways and new ideas.

One developer summarized the sense of pessimism and inertia by describing a slow-moving, self-reinforcing cultural cycle. First, the existing houses and patterns of land uses and their accompanying laws and regulations dominate public expectations and private demand. People want what is familiar. Then, because the public demand is interpreted by developers, planners, and regulators as what is familiar, they too continue to repeat the established patterns. So cycles of development tastes and formulas are reinforced by inertia, and efforts to break the mold are penalized by delays.

Yet despite the discouragement at the new anticommunity fearfulness and the weight of cultural inertia, the group accepted the assertion that opportunities for change exist and identified quite a number of such possibilities. The landscape architect cited her own experience with a demand that the customary engineering of street storm water be changed. A number of streets in the county needed resurfacing, but a tight budget provided the chance to suggest that officials abandon the usual high concrete curbs and gutters and instead replace them with curbless edges that would slow the runoff.

So in counterimposition to the weight of the past—the excessively wide streets, the expensive curbs, the overpaving, the established storm-water and sewer system, which sometimes floods and pollutes—the group arrived at the idea that infrastructure rebuilding and repair offer opportunities for innovative changes.

Municipal infrastructure of all kinds requires periodic major repair and rebuilding. A 50-year cycle is common. This process is going on all over the metropolis all the time. Here, the group thought, were opportunities for fresh design and novel construction. The possibility also occurred to some that the housing filter itself—the social process whereby aging neighborhoods serve successively lower-income residents—might provide another redesign opportunity. One developer was particularly keen on the need for built-out neighborhoods to be modernized. Accordingly, one could imagine that each year a small part of the metropolis would have its structures and lots achieve more contemporary standards and its infrastructure adapted to make more use of natural systems. The financing of, and potential political support for, such a desirable process was, however, not discussed.

The New Urbanism and Landscape Ecology

During the past several years the New Urbanism movement among architects and city planners has paralleled the urban thrust of some landscape ecologists. Both groups are seeking substantial changes in the building practices of American metropolitan regions. Both seek to better harmonize the needs of human settlements with the needs of natural systems. The former addresses transportation, housing, and site design, and the latter brings landscape architecture and ecology to the task of reforming established practices in civil and sanitary engineering.

New Urbanism has the potential to affect the full environmental list. By discouraging too much reliance on automobiles for transportation, New Urbanism addresses global warming and air pollution. By stressing the use of recycled products in new construction, New Urbanist projects might protect forests and other natural resources. Also, density is one of the New Urbanists' major tools for reform. They propose a number of types of dense, clustered, mixed-use neighborhoods that would lessen the need for residents to use their automobiles.

The New Urbanists place these new site and structure criteria within the context of architecture's and city planning's traditional American concerns for fostering a sense of community and community participation among residents. Whether the New Urbanist program is for the refashioning of an old neighborhood or the building of a new one, the pathways of the settlement are intended to promote sociability among the residents. For the moment this goal seems out of step with current fashions. It is a goal that developers in our group reported that the buying public was abandoning.[10]

The landscape architect in the group represented well the new urban initiatives of her design specialty. The management of an urban and suburban watershed was her professional concern. This particular watershed had been built out after World War II, and now its lakes and streams suffer from pollution, excess nutrient loading, and periodic flooding. The work on this watershed highlights the biological skills needed in the difficult tasks of dealing with metropolitan nonpoint-source pollution. As a group the watershed proponents are part of a national clean-up effort that includes the Chesapeake Bay project, the Great Lakes initiative, the EPA effort to restore the ocean estuaries, and river improvements everywhere. Like urban air, urban streams have the wonderful property of revealing what people are doing on their land.

The landscape architect brought to our attention three dimensions of landscape ecology that connect to the concerns of New Urbanists, developers, and planners. The first dimension is cost. A water-management design altered to make use of natural systems can often be cheaper to build and manage than a con-

ventional engineering design. In the experience of the St. Paul area, the high costs of traditional specifications had made the watershed managers willing to explore and later undertake the methods of landscape ecology. All across the country the cost question is driving a reassessment of big infrastructure projects, so far with mixed ecological results.

The second dimension concerns the ecology of human health. Clean water, clean air, and clean food seem to be necessities that might set their own standards for human consumption. But the complex chemical soup and high energy processing of the modern metropolis have complicated the problems of environmental assessment. Currently there are suspicions that many aspects of today's metropolitan environments are injuring human health, but long-term studies will be required to pinpoint the dangers and to seek their remedies. In the long run, landscape ecology, with its emphasis on natural systems, may prove helpful to these concerns.

The third dimension is human values. What do people want for their settlements? The landscape architect stressed the fact that science cannot set policy by itself. Maps of resources to be protected, land to be cleaned up, and sites suitable for development cannot by themselves tell the public what must be done. There are tradeoffs. If a dense settlement is established here, then its runoff will damage that stream over there. Yet allowing such damage may be a good way to preserve an even more valuable river somewhere else in the region. Landscape ecology decisions almost always involve making such tradeoffs. They are decisions that depend on human values and goals. It became apparent that, in this context, the role of governments at every level, from the federal to the local, should be to collect as much information as possible about the environments of a metropolis and its natural systems. Then these governmental bodies should make that information available to the public so that voters can use their values to make the tradeoff decisions.

The Problem of Politics

The subtext of our session's discussion about ecology and development was clearly the real-world realm of politics. What should be done ecologically and what is most desirable socially often collide with regulatory systems in place. Most of our developer informants could cite chapter and verse about regulations that got in the way of both sociable land planning and efficient development. And while it is easy to dismiss some of this as the complaint of an industry that would prefer to be left alone to do business, this group's sensible observations on the standards required by municipal concerns about automobiles belied this kind of critique.

The regulatory framework within which most urban and suburban development proceeds is specific about many things but generally amounts to prohibitions *against* what is most feared rather than prescriptions *toward* what is most desired. Thus, it is difficult for most municipalities to legislate criteria that would lead toward positive community interaction, although the requisite front porches and sidewalks written into some of the New Urbanists' zoning codes are a step in this direction.[11] The group observed that the levels of regulatory intervention are always increasing, largely in response to fashion and class expectations. These increasing standards become normative and are then codified as necessary for life safety concerns. So, we arrive at subdivision standards that, through excessive street-width and building-setback requirements, place neighbors across the street from one another but in reality nearly a half-block apart. It should come as no surprise that people may fear their neighbors if they cannot even see them, especially if everyone is going in and out of the area only by car.

A related aspect of regulatory concern is that rarely does any regulation expire and seldom are they reviewed for consistency with changing conditions. Few municipalities take new ecological considerations into account when reviewing development proposals, even where the citizenry is informed and active. It is also not unusual for municipalities to have zoning ordinances with multitudinous amendments, which produce an environment in which the opportunities for political skullduggery increase dramatically—a common example occurs when council members issue special permits for developments, which then escape normal review processes.

Opportunities for Convergence between Development and Landscape Ecology

If development has not thought much about landscape ecology, and if landscape ecology has only considered the negative aspects of development, is there any hope for these diverse perspectives to converge in a way that would yield socially and environmentally better housing choices? Surprisingly, our answer to this is, "very likely," but only if we can change the way we usually do business at the local and metropolitan levels.

Landscape ecologists are intently focused on issues of scale, which are also a cultural concern. But if the only standard for improved ecological function is the "big project" (major metropolitan wetland, river corridor, etc.), many opportunities for more ecologically attuned small-scale development will be missed. Most urban and suburban development still occurs at something smaller than a "patch" level—subdivisions of 50 to 100 houses or redevelopment parcels of one to four city blocks.

The small projects at these scales have to add up to something if ecological improvement is ever going to take hold within metropolitan areas. While there is no current mechanism for integrating small-scale developments into necessary big metropolitan projects, a number of accredited examples of reduced paving requirements, disconnected drain spouts, and wet backyards connected by wildlife corridors would, over time, amount to an important ecological gain for any metropolitan area.

The Good News and the Bad

With respect to the tension between what developers want to do, and can do, and what landscape ecologists call for, there is both good news and bad. On the negative side of the ledger we find these concerns:

• Developers think that for the most part the public gets what it wants from its housing choices (apart from the low-income households, most are reasonably satisfied).

• The public perceives urban and suburban landscapes as adjuncts of housing decisions—lot sizes, front yards, back decks, and the presence or absence of sidewalks are all clues that orient people socially and economically to their surroundings.

• The public is perceived as being hostile to strangers and fearful of one another (individual subdivisions oppose public trails through their property; in cluster developments, people do not want to share front entries).

• City administrators fear risk taking, and local councils are often unstable and lacking leadership (the conclusion to draw here is that developers could be expected to do much more, but no one asks).

• There is a general fragmentation of specialists within the regulatory environment, so that the water person may not communicate with the street person, who may have little contact with the senior planner.

On the positive side of the ledger are the following:

• At least some developers believe that high-density living can be successfully built and marketed (in both cities and suburbs).

• They also believe that there are many opportunities for change within the current development system, starting with tightening up prescriptions for road width and moving toward a greater tolerance for mixed use than most city codes allow.

• Some developers are concerned about the impacts of the automobile on what they do—they see the expectation of one house per half acre or acre as defeating any opportunity for developing a sense of community, because people are too spread out and must drive to everything they do.

• Some also see looming demographic changes as major opportunities for doing things differently in the future—this includes the prospect of the aging baby boomers choosing denser living environments, as well as the propensity for single-female households to choose denser housing.

What all of this adds up to is a situation that would be ironic if it were not so debilitating. Developers claim that they want to build communities of denser housing but face opposition from local councils, and that part of the problem with denser housing patterns is that people are so wedded to notions of privacy that they do not want to share anything with their neighbors. If we cannot get the political process to recognize changing economic and social realities, and if we cannot get people to recognize the commonality of their interests, there is little chance that we can in fact build socially and environmentally better communities.

But the sensible congruities between developers and landscape ecologists expressed in our group should not be lost to us out of fear and ignorance. The prospects for our metropolitan future envisioned by many of our informants are too valuable to languish without further public education and discussion. If we do in fact have a metropolitan present that evolved unquestionably from the past, we need to start working toward a possibly much-improved future as soon as possible.

Conclusion

It would seem that at least some of the builders of the modern metropolis do not see themselves as obstacles to the refashioning of these settings in forms that would enhance sustainability and increase compatibility with existing natural systems. Instead it seems that the science and the art of landscape ecology must find new ways to help Americans to value and take pleasure in working with the natural processes around them instead of obliterating whatever stands in the path of development. Landscape ecology will also have to confront embedded contradictory regulations if suitable architecture, sensible land planning, and appropriate ways of maintaining metropolitan settlements are to take hold. Surely a beginning step toward such a desirable outcome is more and better communication between those who build our metropolitan environments and those who worry about the sustainability of those same environments. The conclusions reached here indicate that all of us have a major stake in improved communication and understanding around these often contentious issues.

Notes

1. U.S. Bureau of the Census, Statistical Abstract of the United States, 1992 (Washington, D.C.: U.S. Government Printing Office, 1992), table 30.

2. R. T. T. Forman, *Land Mosaics: The Ecology of Landscapes and Regions* (Cambridge: Cambridge University Press, 1995), pp. 450–505; and W. E. Dramstad, J. D. Olsen, and R. T. T. Forman, *Landscape Ecology Principles in Landscape Architecture and Planning* (Covelo, Calif.: Island Press, 1996); M. J. McDonnell and S. T. A. Pickett, *Humans As Components of Ecosystems: The Ecology of Subtle Human Effects and Populated Areas* (New York: Springer-Verlag, 1993). The wildlife conservationists took up urban concerns some years earlier; K. Stenberg and W. W. Shaw, eds., *Wildlife Conservation and New Residential Developments*, Proceedings of a National Symposium on Urban Wildlife, January 20–22, 1986, Tucson, Arizona (Tucson: University of Arizona, 1986); L. W. Adams and D. L. Leery, eds., *Wildlife Conservation in Metropolitan Environments*, Proceedings of a National Symposium on Urban Wildlife, November 11–14, 1990, Cedar Rapids, Iowa (Columbia, Md.: National Institute for Urban Wildlife, 1991).

3. See, for example, D. Karasov, "Politics at the Scale of Nature," chapter 7, this volume.

4. P. Calthorpe, *The Next American Metropolis* (New York: Princeton Architectural Press, 1993); W. Fulton, *The New Urbanism: Hope or Hype for American Communities?* (Cambridge: Lincoln Institute of Land Policy, 1996); M. Hough, *City Form and Natural Processes* (London: Croom Helm, 1984); M. Hough, *Cities and Natural Process* (London: Routledge, 1995).

5. The participants in this group, apart from the authors, were Larry Laukka, Knut Horneland, Peggy Lucas, and Michael Lander (all developers); Gordon Hughes and Dan Cornejo (planners); Sherri Buss (landscape architect); Mike Cronin (land-use consultant); and Jim Asbury (realtor).

6. U.S. Bureau of the Census, Metropolitan Data Book (Washington, D.C.: U.S. Government Printing Office, 1991), tables D and E.

7. For traditional ecological approaches, see I. S. Zonneveld and R. T. T. Forman, eds., *Changing Landscapes: An Ecological Perspective* (New York: Springer-Verlag, 1990); R. F. Nash, *American Environmentalism*, 3d ed. (New York: McGraw-Hill, 1990). For the new urban efforts, see R. H. Platt, R. A. Rowntree, and P. C. Muick, eds., *The Ecological City: Preserving and Restoring Urban Biodiversity* (Amherst: University of Massachusetts Press, 1994); and W. E. Dramstad, J. D. Olsen, and R. T. T. Forman, *Landscape Ecology Principles in Landscape Architecture and Planning* (Covelo, Calif.: Island Press, 1996).

8. *Journal of Watershed Preservation Techniques*, 1 (fall, 1994): 100.

9. Comments made by Larry Laukka, participant in focus group, August 24, 1995.

10. See R. G. Arendt, *Conservation Design for Subdivisions: A Practical Guide to Creating Open Space Networks* (Covelo, Calif.: Island Press, 1996); P. Calthorpe, *The Next American Metropolis* (New York: Princeton Architectural Press, 1993); S. Van der Ryn and P. Calthorpe, *Sustainable Communities* (San Francisco: Sierra Club Books, 1986); A. Duany and E. Plater-Zyberk, *Towns and Town-Making Principles* (New York: Harvard Graduate School of Design/Rizzoli, 1991); R. Cervero, *Suburban Gridlock* (New Brunswick, N.J.: CUPR, 1986); R. Cervero, *America's Suburban Centers* (Washington, D.C.: U.S. Department of Transportation, 1988); and R. Cervero, *Transit-Supportive Development in the U.S.* (Berkeley: University of California Institute of Urban and Regional Development, 1994).

11. Duany and Plater-Zyberk, Towns and Town-Making Principles.

Recommended Reading

Calthorpe, P. 1993. *The Next American Metropolis*. New York: Princeton Architectural Press.

Dramstad, W. E., J. D. Olsen, and R. T. T. Forman. 1996. *Landscape Ecology Principles in Landscape Architecture and Planning*. Covelo, Calif.: Island Press.

Duany, A., and E. Plater-Zyberk. 1991. *Towns and Town-Making Principles*. New York: Harvard Graduate School of Design/Rizzoli.

Forman, R. T. T. 1995. *Land Mosaics: The Ecology of Landscapes and Regions*. Cambridge: Cambridge University Press.

Fulton, W. 1996. *The New Urbanism: Hope or Hype for American Communities?* Cambridge: Lincoln Institute of Land Policy.

Journal of Watershed Preservation Techniques, 1 (fall, 1994): 100.

Nash, R. 1990. *American Environmentalism*, 3d ed. New York: McGraw-Hill.

Platt, R., R. A. Rowntree, and P. C. Muick, eds. 1994. *The Ecological City: Preserving and Restoring Urban Biodiversity*. Amherst: University of Massachusetts Press.

Spirn, A. W. 1984. *The Granite Garden*. New York: Basic Books.

Van der Ryn, S., and P. Calthorpe. 1986. *Sustainable Communities*. San Francisco: Sierra Club Books.

7 | Politics at the Scale of Nature

DEBORAH KARASOV

DEBORAH KARASOV is a geographer and landscape architect who has held positions at the Walker Art Center, the National Endowment for the Arts, the American Academy in Rome, and the Minnesota Department of Natural Resources. Currently, she is working with artists, designers, and restoration ecologists in collaborative projects in Minneapolis–St. Paul.

THE EAGLE CREEK WATERSHED in Minnesota is one of many wild patches across the country threatened by suburbanization and exurban growth. These patches are significant and conspicuous on a local scale and yet have an equally important place within the larger landscape, even if it cannot be readily perceived. These patches are important for biodiversity and for human experience. On a national level, we may think that Eagle Creek is insignificant, hardly important compared to the Rocky Mountains or the California grasslands. But every wild patch has its ecological and educational function. Eagle Creek is connected to the Minnesota River basin, to its migratory corridor and transitional habitat, and ultimately to the Mississippi River.

Fundamentally, this chapter shows that the most effective means of preserving the landscape is for people to take responsibility for the particular place where they live, and for the state to take responsibility for larger questions of biodiversity. Unless we can get communities to learn and care about the wild patches of their own landscape, we do not have much hope in the future for environmentally ethical behavior on a cultural level. Our children's ethical framework with regard to landscape—and ethics here are broadly conceived to include political action—will be shaped in large part from the lived experience in particular places. It is there that we develop our concept of home, which should include our home on earth. It is there that we come to accept a politics of connection.

In this country, in less than half a century, our communities have been imposed on by freeways, shopping malls, and commercial strips, creating haphazard sprawl. The effect is not only complete destruction of the former landscape but also the destruction of place as a source of local connections. More planners in these areas need to understand the importance of creating a process for the community to understand and have a say in the future of its place.

Tragically, the destruction of nature in urban areas means that future generations may be inhibited in becoming place-centered. If by some fairly young age children have not experienced nature as a friendly place, a place for adventure and imagination, their attachment toward places may not take hold as it might have. An opportunity will have passed. Our land planners are creating urban parks, greenways, and river trails, but more often than not these land uses are far from the neighborhoods where children live. For a respect or love of nature to take hold, children need contact with nature not only during a school field trip or at summer camp, but also during hours of play in nearby pockets where nature has been protected or allowed to recover.

This story is a plea for those natural places close to home, for making those natural places an integral concept of our home. Minnesota is considered by many as having some of the most comprehensive land-use regulations and environmental protections. Thus, although regulations do vary from state to state, Minnesota is a good place to evaluate the environmental effects and regulation of sprawl. The results are typical: Homeowners often do not understand their place in the wider landscape context. Thus, while homeowners are focused on their private interests, the wilder areas of their landscape are developed, parcel by parcel.[1]

Our current political system is not set up to assess the value of those places. I say politics, because our environmental system is political. What is required is a different scale of analysis and different political concepts. Nor is anyone watching out for these small urban places; they do not register in our environmental legal structure. And so, perhaps, the environmental challenge ahead is in fact a political challenge.

The Many Scales of the Eagle Creek Landscape

Dan Callahan is a young father of four who was unable to save an urban wild area. Callahan grew up on the bluffs of the Minnesota River, 16 river miles from its confluence with the Mississippi, hunting pheasant and discovering beavers. At the age of 13, he had no inkling that the place where his grandfather used to fish trout, where he himself fished trout not a half an hour from the urbanizing edge of the Twin Cities, would be one of the most controversial topics of the 1995 Minnesota legislative session. At 13 he was aware only that Eagle Creek, a tributary of the Minnesota River, was a special place, an area of native prairie, boiling springs, wet meadows, and old-growth woods. Even poised as it was in the path of the fast-growing suburbs of the postwar era, Callahan could not imagine that this special place would ever be in danger of extinction through development.[2]

The special place called Eagle Creek is the only tributary of the Minnesota River that is of a quality capable of supporting naturally reproducing brown trout (see figure 1). Trout need cold, clean, pure water in order to survive. Eagle Creek is fed along its course by groundwater (artesian) springs that maintain its coldness. The creek has endured with relatively pure water quality due to its small watershed, approximately one-square-mile in area, the majority of which is still undeveloped. In contrast, the Minnesota River is considered one of the state's most polluted waterways and one of the greatest sources of pollution for the Mississippi River, which it joins.

The artesian springs of Eagle Creek create another unique phenomenon, Boiling Springs. In these springs quicksand erupts when pushed up by the underground springs. Two known occurrences exist within Eagle Creek.

The creek and its watershed encompass a number of plant communities and provide habitat for numerous plant and animal species. The stream supports 22 fish species, including wild

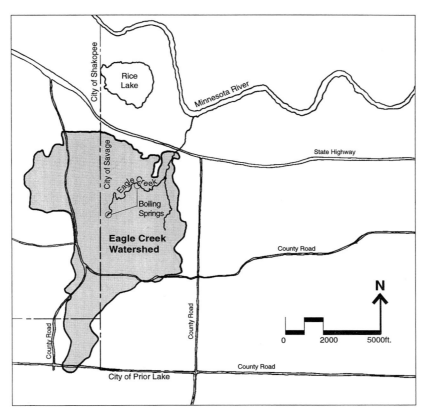

Figure 1. Eagle Creek Watershed bounded by a grid of roads.

brown trout and American brook lamprey. The latter is the only example found in the last 50 years within the 17,000-square-mile Minnesota River valley. It is a nonparasitic fish, which is listed as a state species of special concern. The wild brown trout were last stocked by the Minnesota Department of Natural Resources in 1978, replacing brook trout that are more easily fished, and in this way Eagle Creek became the habitat for the only naturally reproducing brown trout population in the Minnesota

River valley. Beyond the creek proper are wetlands and fens, called the Savage Fen complex, which contain waterfowl and provide a stopover for hundreds of migratory birds. The uplands include old-growth woods and grasslands of native prairie plants with pheasants and grouse. The Eagle Creek watershed adjoins the Minnesota Valley National Wildlife Refuge.

The Eagle Creek watershed thus has value as a patch of urban wilderness and of regional biodiversity. But the city of Savage, within whose jurisdiction Eagle Creek falls, had development plans for the area. In 1993, the city approved 500 homes, covering 300 acres of the watershed, almost half of the Eagle Creek watershed. In future years, a commercial-industrial area would cover an additional 100 acres. With both residential and commercial development, about 31 percent of the land would be covered with pavement and buildings. Studies show that when more than 12 to 15 percent of a watershed is impervious surface, all the cold-water plant and animal species are likely to be lost due to runoff, rainwater diversion, evaporation, warming, and other factors.[3]

Callahan is a member of the small environmental group, Trout Unlimited, that tried to modify Savage's growth plan. When he first joined Trout Unlimited, he started doing research on metropolitan trout streams. He found out that seven of the thirteen trout streams in the metropolitan area had been lost from pollution, unregulated fishing, and development. A major problem facing these cold-water bodies is disruptions in groundwater transport affecting rates of supply.

Trout are very sensitive to environmental changes, and even small alterations to their habitat can be lethal. For example, they require higher concentrations of oxygen than most other fish, and raising temperatures in lakes and streams reduces their capacity to maintain high oxygen levels. Development results in more surfaces—streets, roofs, driveways—that are impervious to water. Rather than seep into soil, water runs off such surfaces and surges into trout waters, raising their temperatures.

The state's Department of Natural Resources considered the city's mitigation plan for the proposed development to be innovative and considerate of ecological issues in its analysis. In the plan nearly all of the runoff from the newly developed watershed would be diverted away from the stream through a collector system that would carry the runoff to primary treatment ponds and wetlands, an alternative that is becoming more widely adopted. However, while reducing pollution to the stream, this plan also assumed that the diverted runoff was not important for the groundwater supply to the creek. Local environmentalists disagreed. What this plan failed to account for was the proportion of current runoff that infiltrates the soil and contributes to the stream as groundwater.

A professor at the University of Minnesota Department of Fisheries and Wildlife confirmed that the assumptions in the city's mitigation plan were incorrect. He concluded that the effects on the creek from the reduction of water supply due to runoff diversion, the contaminants in industrial runoff, and the addition of wastes from the backyards of single-family dwellings could not be ignored.[4] Further, all other new activities—roads, bridges, paved areas—in the basin would have effects, large and small.

Before Trout Unlimited stepped in in 1994, the only environmental issue addressed in regard to the Savage development was the one legally imposed for the Savage Fen watershed, which is next to the Eagle Creek watershed. The Minnesota Wetlands Conservation Act identified calcareous fens for protection and required Department of Natural Resources–approved Fen Management Plans for any project that might cause adverse impacts to such wetlands. Many states have similar wetland protection provisions. Savage's proposed sewer-extension project—the initial step to prepare for development—had the potential to affect the fen because it was located within the preliminarily defined groundwater recharge area for the fen.

Trout Unlimited's members were surprised that there was not more concern about the Eagle Creek watershed as a whole, especially given the resources there. The watershed offers one of the few migratory connections between the upper bluffs and the Minnesota Wildlife Refuge on the river, and Savage Fen is one of the best calcareous fens in the state. The group argued that the watershed's features may not seem like much when looked at individually, but together the watershed contains a number of important ecological communities that could be restored to something resembling their original state.

However, to staff at the Department of Natural Resources, Eagle Creek watershed was debilitated, a view of urban watersheds shared by many natural scientists. Even though it was the last stream in the valley to support a naturally reproducing population of brown trout, the creek was not the kind of resource the fisheries staff typically concerned itself with. In this state and others in the Midwest, the artificially stocked lake of species like bass and walleye is the main focus of fisheries management. Other field sections of the agency were not aware of Eagle Creek. It was too small an area, too much of it was private land, and it was at the edge of the metropolitan area. They had not done vegetation surveys, animal surveys, or archaeological surveys. As Callahan noted, "No one knew about Eagle Creek; that's what killed it."

The Recurrent Players in Local Politics

Savage, like many towns along the Minnesota River valley, was formerly a farming community. In 1866 the town of Hamilton was established as a steamboat landing, which became the city of Savage in the 1900s. After the east–west railroad was constructed through the valley, the early community gradually assumed the economic structure of a typical midwestern farm trade-service center of the nineteenth century, and a system of farm-to-market roads was established within the surrounding hinterland.

Historically, the land-use pattern of the area showed a sharp division between the urbanizing area "below the bluff" and the solidly agricultural area "above the bluff." The lower land was carpeted with "small-town" housing densities and regional transportation lines, while virtually no nonrural uses existed above the bluff before World War II. Much of the residential develop-

ment that had occurred above the bluff since was unplanned and uncontrolled and had developed without essential urban services such as sewer and water.

In 1978, Savage hired its first city administrator, who set out to make the city's development more like that of other suburbs. His first step was to extend the sewer and water lines south over farm area, an $8 million system financed with municipal bonds. The next expansion of sewer lines was in 1990, when 2,600 acres were approved, including the Eagle Creek watershed. In most cities, the sewer line extension (the first step in extending other metropolitan services) is the single most powerful tool of metropolitan growth. In Minnesota, all applications for extending this service line go before the Metropolitan Council, a regional planning agency. The council approved both extensions.

With these changes, Savage prepared to become a third-ring suburb of Minneapolis. It was squarely in the path of metropolitan expansion. Patchworked within the rectangular grid framework of county roads and highways appeared the driveways of single-family homes, some in subdivisions, some not. The sprawl was not appreciably different from that seen elsewhere and was made most obvious on the highway by the suburban creep of service stations, fast-food joints, and regional grocery chains. In 1995, the then-current population of 15,000 was expected to grow to 35,000 by the year 2010.

If Savage's development from a small town to a metropolitan suburb is typical, the local politics surrounding that rise are even more so. Some of the residents wanted things to remain rural in character; they did not want the town to grow too much. On the other hand, many of the town's commuters to the Twin Cities wanted the conveniences of retail development, even if they did not grasp the environmental implications of that growth. In the middle were the majority, who, like many residents of suburban communities, struggled to make their payments, commuted to their jobs, drove their children to activities, and were not very active in community issues.

For their part, the various state agencies that have permitting and regulatory review operate only to the extent of their authority. While motivations and interest may differ from agency to agency (and from state to state), most state regulatory agencies understand that developers who purchase property and act in accordance with zoning and environmental regulations have a right to pursue development of their property.

Walking into this local situation was an environmental group that was suspicious and resentful from past experience. In Trout Unlimited's case, the memory that drove their seemingly uncompromising position was that of another trout stream in the metropolitan area, closer to the Twin Cities, which once contained wild brook trout. When the wastewater treatment plant abutting that creek was expanded, the Metropolitan Waste Control Commission maintained that there would be no effect on the trout stream and adjacent fen. In actuality, though, the creek stopped flowing, and despite restoration efforts, nearly seven years later, it has water flow at only about 75 percent of its original flow. Further, the altered water chemistry has made the stream nearly inhabitable for fish.

Trout Unlimited felt "duped" by the deal. When the Savage case came up, the group's position was that it did not care if anyone said Eagle Creek could be protected; they were told that before. To Trout Unlimited, the only way to keep Eagle Creek from changing was to buy it and have it become a natural protection area. Indeed, city staff later came to believe that there was nothing they could do to make the environmentalists happy.

In the fall of 1993, the city of Savage applied for permission to extend the trunk sanitary sewer service to a new area that included Eagle Creek and Savage Fen. City staff said they planned to divert most of the storm water away from the stream and have

a buffer of native vegetation to protect it. Since the landowner's development would not be drawing from the groundwater, they did not envision any disturbance.

Continuing its historical trend, the city's motivation was to enable private development, and most staff believed that could go hand in hand with environmental protection. The city said it needed development or otherwise homeowner taxes would be too high. It claimed that disallowing the Eagle Creek development would mean the loss of $4.2 million in tax revenues per year.[5]

The city simply did not view Eagle Creek as having the same significance that the environmentalists did. By 1994, before the city even finished its environmental review documents, battle lines were formed: environmental interests versus development interests.

The Narrow Scope of Local Politics

Elsewhere in this book, Judith A. Martin and Sam Bass Warner Jr. (chapter 6) point out that developments like those in Savage take place in a regulatory framework that is responding to fashion and class expectations and where landscape ecology is not present in public consciousness. In most cases, regulations are quite specific about many things but generally amount to prohibitions against what is feared rather than prescriptions toward what is most desired. In this regard, Savage's position on Eagle Creek is classic. Under current regulations, the city argued that it must defend the developer who purchased Eagle Creek property and complied with zoning and environmental regulations. The city acted in accordance with the law by supporting development as it came up but did not create a process to talk about larger visions.

Savage made a series of development decisions that trapped it financially, having spent considerable public funds to build roads, sewers, and other utilities to entice developers to the area. Once the works were in place, the city needed more development to pay for the already laid services.

The city did try an alternative form of environmental review, called the Alternative Urban Areawide Review (AUAR), which at least attempted to avoid the usual environmental-development battles. The central feature of AUAR is that the "subject" of the review is not any specific project but rather development scenarios for the scale of an entire geographical area viewed in the long term. However, the situation soon fell to the commonplace, as the local players fell into traditional modes of operation.

Having worked on the AUAR for a year, from 1994 to 1995, the city was proud of the final document. For the first draft they worked with hydrologists, hired top-rated consultants, and used a state-of-the-art groundwater modeling technique. After the first draft, they formed a 17-member advisory panel to respond to public comments, including representatives from Sierra Club, Trout Unlimited, Scott County, and the Mdewakanton Sioux Community.[6] It was a diverse group, which met 10 times for over four hours each time. The AUAR was very complete, the city believed, a good document with three volumes of material.

A neutral party from the Minnesota Office of Dispute Resolution facilitated the advisory panel meetings. Still, many participants felt that the city unsatisfactorily and prematurely concluded the process. The group reached no consensus and had no final vote, and some continued to object after Savage ended the panel. Further, many were concerned that although the completion of the AUAR did not preclude developments being subjected to regulatory review in the future, such review would not be required by Minnesota environmental rules. For Trout Unlimited, the "alternative dispute resolution" was no resolution at all.

In the end, Trout Unlimited felt it had no recourse but to approach the legislature to try to purchase parts if not all of the watershed. Members believed that one reason the legislature approved at least some of the requested money was that the conservation group could show that the information used for the AUAR was inadequate.

Much of the resistance arose from their skepticism related to the city's scale of analysis. Environmentalists felt that the city's studies did not capture the ecosystem-level processes shaping Eagle Creek in the long term. For instance, the abstract, mathematical groundwater model may or may not have been correct for the specific area of Eagle Creek, since the city gathered no additional data on the creek watershed. With further monitoring, accuracy could be achieved, the consulting engineering firm said, but it would take a number of years and be very costly.

The city completed no studies as to what causes the boiling at Boiling Springs, and environmentalists feared that the proposed detention ponds might cut into the impermeable clay layer thought to produce the springs. Nor did the city do studies on the effect of diverting surface water runoff on the temperature and quality of water in Eagle Creek. In short, there were no stream studies or botanical studies (and before Trout Unlimited forced the issue in the AUAR process, no surveys of Native American burial grounds).

Meanwhile, the 1995 state legislative fight about purchasing Eagle Creek became a clash between those who would buy the entire watershed and those who saw greater reward in protecting a buffer zone on either side of the creek, while allowing much of the stream's remaining watershed to be developed. In essence, this clash was between those who appreciated the value of the entire watershed for biodiversity and education and those who saw the creek as no different from any other creek.

In the end, over the objections of nearly the entire senate legislative body, the legislature chose the buffer-development route, even though Trout Unlimited contended that Eagle Creek could eventually warm beyond the capacity of its trout and other cold-water life forms to survive.

The Scope of State-Level Concerns

At the same time that the battle over Eagle Creek moved from the local review process to legislative lobbying, the environmental groups (again led by Trout Unlimited) tried another option: appealing to the state agencies with permitting authority. These were the Metropolitan Council, the Minnesota Department of Natural Resources, and the Environmental Quality Board. The environmentalists pleaded with these agencies not to accept the AUAR, since it contained incomplete data and relied on plans and ordinances not yet adopted to mitigate potential adverse environmental effects for the development that was allowed to proceed outside of the 200-foot buffer around the creek. These included a storm-water management plan, fisheries management plan, and comprehensive sewer plan: all promised, none enacted.

The state agency staff met with the city about all of these elements. The city argued that "for the most sensitive environmental issues—the fen and the trout stream—there are additional safeguards in the form of regulations [and permits] by other agencies with strong concerns for these areas."[7] Ironically, then, what these statements meant is that even after the "holistic" AUAR process, environmental review would be on a piecemeal basis through permitting. Moreover, the environmental permitting system did little more to address environmentalists' concerns for ecosystem processes and values.

The attitudes of some state agency staff were telling. One environmental reviewer for the Department of Natural Resources wondered what would be gained by objecting. His department tries to work with the city, and it does not want to ruin that re-

lationship with little to gain. The environmentalists could not prove that development would adversely affect the groundwater system of the creek and springs, and the city could not prove that it would not, so development proceeds. He expressed hope, however, that some in-roads were made in changing levels of awareness and landscape behavior.[8]

Others in the Department of Natural Resources believed that some of the underlying issues about larger natural processes could be handled through different avenues. For example, the water-supply question could be handled through permitting—the Department of Natural Resources simply would not grant a permit for any new wells in the aquifer that feeds Eagle Creek. The AUAR process was over, and the Department of Natural Resources was a legitimate participant in it. Now staff believed that the department had to trust the city and give it time to deal with the mitigation goals.

State personnel also thought that they had been able to extract some good promises from the city and developer, and that the AUAR did allow input on projects not usually subject to environmental review, like small housing developments, roads, storm-water plans, and sewer interceptors. The developer was extremely patient, one state reviewer said. "Remember, while all this was going on he still had to pay the bankers every month. I believe that he has been the easiest developer to work with in the last five years. He says, tell me what to do and I'll do it. I'm not overly concerned about the storm-water questions. These are standard engineering issues worked out again and again."[9]

The Department of Natural Resources assigned a staff member to work with the city on a joint aquatic area management plan. He also acknowledged the deficiencies in the AUAR process related to ecosystem management. But he felt the deficiencies were no more than any of the typical vagaries one finds in any environmental regulation.

Having said that, this staff member thought that the city had made a lot of positive moves. Fifteen acres were now reserved around Boiling Springs; the Department of Natural Resources would restore native communities where possible in the upland areas of the Eagle Creek watershed; the Friends of the Minnesota River Valley offered to work with new lot owners regarding native plant landscaping; and in addition to sponsoring restrictive covenants on pesticides and herbicides, the developer proposed what the state agency believed was an innovative storm-water management plan, diverting nearly all runoff to a primary treatment pond and then to a wetland. These were no small feats. The ugly controversy that began with Eagle Creek is one thing, this staff member said, "I would like to believe that another story is now beginning. . . . Whatever their differences, I have to believe that everyone is approaching this compromise from an honorable point of view."[10]

He also agreed that the question of Eagle Creek is complicated by its many scales and levels—unfortunately in our current system there is no one responsible for coordinating these four levels. The storm-water management plan was a solution to the in-stream or bank-to-bank issue. The department's restoration efforts would address the near-stream or riparian corridor level. The AUAR mitigation plan, which the department believed was somewhat improved through the advisory panel process, was Savage's attempt to address watershed questions—although it considered Savage Fen, Eagle Creek, and Boiling Springs as features in isolation. But the groundwater level was regional by nature—it was the responsibility now of a working group of surrounding communities to address questions like future water supply.

But what was the role of the regionally focused Metropolitan Council in all of this? Simply by moving the urban service area line, the council raised land prices. Surely everyone was aware that there was no remaining trout brook within the areas of urban sewer service. Why was the original extension of the ur-

ban service area line granted? Often the extension of sewer lines is the first step in major pressure on a natural or rural area. Yet these extensions may sometimes be approved because a community argues that it needs growth.

In Savage's case, the impact on the fen, the lack of maps, and the incomplete data about biological diversity were all issues raised five years earlier, in 1990, during the city's initial request for the service area expansion. "I suppose the time clock was running out," a Metropolitan Council staff member said. "We had to accept their assurances that these things would be taken care of through ordinances."[11] The Metropolitan Council Board decided there was not enough justification to deny or reduce Savage's request.

One state hydrologist was alarmed about the development, but his questions were never answered. There were no maps in the AUAR document, he said incredulously, no evaluation of wetlands, no sense of how the city would deal with the overall routing of the storm water into the Minnesota River. Nor was it clear what would happen to the water quality of the creek with runoff ponded and sent into the creek. The mitigation plan discussed only monitoring. But what would happen if the monitoring revealed negative effects, this planner asked. Then what? The settlement ponds could be expanded, but what is their capacity? Could they handle the additional flow without reducing their efficiency in removing suspended solids? What would happen during flood episodes?

Unfortunately the public tends to rely on the larger conservation groups like Sierra Club to deal with such questions. These groups play a primary role in most development improvements when sustained effort is necessary. For example, scientists credit the successful management of the Lake Tahoe Basin as a whole system to the activist organization League to Save Lake Tahoe, which had the membership strength, the enthusiasm, and the political muscle to influence the course of government controls in the basin over a period of nearly three decades. In the case of Eagle Creek, environmental groups felt that, after a point, a continuing effort was not worthwhile relative to larger, intact ecosystems outside of the urban area needing preservation. A small volunteer organization does not have the resources to keep fighting.

One Trout Unlimited member shook his head when talking about the lack of oversight for permit review for the storm-water ponds. "In the one [housing development] . . . they propose to build an earth-and-clay dike between a storm-water basin and the creek to retain runoff events. There will be erosion into the creek for years. I confess that I'm tired; I'm not sure how much more I should fight this. I have other issues to move on to."[12]

In hindsight, most of the state agency staff would agree that the AUAR review process was not perfect. They saw that there were a number of things that could have been done in a better way. Part of the reason for the problems, they said, was the scale and complexity of some of the technical issues involved with the review, which tended to confuse and overwhelm participants with difficult-to-absorb information. Their response is to learn from the experience and make appropriate improvements to the AUAR process.

A Political Void

In the decades ahead, Minnesota will not be the only area with development patterns that lead to controversies like those surrounding Eagle Creek. Officials at the U.S. Environmental Protection Agency believe that the leading environmental issue for the next century is limiting the environmental impacts of random urban growth. Sprawl, agency sources told the Washington newsletter *Inside E.P.A.*, "is the root of many of the nation's most intractable environmental problems."[13] Two-thirds of the United States is privately owned, and the states with the greatest numbers of vanishing species and ecosystems are those that have been subjected to private development. Oliver Houck, former general counsel of the National Wildlife Federation, points out that while mechanisms to preserve biological diversity on private lands exist, in their aggregate they remain dwarfed by the pace of private-land development itself.[14]

An innovation dealing with land development is habitat conservation plans for when urban growth threatens the habitats of single species—such as the study done by environmental planner Timothy Beatley for the Coachella Valley east of Los Angeles.[15] These are positive steps, Beatley notes, but there are no assurances that such species will survive in the long term. Often, as in the Eagle Creek compromise, the plans protect a relatively small portion of native habitat while opening up larger portions for development. The plans may also result in "giving up" on existing species outside of protected preserves. Nor do such compromise plans clarify the general uncertainty concerning levels of stringency in mitigation or the fairness of who should pay for mitigation and conservation. Finally, such compromise plans fail to question or address in any fundamental way the engine driving habitat loss. They do not challenge development trends but find conservative solutions that will allow continued development.

At present suburbanites are talking past one another. For example, in Savage, city officials believe that Eagle Creek is a case study for urban habitat conservation—a compromise to protect the trout and still encourage necessary economic progress. They said the city of Savage not only took steps to prevent adverse environmental impacts from necessary economic growth but also used development-generated tax revenues to restore degraded natural areas and to preserve unique resources.

However, according to Trout Unlimited member Dan Callahan, who opened our story: "Savage won't be using development-generated revenues to do anything but try to mitigate the damage from the development."

I believe that Eagle Creek is a case study in the mismatch of environmental systems and politics. The way nature works requires us to understand the value of landscape on many scales, from the small to the large, from the scale of individual experience to the scale of ecosystem function. Moreover we need the state or some higher level of government to coordinate these many scales of evaluation.

In terms of experience, most people do not view themselves as inhabiting a landscape with an ecological function. Most view green space as small, generic pieces, counted like so many types in a generic city—one regional park, one wildlife refuge, one undevelopable floodplain. For their part, many ecologists value green space only on a large scale. But if large areas remain as the only standard for improved ecological function, we will miss opportunities for more ecologically attuned small-scale development. In the instance of Savage, this thinking prevented the Department of Natural Resources from studying Eagle Creek until provoked by environmentalists late in the discussion.

Conservation groups as well usually focus on the so-called intact, large ecosystems far away from urban areas. But what about changing ways of Americans? Hard-pressed two-earner families or single mothers with two or three children may not be able to go camping in remote wilderness areas.

Point by point, William Romme notes how analogous exurban growth in the mountainous west, parcel by parcel, has dramatically altered the ecosystems, to say nothing of the special qualities that drew people there in the first place (see chapter 8). Loss of biodiversity, fragmentation of habitat, disruption of migration patterns—some of these changes may take place within one gen-

eration. Studies such as his are uncommon, in part because the political system is designed to approve or not approve a single application; cumulative impacts are nearly impossible to grasp. Further, public resource-management agencies have not engaged in landscape-scale studies that cover public *and* private land. In this way, we continue to concentrate only on the islands of protected lands, albeit vital in themselves, while allowing the remaining "compromise" landscapes, as ecologist Eugene Odum would call them, to deteriorate. Romme argues that the cumulative impacts of these compromise landscapes are detrimental. One might add that because such landscapes are near where more than 75 percent of the population live, they are the key to educational opportunities oriented toward cultural change.[16]

Conclusion

We must change the political culture behind controversies like that over Eagle Creek. Just as we make progress in developing landscape ecology principles—and, practically, in implementing sustainable landscapes—we must make cultural progress in our politics and solutions to environmental conflicts. Just as we count the acres of preserved habitat or decreasing rates of pollutants, we must count the innovations in politics, the number of community organizations that alter their mission to embrace the nonhuman to create, for example, a process whereby the community can come to understand its place in the Minnesota River valley system and children can learn the history of the valley. The shift in our attention is essential. Our children's ethics arise in part from their lived experience in a region, and they form the raw stuff out of which they craft a sense of that place.

Contemporary debates like that over Eagle Creek persist because we fail to step back, to change our environmental systems and political arenas to address the many scales of the landscape—

even the scale of the biosphere. Process is the key, and it is worth repeating Martin and Warner's conclusion in this regard. If we cannot change the political process, there is little chance that we can in fact build socially and environmentally better communities.

Poet–politician Václav Havel argues that we are losing our ability to discuss the things we have in common, including our place within the biosphere. The answer he says is to

> reconstitute the natural world as the true terrain of politics. . . . We must draw our standards from our natural world, heedless of ridicule, and reaffirm its denied validity. We must honor with the humility of the wise the bounds of the natural world and the mystery which lies beyond them admitting that there is something in the order of being which evidently exceeds all our competence.[17]

What would it mean to have politics at the scale of nature? If we were to draw our standards from our natural world, our politics would reflect the fact that all the scales of biodiversity, including the scale of personal experience, are vitally important. It would also mean that state agencies need to work conservatively when we do not completely understand natural processes, like the groundwater system of Eagle Creek. Moreover, we need to save remnant ecosystems in order to research those processes.

Not only did the current environmental legal system not discuss such values in the case of Eagle Creek, it is incapable of doing so. If we learn from controversies like Eagle Creek, though, we will soon learn to act on all scales, spatially and temporally.

Notes

1. R. H. Platt and G. Macinko, *Beyond the Urban Fringe: Land Use Issues of Nonmetropolitan America* (Minneapolis: University of Minnesota Press, 1983).

2. Information and quotes from Dan Callahan are from interviews during the month of January 1996.

3. D. B. Booth, "Urbanization and the Natural Drainage System: Impacts, Solutions, and Prognoses," *Northwest Environmental Journal* 7 (1991): 93–118; D. B. Booth and L. E. Reinelt, "Consequences of Urbanization on Aquatic Systems: Measured Effects, Degradation Thresholds, and Corrective Strategies," in *Watershed 1993: Proceedings of a National Conference on Watershed Management*, Alexandria, Va., pp. 500–545.

4. T. F. Waters, "Effects of Urbanization in the City of Savage on Trout Habitat in East Branch Eagle Creek," unpublished paper, prepared for Trout Unlimited, 1995.

5. D. Rebuffoni, "Savage Land Issue Will Be Mediated," *Star Tribune*, November 11, 1994.

6. The following organizations and individuals served as advisory panel members: city of Savage; city of Shakopee city planner; Army Corps of Engineer ecologist; Scott County planning director; two local developers, including Klaas Van Zee; Lower Minnesota River Watershed District engineer; Minnesota Department of Natural Resources environmental review supervisor; Metropolitan Council senior planner; Minnesota Department of Transportation planner; Minnesota Pollution Control Agency environmental planner; Savage Chamber of Commerce; Shakopee Mdewakanton Sioux Community; U.S. Fish and Wildlife Service biologist; and representatives from Audubon, Sierra Club, Trout Unlimited, and Friends of the Minnesota River Valley.

7. G. Downing, environmental review coordinator, Environmental Quality Board, Letter to Elizabeth H. Schmiesing, Faegre & Benson, May 12, 1995.

8. This and other quotes from interview with Tom Balcom, Department of Natural Resources, January 10, 1996.

9. This and other quotes from interview with Bill Penning, Department of Natural Resources, January 11, 1996.

10. This and other quotes from interview with Dirk Peterson, Department of Natural Resources, December 15, 1995.

11. This and other quotes from phone interview with Metropolitan Council staff member Richard Thompson, January 4, 1996.

12. This and other quotes from interview with Rob Buffler, then vice president of Trout Unlimited, January 5, 1996.

13. "Inside E.P.A.," quoted in *Metropolis*, October 1996, p. 19.

14. O. A. Houck, "Foreword," in *Biodiversity and the Law* (Washington, D.C.: Island Press, 1996), p. xiii.

15. T. Beatley, *Land Development and Protection of Endangered Species: A Case Study of the Coachella Valley Habitat Conservation Plan*. Prepared for the National Fish and Wildlife Foundation, Washington, 1990.

16. U.S. Bureau of Census Statistical Abstract of the U.S., 1992 (Washington, D.C.: U.S. Government Printing Office, 1992), table 30.

17. V. Havel, *Living in Truth* (London: Faber & Faber, 1990), p. 149.

Recommended Reading

Jackson, W. 1994. *Becoming Native to This Place*. Lexington: University Press of Kentucky.

Orr, D. 1994. *Earth in Mind: On Education, Environment, and the Human Prospect*. Washington, D.C.: Island Press.

Tall, D. 1993. *From Where We Stand: Recovering a Sense of Place*. Baltimore: Johns Hopkins University Press.

8 | Creating Pseudo-Rural Landscapes in the Mountain West

WILLIAM H. ROMME

WILLIAM H. ROMME is a plant ecologist on the faculty of Fort Lewis College in Durango, Colorado. He has conducted extensive research on forest fire ecology and ecological history in Yellowstone National Park and in the mountains and plateaus of the southern Rocky Mountains. He serves on the Science Council of the Greater Yellowstone Coalition.

THE HUMAN POPULATION of the Rocky Mountain region is growing at an extraordinary rate. Colorado, for example, was the fourth-fastest-growing state in the United States between 1993 and 1994, with an annual growth rate of 2.6 percent per year.[1] Several Colorado counties containing major ski resorts grew at 8.5 percent per year from 1960 to 1990.[2] The current population in Colorado is 3.7 million, and if present trends continue, the population will grow to 5 million in the next 25 years. Although the West has a long history of transient economic booms followed by busts, the changing economics and demographics of the region and the nation indicate that this boom is likely to last for a long time. The West is undergoing a massive economic shift from dominance by extractive industries and agriculture to an emphasis on tourism, second-home development, and retirement based on income earned outside the region.[3] There is widespread concern that this rapid population growth will seriously degrade the special aesthetic qualities and ecological integrity of the western landscape.

The concern is not just about the actual numbers of people but also (or even primarily) about the patterns of land development that are occurring.[4] Many landscapes of the mountain West, especially those in very scenic areas such as the foothills of the mountains, are being rapidly transformed from predominantly rural and wildland systems into exurban landscapes. Although a variety of development patterns is occurring, one of the most popular designs is widely dispersed homes on large lots, typically 1 to 35 acres in size. Most of the residents of these new developments commute daily by automobile into nearby towns to work or do business, and many people drive into town and home again several times a day. A large percentage of residents are retired or work in their homes through telecommunications connections to centers of business and industry located all over the country. I call these developments "pseudo-rural" landscapes because they lack the high population density and socioeconomic diversity that characterize urban areas, yet at the same time, aside from low density, they also lack nearly all traditional rural qualities—for example, people making their living by working on the land.

State and county governments are attempting to manage the rapid growth now taking place, but there is widespread sentiment that the present form and level of growth management are not adequate to protect the special qualities of the West that make it a desirable place to live. In Colorado, many counties attempt to regulate growth with a permit process that requires county review and approval of new developments. However, in the absence of a plan to guide individual decisions, counties have few concrete criteria on which to base a decision to approve or not approve any specific application. In particular, consideration of the cumulative or regional impacts of individual developments is nearly impossible under the current permit process used in many counties. Thus, the tendency is to approve every proposed new development unless it can be shown that the new development lacks a technical requirement such as road, water, or sewer access. Moreover, the county review process is only required for certain types of proposed subdivisions; for example, those that create individual parcels of 35 acres or larger in Colorado or 160 acres in Montana are exempt from the county review process—a major reason for the great number of 35-acre lots now being sold in Colorado. One of the most pressing needs today is for good plans to guide development in the rural West. To be effective, plans must be based on the best available ecological information and must have wide public support.

Landscape ecology can contribute significantly to better planning and growth management in the American West and elsewhere. By integrating concepts and empirical data from both natural and social sciences, by explicitly dealing with the structure and function of large heterogeneous land areas (kilometers in extent), and by embracing human-dominated as well as natural areas, the new synthetic approach of landscape ecology can help us to better conceptualize land-use issues and to suggest constructive solutions.[5] Therefore, my objective in this chapter is to apply the concepts of landscape ecology to the broad questions of growth and land development in La Plata County, Colorado, an area that is representative of much of the American West today. From Montana to southern Arizona, extensive areas that until recently were rural or wildlands now are being transformed into pseudo-rural landscapes of the kind I describe in La Plata County. Although the details of my analysis are specific to this location, I expect that many of the problems and solutions identified for this area will be generally applicable throughout the West.

The Landscape Ecology of La Plata County, Colorado

La Plata County encompasses some 1.08 million acres of remarkably scenic country in southwestern Colorado (figure 1). It includes semi-arid mesas and canyons of the San Juan Basin, rugged alpine landscapes of the San Juan Mountains, and broad fertile valleys along the La Plata, Animas, Florida, and Los Pinos rivers, all major tributaries of the San Juan River and ultimately of the Colorado River. Elevation ranges from 1,500 to over 3,900 meters. Natural vegetation at the lower elevations is a mosaic of pinon pine and juniper woodlands, dense mountain shrublands of Gambel oak and serviceberry, and sagebrush grasslands. At middle elevations are extensive forests of ponderosa pine and Gambel oak. The high mountains are covered by dense forests of Engelmann spruce, subalpine fir, Douglas-fir, and trem-

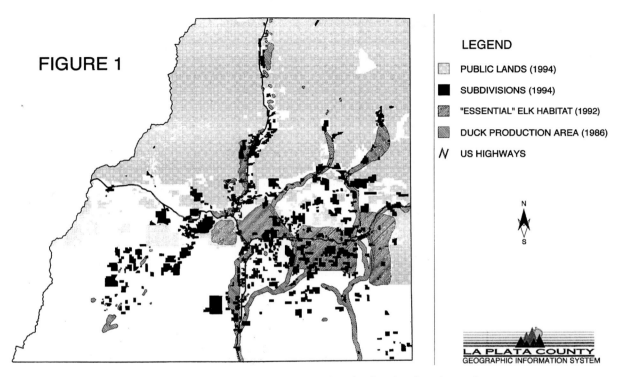

FIGURE 1

LEGEND

- PUBLIC LANDS (1994)
- SUBDIVISIONS (1994)
- "ESSENTIAL" ELK HABITAT (1992)
- DUCK PRODUCTION AREA (1986)
- US HIGHWAYS

Figure 1. Map of La Plata County, Colorado, showing locations of important wildlife habitats and residential subdivisions. (Data provided by the Colorado Division of Wildlife and La Plata County Planning Department; map produced by Alan Andrews, La Plata County Planning Department.)

bling aspen.[6] The region is famous for its spectacular scenery, abundant wildlife, cultural diversity (including both extant and prehistoric Native American cultures), and relaxed way of life.

The human population of La Plata County was estimated at 38,364 in 1995 (Peter Holton, La Plata County Planning Department, personal communication), but it is growing at about 3 percent per year—comparable to growth rates in Africa. Between 1990 and 1994, the county's population increased by 4,600 people (a 14 percent increase in 5 years), and there were 1,927 housing starts. Eighty percent of the population growth is occurring in unincorporated areas outside of existing communities. This population growth is fueled not by local birth rates but by immigration from other states, especially California and Texas.

In the following sections I develop eight concepts from landscape ecology and apply them to the issue of growth in La Plata County. These eight concepts are organized into groups related to (1) biodiversity, (2) energy and materials in ecosystems, (3) natural disturbance, and (4) human social, economic, and political systems. Several of these concepts are derived at least in part from principles of conservation biology, ecosystem ecology, and other fields, because landscape ecology is a synthetic approach that incorporates a wide range of perspectives and subject matters.[7]

Landscape Ecology Concepts Related to Biodiversity

1. *Landscape structure, that is, the kinds, extent, and spatial arrangement of ecosystems within a geographic area, has a critical influence on biodiversity.* Landscape structure refers to the kinds of elements or ecosystems of which the landscape is composed, for example, forests, wetlands, towns, streams, and roads. It also may refer to more subtle ecological units, such as north- and south-facing slopes at various elevations on different geological substrates. Landscape structure also deals with the distribution and specific locations of the various landscape elements, for example, whether the forests are all in one clump or are scattered throughout the landscape.[8] Biodiversity has at least three components: (1) genetic heterogeneity within and between populations; (2) species richness (number of species), evenness (relative abundance of each species), and composition; and (3) the variety and spatial extent of biotic communities and ecosystems (Noss and Cooperrider 1994).[9]

One major determinant of landscape structure is the underlying variation in geology, topography, and elevation, which creates a variety of habitats. La Plata County contains a great range of natural habitats and supports a high diversity of species, communities, and ecosystems. Some habitats and their associated biotic communities are extensive and widespread, for example, the midelevation forests of ponderosa pine and Gambel oak and the dense shrublands of oak and serviceberry. Others are rare and localized, such as natural ponds and wetlands.

One important task in developing a plan to maintain biodiversity is to map the specific locations of rare or unique habitats, species, and ecosystems and then to devise means of preventing or ameliorating destructive development in these special areas. The rare and unique habitats, which contribute greatly to the biodiversity of the landscape, may be highly vulnerable to destruction or degradation because of their rarity and their close association with particular geological or topographical features. In La Plata County, for example, there exists only one natural, perennial pond of relatively large size (greater than an acre) at lower elevations, referred to locally as Turtle Lake or Chapman Lake. Formed by natural landslide deposits on the northwest shoulder of Animas City Mountain and lying just outside the city limits of Durango, this shallow, productive pond supports an unusual aquatic and wetland community, including turtles, frogs, and other animals that are rare and restricted in the semi-arid environment of southwestern Colorado. Most of the pond is on private land, and although the present owner wishes to protect it, the area has no formal protection. Moreover, the adjacent meadows and wetlands are now covered with "for sale" signs, so the future of the pond's watershed is uncertain.

Another example of a rare and unique landscape element that adds to biodiversity in La Plata County is a series of glacial moraines dating from the Pleistocene that are located at the north edge of Durango. The dry, gravelly, south-facing slopes on these moraines support a population of nipple cactus numbering in the hundreds or low thousands. The nipple cactus, which produces showy pink flowers every June, is an uncommon species in La Plata County, usually occurring as only a few scattered individuals in an area. Thus, the population on the Durango moraines probably represents a substantial portion of the county's entire population of this species and certainly is one of the greatest concentrations of individuals. The future of this population is uncertain, however, since the moraines (all in private ownership) are now being rapidly covered with new houses, yards, driveways, and commercial facilities.

Species diversity—that is, the number of native species in a biotic community—tends to decrease as one moves to higher elevations in the southern Rocky Mountains. In southwestern Colorado, for example, there are roughly a dozen species of reptiles and amphibians at 1,650 meters but only two species at 3,000 meters.[10] Organisms at lower elevations experience drought stress, but those at higher elevations are subjected to cold temperatures and short growing seasons. Plant and animal species have been able to evolve a remarkable variety of adaptations to drought, but the temperature limitations apparently are harder to overcome, and species richness is reduced as a result.[11] Since low-elevation landscapes generally support greater species diversity than high-elevation landscapes, habitat degradation at the lower elevations is especially critical.

Species composition also is very different at high and low elevations; many of the kinds of organisms found in the foothills and basins cannot survive in the high mountains and vice versa. Much of the high-elevation portion of La Plata County is federally owned and managed by the San Juan National Forest and the Bureau of Land Management, but nearly all of the low-elevation lands are private or within the Southern Ute Reservation. Although there are important biodiversity issues related to management of the high-elevation public lands, I will not deal with

those in this chapter. Rather, I wish to emphasize the pivotal role that private landowners and developers play in determining what happens to biodiversity in La Plata County and similar areas throughout the West.

Spatial patterns of biodiversity in La Plata County have not been studied in great detail, and we have little information about the distribution, abundance, and demographic status of and threats to the vast majority of species and biotic communities within the county or region. However, we do have information about critical habitats of several native wildlife species that are conspicuous and highly valued by residents and visitors (data from the Colorado Division of Wildlife). The GIS (geographic information system) specialists working for La Plata County have evaluated the spatial distribution of these key wildlife habitats in relation to land ownership (table 1) and residential subdivisions (table 2). The results, described in the following paragraphs, show that the current transformation of La Plata County from a rural landscape of wildlands and agricultural fields into an exurban landscape of housing subdivisions poses a serious threat to the long-term viability of these wildlife populations. This is in large part because the portions of the landscape that developers and home buyers find desirable are often the same lands on which wildlife depend for critical stages in their life history.

Waterfowl breeding areas (duck production areas in figure 1 and tables 1 and 2) are the shallow ponds and marshes of the county, which harbor a great variety of very habitat-sensitive species in addition to the more obvious ducks and geese. These wetland species include turtles, frogs, marsh wrens, sandpipers, crayfish, water striders, rushes, sedges, and many other inconspicuous but ecologically important plants, invertebrates, and vertebrates that together contribute a major component of the biodiversity of the county. Wetlands of this kind are rare in this generally arid landscape, occupying only 5 percent of the total

Table 1. Distribution of Important Wildlife Habitat Among Public, Private, and Tribal Lands

Habitat category	Public lands[a]		Private lands		Tribal lands	
Duck production areas[b]	6,600	(13%)	32,562	(66%)	9,955	(20%)
Waterfowl winter habitat	138	(1%)	18,638	(72%)	7,102	(27%)
Waterfowl winter concentration areas	212	(1%)	16,917	(67%)	8,071	(32%)
Bald eagle winter habitat	9,404	(10%)	64,832	(69%)	19,272	(21%)
Bald eagle winter concentration areas	456	(4%)	7,915	(70%)	3,013	(26%)
Elk winter range	157,827	(21%)	414,229	(56%)	167,707	(23%)
Elk severe winter range	24,383	(11%)	162,720	(72%)	37,338	(17%)
Elk winter concentration areas	22,883	(26%)	61,813	(71%)	2,907	(3%)
Essential elk habitat[c]	15,177	(23%)	47,702	(73%)	2,907	(4%)
Mule deer winter range	57,058	(10%)	372,148	(62%)	167,552	(28%)
Mule deer severe winter range	17,287	(8%)	157,431	(69%)	52,350	(23%)
Mule deer winter concentration areas	13,659	(11%)	75,876	(60%)	37,376	(29%)
Black bear concentration areas	166,253	(58%)	114,326	(39%)	7,961	(3%)

Sources: Habitat data are from Colorado Division of Wildlife, and GIS analyses are from La Plata County GIS Department.

Notes: Numbers in the table are acres followed in parentheses by the percentage of all habitat of that category within the county.

[a]Public lands include National Forest, Bureau of Land Management, and state lands.

[b]Duck production areas are wetlands where waterfowl can breed in the summer.

[c]Essential elk habitat is a synthetic category defined as the overlap of elk winter concentration areas and severe winter range.

county area (figure 1). Two-thirds of the county's wetlands are found on private lands (table 1), and 12 percent of the 49,000 acres of wetlands in the county were within the boundaries of subdivisions as of 1995 (table 2).

Winter habitat for waterfowl is less extensive than summer habitat because many small ponds and marshes freeze over during winter. Most critical to maintaining winter populations are a few areas where the birds tend to concentrate, such as along the

major rivers and around a few ice-free ponds (figure 1). These habitats are found predominantly on private lands (72 percent); public lands contain only 1 percent of the ice-free waters in the county in winter (table 1). As of 1995, 16 percent of the winter concentration areas for waterfowl lay within subdivisions (table 2). Bald eagles, which also winter in La Plata County, tend to concentrate in the same kinds of areas as waterfowl; 70 percent of bald eagle concentration areas are on private land (table 1). In

Table 2. Total Acreage of Important Wildlife Habitats in La Plata County, Colorado, and Area Occupied by Subdivisions As of 1995

Habitat category	Total acres in county	Percentage of county	Acres occupied by subdivision	Percentage of habitat area within subdivision
Duck production areas[a]	49,115	5	6,047	12
Waterfowl winter habitat	25,878	2	1,754	7
Waterfowl winter concentration areas	25,199	2	3,954	16
Bald eagle winter habitat	93,511	9	12,618	13
Bald eagle winter concentration areas	11,384	1	689	6
Elk winter range	740,795	68	62,658	8
Elk severe winter range	224,460	21	28,095	13
Elk winter concentration areas	87,580	8	14,645	17
Essential elk habitat[b]	65,786	6	10,598	16
Mule deer winter range	597,789	55	54,714	9
Mule deer severe winter range	227,253	21	25,898	11
Mule deer winter concentration areas	127,674	12	7,439	6
Black bear concentration areas	288,781	27	20,215	7

Sources: Habitat data are from Colorado Division of Wildlife, and GIS analyses are from La Plata County GIS Department.

Notes: Subdivision acreage does not include "minor exempt subdivisions," which together affect nearly as much land as the major subdivisions referred to in this table.

[a]Duck production areas are wetlands where waterfowl can breed in the summer.

[b]Essential elk habitat is a synthetic category defined as the overlap of elk winter concentration areas and severe winter range.

1995, 13 percent of total eagle habitat and 6 percent of eagle concentration areas were occupied by subdivisions (table 2).

Elk and mule deer, prized by hunters and wildlife enthusiasts alike, are highly conspicuous residents of southwestern Colorado. To many residents and visitors, the elk are an important symbol of the wild Rocky Mountain landscape.[12] Mule deer occupy lower elevations throughout the year, but elk tend to summer in the lush meadows and forests of the San Juan Mountains and migrate to lower elevations in winter, when deep snow covers the forage of the high country. Numbers of elk and deer are controlled more by the limited availability of winter forage than by the relatively abundant summer forage. Although a large proportion of the county is potential winter habitat for deer and elk (table 1), the animals tend to concentrate in a few areas where forage production and snow conditions are especially favorable (figure 1). Important concentration areas include some of the major river valleys and certain south-facing slopes where snow melts relatively quickly. Other parts of the county provide habitat for deer and elk during severe winters; areas where forage is still available during severe snow conditions include steep south-facing slopes at middle elevations as well as the semi-desert lower elevations in the southern part of the county (figure 1). Some of these sites (but not all) produce relatively little forage because of unfavorable conditions for plant growth, and the animals tend to feed elsewhere when possible; but in severe winters the availability of these habitats means the difference between major die-offs and survival of elk and deer.

Perhaps the most crucial winter habitat for elk is those lands representing both winter concentration areas and severe winter habitat. The GIS was used to identify the places where these two conditions overlap, and the new synthetic category so produced is referred to as "essential elk habitat." Sixty to 70 percent of elk and deer concentration areas, severe winter habitat, and essential elk habitat in the county are found on private lands (table 1). As of 1995, 17 percent of elk concentration areas and 6 percent of mule deer concentration areas were within the boundaries of subdivisions; 13 percent of severe winter habitat for elk and 11 percent for deer were occupied by subdivisions; and 16 percent of essential elk habitat was within subdivisions (table 2, figure 1).

Black bears range widely over the mountains and foothills of southwestern Colorado, but they tend to concentrate in areas of moderate elevation, where food supplies, such as acorns and berries, are most abundant.[13] These habitats are found mostly on public lands (58 percent), but nearly 40 percent are on private lands (table 2). Seven percent of black bear concentration areas were occupied by subdivisions in 1995 (table 2).

As table 2 shows, subdivisions now occupy from 6 to 17 per-cent of various kinds of important wildlife habitat in La Plata County. At first glance, subdivisions might appear to have had little impact on biodiversity to date, since from 83 to 94 percent of the habitat in each category remains undisturbed. However, the actual impact of subdivisions is substantially greater than is indicated by the numbers in table 2 because many subdivisions lie adjacent to, but not on top of, important units of wildlife habitat. For example, developers do not build homes within large wetlands or floodplains, but they often build right up to the edge of the wetland or floodplain. An adjacent subdivision, with its associated human disturbance, cats and dogs, and habitat alteration, may preclude successful breeding by waterfowl or peaceful winter foraging by elk nearly as effectively as a development directly on top of the habitat parcel in question.[14] Subdivisions may also be barriers to migration of animals between patches of suitable habitat or between summer and winter range.

Another important reason why the numbers in table 2 are probably unduly optimistic is because growth is continuing apace. In 1995, the La Plata County Commission approved a 244-unit subdivision for 962 acres lying within one of the larger blocks of previously undeveloped elk winter concentration area, and a comparable number of lots are approved every 18 months as part of "minor exempt subdivisions," those involving fewer than four lots and not requiring any assessment of cumulative impacts by the county planning department. Moreover, if the growth rates of the early 1990s continue, the county population will double in 20 to 25 years. If development patterns continue as they have, then we can roughly estimate that habitat impacts also will double within 20 to 25 years. If we double the numbers in the last column of table 2 to project the effects of a doubling of the county's human population, we find that by 2020—if current trends continue—approximately one-fourth of the county's waterfowl breeding areas, one-third of the waterfowl winter concentration areas, one-quarter of the elk severe winter range, and one-third of elk winter concentration areas will lie within subdivisions. An additional unknown but probably large percentage of these habitats will lie immediately adjacent to subdivisions. The exact implications of such a situation are difficult to predict; wildlife numbers may gradually decline, or they could remain relatively high until some threshold of habitat availability is crossed, after which populations could plummet precipitously. What does seem certain, however, is that much of the wildlife and native biodiversity that we now value in La Plata County, and often take for granted, could become quite scarce within the next human generation.

The purpose of these projections is not to accurately predict the future of biodiversity in La Plata County. Such prediction is impossible because there are too many critical variables that cannot be known with certainty. Rather, the purpose of this analysis is to demonstrate the crucial importance of the spatial relationships between human development patterns and the habitat that maintains biodiversity. The results further suggest that our present course is leading to a future that many will find undesirable, and one that can be avoided by making better choices about land use today.

2. *The size, shape, and juxtaposition of habitat patches within the landscape may be as important as the total extent of habitat in determining the population size and viability of sensitive species.* The leading cause of species extinction in the world today is loss of habitat;[15] therefore, habitat preservation is a centerpiece of any conservation strategy. However, even a large total acreage of a particular kind of habitat may not maintain all of the species that depend on that habitat if the individual patches of habitat are too small or too isolated within a sea of development. A major threat to our native biota is fragmentation, that is, the breaking of a for-

merly extensive habitat into small patches or the perforation of a residual large patch with roads and other anthropogenic features.[16]

Fragmentation actually can increase species richness (total number of species), because it creates new kinds of habitats. For example, creating openings within an extensive unbroken forest allows a mixing of species adapted to open lands with species of the closed forest. However, the goal of conservation biology is not simply to maximize the number of species in a landscape, because all species are not equivalent in terms of their contribution to ecological function and integrity. Many of the species that invade the openings in a fragmented forest are generalists that can thrive in a wide range of habitats and are not in need of conservation measures. But the activities of these wide-ranging species may threaten the long-term survival of specialized forest species that have narrow habitat tolerances, whose numbers are declining in North America. Species that can persist only away from habitat edges or that require a large patch for a critical stage in their life history are termed *interior species*. Species that do not require large patches and can thrive in disturbed areas or along the margins of natural habitat are called *edge species*. Nearly all interior species in southwestern Colorado are native to the area, and many are rare or threatened. In contrast, most edge species are common across much of the West, and many are exotic species that were introduced from elsewhere.

Predation and brood parasitism by edge species are two important causes for the decline of interior vertebrate species, especially birds, following habitat fragmentation.[17] Birds that nest on the ground or in low bushes (e.g., hermit thrush, orange-crowned warbler, and green-tailed towhee) are especially vulnerable to predators that penetrate forests or shrublands from the surrounding open lands. Examples of these nest predators include native species like raccoons, striped skunks, and magpies, as well as introduced species like domestic dogs and cats.[18] Since the predators tend to remain near the edges of dense forest, birds nesting away from edges are more likely to be successful in rearing their young. Those that attempt to nest near the edge or within a tiny patch of forest where there is no real interior may suffer complete loss of their eggs and young to predators. In deciduous forests of the eastern United States, substantial egg predation was observed as far as 600 meters in from the forest edge.[19] This finding suggests that a forest patch must be greater than 1,200 meters across to provide an effective interior habitat where ground nesters can escape predation from edge species. Moreover, in two forest patches of the same total acreage, a round- or square-shaped patch has more interior habitat than a linear or convoluted patch.

Most of the research on effects of forest fragmentation on birds has been done in eastern deciduous forests, and some specific recommendations about the size and shape of remnant patches of native habitat may not be applicable to the coniferous forests and other distinctive ecosystems of the West.[20] Nevertheless, the studies in eastern forests clearly indicate that we must be concerned with the size and shape of the patches of natural forest and shrubland that we leave when carving up the landscape for new subdivisions: Even if the total acreage of natural forest or shrubland remains high, its conservation value may be nil if the entire area of natural habitat is easily accessible to predators from the openings that are created. We also have an urgent need for research on the specific effects of habitat fragmentation on western ecosystems.

A major nest parasite in La Plata County and elsewhere is the brown-headed cowbird. This species does not build its own nest or care for its own eggs but lays its eggs in the nests of other birds, which then unwittingly raise the young cowbirds—often to the detriment of their own offspring.[21] Cowbirds thrive in nonforested lands, especially where cattle are present, and cowbird parasitism can significantly reduce the reproductive success of host species for a distance of at least 200 meters into adjacent deciduous forests in the eastern United States.[22] The overall impact of cowbirds on forest birds in southwestern Colorado is not known at present, but studies initiated recently indicate that it may be substantial. Joseph and Catherine Ortega (personal communication, 1995) found that 70 percent of warbling vireo and 80 percent of solitary vireo nests were parasitized by cowbirds in a riparian woodland adjacent to agricultural fields in rural La Plata County.

The effects of fragmentation on plant species have received much less attention than the effects on animals, and it is difficult to generalize about the mechanisms or even the magnitude of fragmentation effects on plants. This is a topic on which research is urgently needed. Two important ways in which habitat fragmentation may affect native plant diversity and population viability are by facilitating invasion by competitive, nonnative weeds and by blocking seed and spore dispersal or movement of pollinators. Both of these mechanisms, which involve connections between patches rather than patch size and shape per se, are discussed in the following section.[23]

3. *Connections between patches in the landscape play a critical role in biodiversity, both for maintaining viable populations of desirable native species and for spreading disturbance and undesirable species.* Many vertebrate species in the Rocky Mountain region are migratory, moving from summer habitats in the high mountains to winter ranges at lower elevations or latitudes. Only a handful of species of mammals and birds (e.g., pika and white-tailed ptarmigan) spend the winter in the harsh environment above the timber-

line.[24] More species are able to endure winter in the forested portions of the mountains, but a great many native animals are entirely dependent on being able to reach suitable winter habitats at the lower elevations. Landscape structure plays a key role in facilitating or disrupting these natural migration patterns.

We have little specific information on critical migration routes for most species in La Plata County. Migration patterns of elk and mule deer, however, are reasonably well known because of their status as game animals. Elk prefer to follow sunny slopes and gentle topography, and they avoid steep, north-facing slopes with deep snow (A. W. Spencer, personal communication, 1995). Their large size makes them a hazard to motorists when they cross major highways. Every winter many elk are killed and many automobiles demolished when the two collide. Because they have no alternatives, the animals continue to migrate from summer to winter habitats, but this movement is becoming more difficult and dangerous for both elk and humans as their traditional movement corridors become obstructed by subdivisions and strip development along highways.

In addition to the effects of landscape structure on seasonal migration, the distribution and connections between suitable patches of habitat influence the movement of breeding animals and hence gene flow within a population, as well as the dispersal of young animals.[25] Some species are able to move freely throughout human-altered landscapes, but others are blocked by seemingly innocuous landscape features.[26] One of the most important barriers to animal movement is roads. Many small mammals, amphibians, and invertebrates appear unwilling to cross even a small dirt road.[27] Thus, bisecting a large patch of natural habitat with a road to service a few homes on large lots may effectively divide a population of sensitive animals into two isolated subpopulations—and the smaller and more isolated a pop-

ulation, the greater the risk of extinction via inbreeding, demographic changes, and natural disasters. Unfortunately, we have almost no specific information on the magnitude of these kinds of effects in La Plata County. Nevertheless, maintaining connections between patches of suitable habitat is an important component of maintaining viable populations of native species.

But connections between patches of *disturbed* ground may actually be a threat to native species.[28] Some plant species of open, disturbed habitats are very aggressive and may be capable of competitively displacing the natives—especially in the presence of chronic disturbance by livestock grazing, fertilization, or soil disruption.[29] Good examples of competitive plant invaders in La Plata County are cheatgrass, leafy spurge, gray-spotted knapweed, and muskthistle—all natives of Eurasia. I have watched many roadsides and overgrazed pastures being overtaken by these species within a period of a few years. These and other aggressive, nonnative species are extremely difficult to eradicate once they become established. The best strategy for noxious weed control is to prevent their becoming established in the first place, and the spatial distribution and connectedness of disturbed ground (i.e., landscape structure) is a major determinant of weed spread and establishment.

Landscape Ecology Concepts Related to Energy and Materials in Ecosystems

4. *Different energy sources and uses have different costs and impacts on ecosystems.* Natural ecosystems are powered primarily by solar energy that is harvested by plants and moves through food webs to support the entire biotic community. Solar energy in this setting is a perpetual energy source with few adverse side effects. In contrast, the pseudo-rural landscapes being created in the

mountain West today are fueled almost exclusively by fossil energy sources that are nonrenewable and are associated with substantial costs and environmental impact. The transportation system, based on frequent, long-distance travel by automobile, depends entirely on uninterrupted supplies of gasoline from sources outside the county and the region. Most existing as well as new homes are heated with natural gas, which is produced locally in La Plata and some other western counties but is nevertheless a nonrenewable carbon-based fuel. Other homes are heated with electricity generated by large coal-fired power plants, with propane, or with firewood.

The global ecological effects of fossil-fuel consumption are too well documented to require further elaboration here. What is striking about the current development patterns in the West is the degree to which the undesirable aspects of a fossil-fuel economy are being utterly ignored. By dispersing homes over large areas, we are committing ourselves to a long-term dependence on private automobiles, since alternative forms of transportation like buses, bicycles, or walking are impractical in this kind of a setting. Most remarkable is the continued reliance on traditional fossil-fuel-based heating systems in one of the best regions in the country for passive solar heating. Although there are notable exceptions, very few of the new homes being built in La Plata County explicitly incorporate passive solar features in their architectural designs, even though effective technologies have been available and well understood for over 20 years.

5. *Both desirable and undesirable substances cycle through ecosystems at variable rates; resources may be available only in finite supplies, and pollutants may disappear slowly.* A major limiting resource in a semi-arid environment like southwestern Colorado is water.[30] Most of the new homes being built on large lots are serviced by individual wells, since a central water supply system is cost pro-

hibitive with this kind of landscape design. The number of wells in La Plata County has been growing exponentially since the 1970s (figure 2). Questions are now being raised about just how much water is available in the county and whether future home builders will have an adequate supply. There is also concern that new wells may deplete the water supply in older wells and springs, with as yet undetermined legal or ethical consequences. Developers are now required to demonstrate the presence of adequate water for new developments, but the actual groundwater supply is not known precisely, and in practice it is difficult for the county to deny a proposed development on the basis of its impact on the groundwater resource.

The wide dispersion of homes in La Plata County also makes it impractical to collect sewage for treatment at a central facility. Therefore, most new homes have an individual sewage disposal system. There is likely some threshold in density of septic tanks after which well-water pollution becomes highly probable, but where this threshold may lie is not known. In addition to septic tanks, there are numerous small sewage lagoons in La Plata County, which are thought by some to be a health hazard and to breed mosquitoes (Peter Holton, La Plata County Planning Department, personal communication, 1995). The county must also deal with other sources of water pollution, for example, salty wastewater associated with natural gas production that may be injected accidentally into clean groundwater aquifers and contaminate wells, springs, and seeps.

The cumulative impacts of these various forms of water pollution, as well as the spatial features of their sources and movements through the hydrologic systems of La Plata County, are not well understood at present, which hampers efforts to regulate water consumption and pollution. Moreover, many new home buyers are unaware of the hydrologic system that supports their supply of clean water and their disposal of wastes; hence,

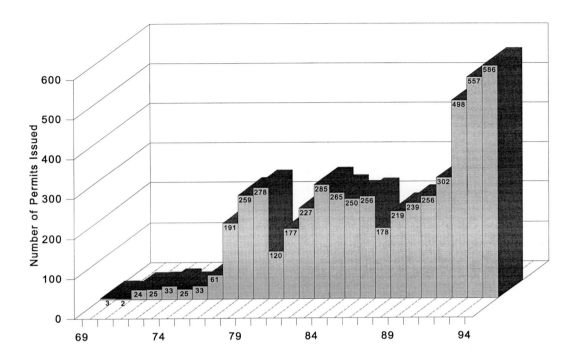

Source: Colorado Division of Water Resources

Figure 2. Number of water-well permits issued annually in La Plata County, Colorado, from 1969 to 1994. (Data and figure provided by Peter Holton, La Plata County Planning Department.)

they will suffer unpleasant surprises if the system proves inadequate.

Landscape Ecology Concepts Related to Natural Disturbance

6. *Natural disturbances such as fires and floods—when occurring within their prehistoric range of variability in frequency, extent, and intensity—have an essential regenerative effect on ecosystems.* Recent ecological research has shown that natural disturbances such as floods and fire are essential to the long-term integrity and function of many ecosystems. For example, periodic low-intensity fire, occurring at intervals of 5 to 40 years, formerly maintained rapid nutrient cycling and high biodiversity in the ponderosa pine forests that cover a large portion of La Plata County. Euro-American settlers disrupted this natural fire regime beginning in the late 1800s, and today most ponderosa pine forests in the

county have not burned for over 100 years—a fire-free interval far longer than ever occurred in the previous several centuries. These stands now have excessive numbers of small trees and abnormally deep layers of dead organic matter on the forest floor.[31] When fires do occur today, they tend to be hotter and more damaging than prehistoric fires because of the unusually high fuel levels that have developed over the past century. Recognizing these undesirable changes, public-land management agencies are now attempting to restore the natural ecological role of fire by intentionally setting fires during weather conditions when fires can be controlled and allowing some lightning-caused fires to burn without interference. This program can ultimately reestablish many of the ecological characteristics and processes that have been lost, as well as reduce the risk of uncontrollable wildfires burning through heavy fuels.[32]

These well-intentioned fire-management efforts are being seriously constrained, however, by the building of expensive new homes in ponderosa pine forests, pinon-juniper woodlands, and native shrublands—all of which were historically rejuvenated by periodic fire. Architects and developers generally do not think about wildfire in designing homes and subdivisions, and as a result many of the new homes in La Plata County are considered by firefighters to be indefensible if a wildfire occurs under hot, dry weather conditions.[33] This development pattern has two undesirable consequences. First, many people have unwittingly put their lives and property at risk. Second, managers are under pressure to prevent fires that would benefit the land because those fires pose a threat to the exurban development occurring within the ecosystem. In fact, because it can be difficult to stop a prescribed fire precisely at the border between national forest and private land, ecologically beneficial fires burning on public lands are often suppressed because they may threaten homes and structures on private lands just across the border.

Most counties prohibit building on floodplains but have almost no restrictions on building homes in fire-dependent ecosystems. This is due in part to previous lack of understanding about fire ecology but also to a perception that we can control wildfire with modern fire-fighting technologies. We are growing increasingly aware that we cannot eliminate fire from many kinds of ecosystems; all we can do is postpone it, with often disastrous effects because of the accumulation of fuels in the absence of fire.[34] There is also growing recognition that fire is an ecological process essential to the long-term integrity and function of many ecosystems. A well-crafted plan will incorporate the best available information about spatial patterns in fire history and fire ecology throughout the county and will regulate home building accordingly to protect human values as well as allow essential ecological processes like fire to continue to operate.

Landscape Ecology Concepts Related to Human Social, Economic, and Political Systems

7. *Landscape structure influences costs and opportunities for providing basic services to people.* Social and economic costs are associated with any kind of landscape plan. Nevertheless, dispersing homes in large lots over an extensive land area maximizes the cost per person of providing utilities, law enforcement, road maintenance, school buses, and other services. It would be far more efficient and less expensive, for example, to run electrical lines and a school bus to a cluster of homes than to the same number of homes scattered over a square mile. An ethical issue that has received surprisingly little attention in the West is the question of who should pay the costs of dispersed home development. At present, the property taxes paid by new residents and the development fees paid by developers together are usually less than the costs incurred by La Plata County government for providing services to new subdivisions (Wayne Bedor, La Plata County Government, personal communication, 1995). Thus, ex-

isting residents are in effect subsidizing the exurban sprawl now taking place.[35] A recent study in Gallatin County, Montana, reached a similar conclusion: County government had to spend more money than it received from dispersed residential lands but received more than it spent for agricultural and open lands (M. Haggerty, Montana State University, personal communication, 1996).

The consequences of our choices regarding landscape planning will be with us for a long time. For instance, we are now essentially ruling out the possibility of efficient public transportation even in the future, because our new housing is being developed at such low density. If the country ever experiences a serious gasoline shortage, we may regret having locked ourselves into a transportation system that depends so completely on private cars. If energy prices rise substantially for any reason, we may wonder why we passed up the opportunity to install solar heating in our new homes rather than rely on traditional non-renewable energy sources.

8. *Landscape structure both influences and reflects human values and aesthetic experiences.* Spreading people over a huge area remote from stores, schools, and other services means that people have to drive a great many miles every day, which of course leads to traffic congestion in the major business centers and along the major highways leading into those towns. La Plata County's road system was designed in the early twentieth century for a sparse, predominantly agricultural population that made one or two trips to town per week; it is woefully inadequate to handle the ever-increasing volume of traffic of the 1990s (Shirley Baty, La Plata County Commissioner, personal communication, 1995).

In Durango, the largest community in La Plata County and the major business center, long-time residents have observed that a qualitative change in traffic seems to have occurred in the early 1990s: the city streets used to be crowded with tourists in sum-mer and during ski season but were relatively quiet in the spring and fall; now they are crowded year-round with commuters from outlying areas of the county. In summer 1995 the county experienced a slump in tourist visitation, but the roads were as crowded as ever, and traffic actually became gridlocked on several occasions—a distressing experience for people who moved here in part to escape just these kinds of traffic conditions.

This subjective experience of having crossed a threshold in traffic conditions is supported by quantitative data from the county clerk's office (figure 3) showing that the vehicular population in La Plata County is growing even faster than the human population, and that since about 1990 the number of vehicles has exceeded the number of humans. A major reason for the rapid growth of automobile numbers is, of course, the widely dispersed pattern of residential development that requires multiple vehicles and multiple trips daily for each household. Studies and plans are in progress for widening roads and improving intersections, but these kinds of improvements are unlikely to reduce traffic congestion if the number of vehicles and trips continue to grow as they have in the last decade. In fact, as Judith A. Martin and Sam Bass Warner Jr. point out, the needs of automobiles often drive land-use and development decisions (see chapter 6).

A low-density, exurban landscape design may have important social as well as environmental effects. Architects Andres Duany and Elizabeth Plater-Zyberk point out that most of the suburban landscapes that have been created in America since World War II tend to segregate families by economic class and to isolate people by making it difficult to go anywhere except by private automobile.[36] The expensive houses now being built on large lots in the mountain West have these same effects but on an even grander scale. The large lots and lack of sidewalks discourage visiting with, or even knowing, one's neighbors. Affordable housing is almost nonexistent in most of the new subdivisions, some of which are surrounded with fences, gates, and security guards

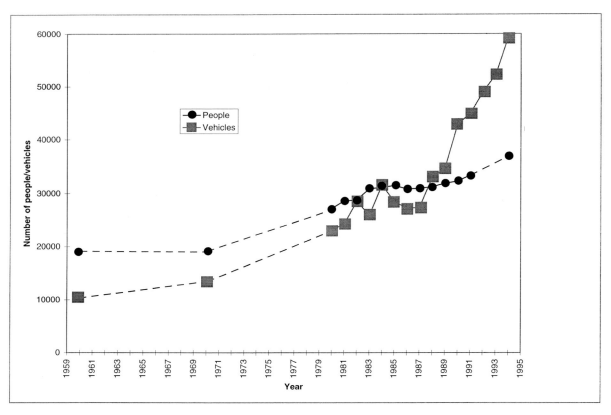

Figure 3. Number of people and of vehicles (including cars, trucks, trailers, and recreational vehicles) in La Plata County from 1960 to 1994. (Data provided by Linda Daly, La Plata County Clerk's Office.)

to keep out "undesirable" people. People with low-paying service jobs increasingly cannot afford to live in the upscale communities where they work, so they commute long distances or camp in nearby national forests.[37] There generally are no services at all within the well-to-do subdivisions, only large houses, roads, and driveways; so even wealthy people must drive into town for everything from groceries, medical care, and entertainment to school and activities for children.

I suggest that such a pattern of housing people is destructive not only environmentally but socially as well. This pattern is another reason for referring to such development as a pseudo-rural landscape: Houses occupy only a small proportion of the land area, as in a true rural setting, but the "community" has none of the cohesiveness or shared purpose of a viable rural populace. Indeed, what kind of community spirit and sense of working together for a common cause could possibly be fostered under such fragmented conditions?

Alternative Landscape Designs for the Mountain West

To slow development by limiting the number of people moving into the scenic landscapes of the Rocky Mountain region is probably not feasible, given the demographic and economic changes that are now occurring in the United States.[38] In fact, to try to stop growth may not be ethically right, since to do so would quickly accelerate the social stratification that we now see by hugely inflating the prices of available homes and land. Moreover, even the long-time residents of the West or their ancestors were once newcomers to this region. However, I believe that it is appropriate to regulate the patterns of land development and housing that accommodate these immigrants who come here seeking a more aesthetically rewarding life. Indeed, I would argue that we have an ethical obligation to reduce the impacts of growth, because the West is a sublime landscape of national and even international significance, a place where people can come for spiritual and aesthetic rejuvenation.[39] The present pattern of growth appears to be destroying many of the qualities that make the West a special place, and there is no obvious reason why we should have to accept this kind of destruction.

There are many alternatives to the present pattern of exurban development.[40] An obvious design is to create clusters of new homes within a small portion of a large tract of private land and then designate the remaining land as open space with some form of binding, protective covenant. Well-designed clusters of homes would provide their owners with the open space and scenery

that they desire, as well as a few close neighbors and a chance of belonging to a community. The houses could also be designed to fit in with and take advantage of the local environment, for example, by incorporating passive solar-heating features. The cluster of homes would constitute a "high-density" development locally, but the open space thus maintained would provide genuine wildlife habitat and would enhance biodiversity and scenic beauty. The overall human density, defined in terms of people or houses per square mile, would be low. David Theobald showed that a larger number of homes in a clustered pattern actually caused less habitat fragmentation than fewer homes in a dispersed pattern.[41] A group in La Plata County, San Juan Co-Housing, is currently developing just such a community (Mac Thomson, personal communication, 1995).

But we can be even more creative than this. Another alternative is actually to create several new towns.[42] These would be small towns, complete with grocery stores, schools, daycare services, doctor's offices, coffee shops, and the like. Residents of these new small towns would be able to live and do most of their business in town without having to make several car trips daily to the urban centers. The lands between the towns could remain open for agriculture, wildlife, or scenery. La Plata County contains several small townsites that were viable communities and centers of commerce prior to World War II; these could be revitalized relatively easily.

There are several reasons why these and other kinds of landscape design are not being widely implemented in La Plata County and the mountain West today. Some people distrust the idea of clustering houses because they fear that the open space that is left will later be filled up with additional high-density development. However, a variety of legal arrangements, such as conservation easements and land trusts, are available to protect open space in perpetuity.

Another objection to clustered development or new small

towns is voiced by many realtors and land developers who say that people are moving to Colorado precisely to get away from neighbors—that they really do prefer to live on large isolated lots and drive into town every day. This is undoubtedly true for some newcomers, but it is difficult to assess how widespread this preference is because the consumer is being given few real choices. Most of the new subdivisions being developed are composed of large houses on large lots, and the real estate advertisements (which have grown to an entire section in every Sunday edition of the Durango newspaper) routinely extol the wonders of living in a pristine wilderness adjacent to public land but only 10 minutes from the center of town. If newcomers were informed of the larger implications of pseudo-rural development and given genuine choices, their tastes might be very different.

Finally, the present regulatory structure actually discourages clustering and other creative designs for home development because it usually focuses on specifying minimum lot sizes (acres per house) rather than on controlling overall density (measured as houses per acre or per 100 acres). Although often well intentioned, requirements for larger lot sizes actually accelerate the fragmentation of land and are counterproductive to the goal of maintaining genuine open space and wildlife habitat.[43]

Another objection to any kind of land-use planning is that it may impose on the rights of individual landowners. If the county identifies key wildlife habitats, for example, and then prohibits or restricts subdivisions in those areas, the owners of those lands are denied the opportunity to sell or develop their land for high profits. Similarly, some farmers and ranchers fear that if their property is designated agricultural, they or their children will be forced to remain working in agriculture. A large proportion of the farmers and ranchers in this region are nearing retirement and have children who do not want to operate the family farm or ranch, or are unable to do so because of cur-

rent low prices for agricultural products. There are a number of possible solutions to this problem.[44] One is the idea of transferring development rights. A landowner could sell the development rights on his or her property to another landowner, who would then be allowed to develop an additional number of new homes. The first property would thereby remain undeveloped, while the second property would be developed at a higher density. Both landowners would profit financially, and the entire community would profit by preventing development on lands important for biodiversity or scenic beauty. To implement this kind of solution requires a great deal of education, for most landowners in La Plata County appear to be largely unaware of tools like the transfer of development rights. It also requires leadership from the county government and the building of trust among residents, who tend to be extremely suspicious of any government intrusion into their business.

The present uncontrolled pattern of growth in the mountain West can be viewed as a modern "tragedy of the commons."[45] The "commons" are resources that are used by all members of the community but are owned and protected by no one. In this sense, the commons in La Plata County consist of the sense of open space, unobstructed views, biodiversity, and a rural pace of life—all of which attract people to this beautiful region. At the moment, because each person is pursuing his or her own self-interest without regard for the needs of the whole community, we are rapidly and probably irreversibly destroying the things that make this part of the West a unique and satisfying place to live. The government by itself cannot prevent a tragedy of the commons. Ultimately, a great deal of responsibility falls on individual people—land owners, developers, realtors, purchasers of new homes, and others—to make individual decisions about what they do with the land that enhance and sustain the whole community rather than degrade it. That community includes, at a minimum, all of the human residents of La Plata County; in the best of circumstances the community would be recognized as including the plants, animals, soils, and waters as well as the human residents and visitors.[46] Curt Meine argues that we have drawn our distinctions too sharply between public and private land, between what is useful and what is beautiful (see chapter 3). We need to think instead of the whole, to design communities that fit the natural contours of the land and all of its residents.

If we are to save the special qualities of the western landscape, landowners will have to learn to think not just in terms of their "rights" to exploit the land as they wish but also of their responsibilities to the human and biotic community. Owning property in proximity to the only natural low-elevation pond in La Plata County, for example, should be looked upon as a rare privilege and a sacred trust rather than simply an opportunity for maximizing profits by developing lots.[47] New home buyers need to look beyond their own romantic notions of buying a piece of virgin wilderness and consider the impacts of their individual choice of a home on the scenic beauty, diversity, and ecological integrity of the greater community. As Aldo Leopold stated so aptly, "A thing is right when it tends to preserve the integrity, stability, and beauty of the biotic community. It is wrong when it tends otherwise."[48]

Government can help in this process of choosing what is right by providing information (e.g., locations of critical wildlife habitat) as well as economic and political incentives for good land stewardship (e.g., mediating transfers of development rights). La Plata County now has an excellent opportunity to redirect the patterns and impacts of growth within its boundaries. The county is in the process of developing a plan that will set guidelines and requirements for future development. There have been numerous attempts since 1959 to implement a plan, but all previous efforts have failed through a combination of apathy and outright resistance (Josh Joswick, La Plata County Commissioner, personal communication, 1995). This latest effort may succeed, however, for at least three reasons. First, the county planning commission is working hard to involve people from many different sectors of the community from the earliest stages of planning, to identify problem areas, to obtain input, and to develop a sense of individual ownership in the plan. Second, county residents are becoming keenly aware of the undesirable impacts of the present pattern of growth: traffic and wildlife conflicts have become impossible to ignore. Finally, the makeup of the county's population has changed substantially in the last two decades. Ironically, it may be the newcomers, who came here precisely because they value the area's natural scenic and environmental qualities and can most clearly see the impacts of uncontrolled exurban sprawl, who will have the necessary political will to effect change.

Acknowledgments

I could not have written this essay without the expert assistance of Alan Andrews of the La Plata County GIS Department, who did all of the GIS analyses reported here. Peter Holton and Fred Vanden Bergh, with the La Plata County Planning Department, provided additional essential information and encouragement. Jan Neleigh, chair of the La Plata County Planning Commission, gave me a crash course in planning theory and in the intricacies of the current La Plata County permit system. Jim Garner, with the Colorado Division of Wildlife, provided wildlife data and permission to report those data in this essay. I am grateful to the following people for providing critical reviews of an early draft: Peter Holton, Deborah Kendall, Richard L. Knight, J. Page Lindsey, Ed Marston, Jan Neleigh, Joe Ortega, Phil Shuler, Tom Sluss, L. Preston Somers, Albert W. Spencer, and Mac Thomson. I also benefited greatly from discussions and critical reviews by the other contributors to this book as well as the students and visiting participants in the landscape ecology seminar at the University of Minnesota in winter 1995.

Notes

1. N. T. Hobbes, comments delivered at symposium hosted by R. L. Knight, "Subdividing the West: Implications of Population Growth," 1994. Videocassette available from Office of Instructional Services, Colorado State University, Fort Collins, CO 80523 (cassette number TV09488).

2. D. M. Theobald, "Morphology and Effects of Mountain Land Use Change in Colorado: A Multi-Scale Analysis" (Ph.D. diss., University of Colorado, Boulder, 1995).

3. Hobbes, comments delivered at "Subdividing the West"; E. Marston, comments delivered at "Subdividing the West"; Theobald, "Morphology and Effects of Mountain Land Use Change in Colorado."

4. Theobald, "Morphology and Effects of Mountain Land Use Change in Colorado."

5. R. T. T. Forman, *Land Mosaics: The Ecology of Landscapes and Regions* (Cambridge: Cambridge University Press, 1995).

6. W. H. Romme, D. W. Jamieson, J. S. Redders, G. Bigsby, J. P. Lindsey, D. Kendall, R. Cowen, T. Kreykes, A. W. Spencer, and J. C. Ortega, "Old-Growth Forests of the San Juan National Forest in Southwestern Colorado," in M. R. Kaufmann, W. H. Moir, and R. L. Bassett , tech. coordinators, *Old-Growth Forests in the Southwest and Rocky Mountain Regions: Proceedings of a Workshop* (USDA Forest Service General Technical Report RM-213, 1992), pp. 154–165; L. Floyd-Hanna, A. W. Spencer, and W. H. Romme, "Biotic Communities of the Semi-Arid Foothills and Valleys," in R. Blair, ed., *The Western San Juan Mountains, Colorado: A Guide to the Geology, Ecology, and Human History along the Skyway* (Niwot: University Press of Colorado, 1996), chapter 11; D. W. Jamieson, W. H. Romme, and L. P. Somers, "Biotic Communities of the Cool Mountains," in Blair, ed., *The Western San Juan Mountains, Colorado*, chapter 12.

7. R. T. T. Forman and M. Godron, *Landscape Ecology* (New York: Wiley, 1986); P. G. Risser, "Landscape Ecology: State of the Art," in M. G. Turner, ed., *Landscape Heterogeneity and Disturbance* (New York: Springer-Verlag, 1987); Forman, *Land Mosaics*.

8. Forman and Godron, *Landscape Ecology*; R. T. T. Forman, "Ecologically Sustainable Landscapes: The Role of Spatial Configuration," in I. S. Zonneveld and R. T. T. Forman, eds., *Changing Landscapes: An Ecological Perspective* (New York: Springer-Verlag, 1990), pp.261–278.

9. R. Noss and A. Y. Cooperrider, *Saving Nature's Legacy: Protecting and Restoring Biodiversity* (Washington, D.C.: Island Press, 1994).

10. A. W. Spencer and W. H. Romme, "Ecological Patterns in the San Juan Mountains," in Blair, ed., *The Western San Juan Mountains, Colorado*, chapter 10.

11. Ibid.

12. O. J. Murie, *The Elk of North America* (Stackpole Company and Wildlife Management Institute, 1951; reprint, Jackson, Wyo.: Teton Bookshop, 1979).

13. T. D. I. Beck, "Black Bears of West–Central Colorado," Technical Publication Number 39 (Denver: Colorado Division of Wildlife, 1991).

14. R. L. Knight, G. N. Wallace, and W. E. Riebsame, "Ranching the View: Subdivisions versus Agriculture," *Conservation Biology* 9 (1995): 459–461.

15. P. Ehrlich and A. Ehrlich, *Extinction: The Causes and Consequences of the Disappearance of Species* (New York: Ballantine, 1981).

16. R. F. Noss and B. Csuti, "Habitat Fragmentation," in G. K. Meffe, C. R. Carroll (eds.), and contributors, *Principles of Conservation Biology* (Sunderland, Mass.: Sinauer, 1994), 237–264; Forman, *Land Mosaics*.

17. D. S. Wilcove, "Nest Predation in Forest Tracts and the Decline of Migratory Songbirds," *Ecology* 66 (1985): 1211–1214; J. Terborgh, *Where Have All the Birds Gone?* (Princeton, N.J.: Princeton University Press, 1989); Noss and Csuti, "Habitat Fragmentation."

18. Knight, Wallace, and Riebsame, "Ranching the View."

19. Wilcove, "Nest Predation in Forest Tracts and the Decline of Migratory Songbirds"; Noss and Csuti, "Habitat Fragmentation."

20. K. McGarigal and W. C. McComb, "Relationships between Land-

scape Structure and Breeding Birds in the Oregon Coast Range," *Ecological Monographs* 65 (1995): 235–260.

21. H. Friedman and L. F. Kiff, "The Parasitic Cowbirds and Their Hosts," *Proceedings of the Western Foundation for Vertebrate Zoology* 2 (1985): 225–302; Noss and Csuti, "Habitat Fragmentation."

22. Noss and Csuti, "Habitat Fragmentation."

23. Forman, *Land Mosaics.*

24. Jamieson, Romme, and Somers, "Biotic Communities of the Cool Mountains."

25. Noss and Csuti, "Habitat Fragmentation."

26. K. Henein and G. Merriam, "The Elements of Connectivity Where Corridor Quality Is Variable," *Landscape Ecology* 4 (1990): 157–170.

27. Noss and Csuti, "Habitat Fragmentation"; Knight, Wallace, and Riebsame, "Ranching the View."

28. M. Benninger-Truax, J. L. Vankat, and R. L. Schaefer, "Trail Corridors As Habitat and Conduits for Movement of Plant Species in Rocky Mountain National Park, Colorado, USA," *Landscape Ecology* 6 (1992): 269–278.

29. J. A. Drake et al., eds., *Biological Invasion: A Global Perspective* (Chichester, N.Y.: published on behalf of SCOPE by Wiley, 1989); H. A. Mooney and J. A. Drake, eds., *Ecology of Biological Invasions of North America and Hawaii* (New York: Springer-Verlag, 1986); M. E. Soulé, "The Onslaught of Alien Species, and Other Challenges in the Coming Decades," *Conservation Biology* 4 (1990): 233–239.

30. See, for example, J. W. Powell, "Report on Lands of the Arid Region of the United States, with a More Detailed Account of the Lands of Utah" (facsimile of 1879 edition; Boston: Harvard Common Press, 1983).

31. W. W. Covington and M. M. Moore. "Southwestern Ponderosa Forest Structure: Changes Since Euro-American Settlement," *Journal of Forestry* 92 (1994): 39–47.

32. M. Kaufmann, R. T. Graham, D. A Boyce Jr., W. H. Moir, L. Perry, R. T. Reynolds, R. L. Bassett, P. Melhop, C. B. Edminster, W. M. Block, and P. S. Corn, "An Ecological Basis for Ecosystem Management," USDA Forest Service General Technical Report RM-24, 1994.

33. San Juan National Forest Association, "When Fire Burns," special supplement to the *Durango Herald* newspaper, May 1995, Durango, Colo.

34. Covington and Moore, "Southwestern Ponderosa Forest Structure."

35. K. Kasowki, "The Costs of Sprawl, Revisited," *National Growth Management Leadership Project Newsletter* 3, no. 2: 1, 3–6.

36. A. Duany and E. Plater-Zyberk, "The Second Coming of the American Small Town," *Wilson Quarterly* 16 (1992): 19–50.

37. E. Marston, comments delivered at "Subdividing the West."

38. Ibid.

39. See J. Sax, *Mountains without Handrails: Reflections on the National Parks* (Ann Arbor: University of Michigan Press, 1980), who develops this idea from the writings of Frederick Law Olmsted.

40. Forman, *Land Mosaics.*

41. Theobald, "Morphology and Effects of Mountain Land Use Change in Colorado."

42. Duany and Plater-Zyberk, "The Second Coming of the American Small Town."

43. Theobald, "Morphology and Effects of Mountain Land Use Change in Colorado."

44. R. Arendt, *Rural by Design: Maintaining Small Town Character* (Chicago: Planners Press, American Planning Association Press, 1994); R. L. Knight, "Saving the West: Protecting Open Space." Videocassette available from Office of Instructional Services, Colorado State University, Fort Collins, CO 80523 (cassette number TV09489).

45. G. Hardin, "The Tragedy of the Commons," *Science* 168 (1968): 1243–1248.

46. A. Leopold, *A Sand County Almanac, with Essays on Conservation from Round River* (New York: Ballantine, 1966).

47. C. Meine, "The Oldest Task in Human History," in R. L. Knight and S. F. Bates, eds., *A New Century for Natural Resources Management* (Covelo, Calif.: Island Press, 1995).

48. Leopold, *A Sand County Almanac*, p. 262.

Action across Boundaries

JOAN IVERSON NASSAUER

LANDSCAPE ECOLOGY insistently confronts us with the complexities of connection. Rather than establishing boundaries to separate ecosystems or disciplines, it repeatedly points out their connectedness. Boundaries help us to simplify and to understand; there are fewer pieces and fewer relationships to comprehend and organize. Once we are familiar with the area inside a boundary, whether that area is a particular piece of land (for example, my neighborhood or my farm), or a particular unit of government (for example, my town or my county), or a particular way of thinking about the land (for example, history or geology), we are drawn to stay within that familiar area. Undoubtedly, there are more than enough perplexing situations and questions within it. Why go beyond the boundaries?

Landscape ecology suggests that we should go beyond the boundaries precisely because sufficient answers are unlikely to lie solely within them. Respect for the complexity of the ecological relationships must balance our human propensity for knowing the world by simplifying it. We would be quickly overwhelmed if we were responsible for paying attention to everything, but landscape ecology replaces the burden of environmental omniscience with the possibility of shifting, selective attention. It makes landscape a mobile, amoeba-like fuzzy set with boundaries that grow and shrink and arrange themselves to suit the relevant phenomenon, in which no phenomenon is seen separate from its context.[1]

This book makes it possible to see the boundaries of landscape ecology arranging themselves to extend into cultural phenomena, as expressed by philosophy, literature, social science, design, or art. Sometimes culture will be in the foreground of inquiry, and sometimes it will be context. Its perceived position will shift back and forth, like any ambiguous gestalt figure. The perceptual dexterity of all of us involved in landscape ecology is critical to our success, whether we are making new communities or making discoveries.

Ecosystem Boundaries

The shifting boundaries that characterize landscape ecology are both spatial and conceptual. Flows of energy, materials, and organisms across ecosystem boundaries have defined central questions for landscape ecology from the beginning, but those flows are not the topic of this book, at least not directly. An extensive literature on these aspects of landscape ecology is found elsewhere.[2] But indirectly, scientific knowledge about flows across ecosystem boundaries is found throughout this book. Scientific knowledge provoked nearly all of the book's authors to examine the puzzle of cultural barriers to ecological flows. Chris Faust's photographs teach us how to see the edges that human settlement imposes on natural phenomena. They also suggest that the human intentions behind these patterns range from the loving to the exploitive. More often human intentions have been oblivious to their ecological effects. Curt Meine's critique of the land-ownership grid describes it as both a physical and philosophical obstacle to ecological connections. Several of the authors offer ideas for solutions—from William Romme's suggestions for land-use planning to Deborah Karasov's hopes for environmental education. Science also was the springboard for some of the authors to suggest analogous cultural effects. For example, Marcia Eaton introduces the idea of aesthetic scales that are appropriate only within limits of cultural expectation and understanding.

Each of these essays demonstrates the shifting attention necessary to see landscape ecology whole. The authors shift science and culture from foreground to background to foreground, looking for ways that one impinges on the other. They some-

times look for cultural responses that would use scientific knowledge to make healthier landscapes. They sometimes look for similarities between ecological function and culture—to make better matches between human experience and ecological function. Sometimes they confront us with the ecological consequences of cultural realities.

In a similar way, scientific questions in landscape ecology can sometimes be formulated by beginning with culture in the foreground. For example, knowledge of urban landscape patterns and how those patterns have changed might inform how those patterns can change further to accommodate ecological function, as Judith A. Martin and Sam Bass Warner Jr. suggest here. New possible landscapes that could meet cultural preferences and fill a niche in land economics should be designed and tested for ecological function, rather than testing only more conceptually abstract alternatives for future landscape patterns.[3] Cultural knowledge is necessary to formulating useful scientific questions about the ecological function of novel patterns of cities, suburbs, farms, and forests. Landscape ecology should include an iterative process of ecological and cultural hypotheses being tested and monitored through designs on the land.

Disciplinary Boundaries

If the premise of this book and the beginnings of landscape ecology hold true—if landscape ecology is about ecosystems inhabited by humans—then it must be cultural, biological, and physical in the way it formulates questions. The human as actor must never be set aside, and the intrinsic capacity of the biophysical world to balance itself oblivious to human intention must never be ignored.

Crossing disciplinary boundaries to ask cultural questions informed by science and to ask scientific questions informed by culture may be less a matter of blurring boundaries than of bridging them, in the way that Frank Golley has characterized landscape ecology as a "bridge discipline."[4] A bridge connotes separateness and respect for differences. These were characteristics of the discussion among participants in the seminars that led to this book. Working across disciplines does not mean failing to recognize the knowledge of experts. It means being willing to try to communicate expertise in a credible common language. It also means being willing to respect unfamiliar methods or arguments, which others in one's own discipline might dismiss as "too soft, too imprecise" or "too linear, too formulaic." Most essentially, it means being willing to investigate questions that shift out beyond familiar knowledge or methods.

Around the seminar table, this willingness meant that we turned to one person to get an urban geographer's view of a question, another to get a philosopher's view, or another to get an ecologist's view. Each voice was privileged by its discipline, but no single voice answered the question. To the degree that you can read the voice of one author in another's essay in this book, you know that we were listening to one another, and that we found another discipline's insights valuable in forming our own viewpoints.

Community Boundaries

Contradicting its premise, landscape ecology usually is not used by human communities making landscape decisions. Sometimes the separation of landscape ecology from landscape decisions follows the conceptual divide between theory, art, scholarship, or research and the world at large. In theory, landscapes are simplified to represent them or know them better, but these simple representations must grow to put new insights in place on the land. Each of this book's authors sees the need for careful action

as far too urgent to perpetuate the divide between theory and practice.

More often landscape ecology is not used because of conflicts between the view of landscape as a set of ecosystems and the view of landscape as property, which is the test against which all land-use regulation is measured. As several essays discuss, the conflict stems partly from real differences between boundaries of properties, towns, or counties and ecological flows that move across these political boundaries. These essays suggest interpretations and approaches to this stubborn distinction.

Finally, the failure to use landscape ecology may be the confusing and frustrating result of inadequate attention to culture when expert ecological knowledge is brought to bear on the issues affecting human communities. In the context of implementing landscape ecology, attention to culture means legitimately acknowledging disciplinary expertise and also legitimately acknowledging and using local knowledge and wishes. At the very least it means that people who know about landscape ecology and people who know and feel passionately about their own communities must learn to speak a common language, both literally and metaphorically. Frequently it means helping local people to see beyond the perceptual habits of everyday life to consider implications that are not immediately felt and literally see the way their landscape might be in the future.

To accomplish this real vision of the future, words are seldom adequate; images are the basis for a potent common language of landscape. In the seminars that led to this book, we found that critically discussing what we saw in Chris Faust's photographs helped us recognize when we were talking about the same aspect of the landscape in different ways, and it helped us test and develop our ideas against a more complete background. Experts must integrate their knowledge across disciplines to construct valid, whole images of the future, and experts' discussions should be shared with the larger community. To evoke this kind of shared discussion, citizens should expect to see understandable images of how recognizable places in their local landscapes could change over time. To a large degree, human communities will determine ecological function by the landscapes we choose for ourselves.

The boundaries of landscape ecology must include application of knowledge to real landscapes and learning from real landscapes. Landscape ecology should be as much about doing as it is about thinking. As I. S. Zonneveld defined it, it includes scholarship, research, design, planning, construction, farming, forestry, banking, teaching, politics, and religion.[5] On a different plane from its research, landscape ecology is also about political strategy and advocacy, as Deborah Karasov suggests. It is as much about how human communities make decisions as it is about the disciplinary knowledge and expert judgments that could inform those decisions. Landscape ecology is as much in need of metatheory to help us understand how we—scientists, designers, farmers, realtors, and citizens—act together to shape the land as it is in need of theory to help us understand what we should be making. Every landscape project that transcends traditional political boundaries to address the larger ecological pattern—every watershed management project, every metropolitan or statewide land-use plan, every soil and water conservation plan, every habitat preservation plan—should be seen as a project in building the metatheory of landscape ecology as well as a project in building landscape ecological pattern.

Action across Boundaries

Acting across boundaries demands practiced dexterity in shifting attention among several views of the same landscape. To examine a landscape, we must shift upscale to look at its spatial context and shift downscale to look at the function of the ecosystems nested within it. We must formulate ecological questions by considering cultural possibilities, and we must formulate cultural questions by considering ecological processes. We must be willing to bring research results into the uncertain realm of public decision making, and scientific and scholarly knowledge must be privileged in community decision making for the insights it can lend to making future landscapes. The authors of these essays learned the necessity of the shift and grew practiced in its application. These essays are intended to suggest a further shift, from our insights to larger actions.

What makes such dexterity conceivable and the complexity of landscape ecology credible is the nature of landscape, the unifying skin of the settled planet. Landscapes are only artificially bounded by thought and action. They should be reconnected by the same artifice to allow humans to live with appropriate caution on the earth. For each of us, some landscape is our home and ultimately our living.

Notes

1. T. F. H. Allen and T. W. Hoekstra, *Toward a Unified Ecology* (New York: Columbia University Press, 1992).

2. See, for example, *Landscape Ecology* 1 (1988) and subsequent issues.

3. J. I. Nassauer, "Culture and Changing Landscape Structure," *Landscape Ecology* 10 (1995): 229–238.

4. F. Golley, Remarks at the Ninth National Symposium on Landscape Ecology, Tucson, Arizona, 1994.

5. I. S. Zonneveld, Presidential Address, *International Association for Landscape Ecology Bulletin* 1 (1982): 1.

Recommended Reading

Allen, T. F. H., and T. W. Hoekstra. 1992. *Toward a Unified Ecology.* New York: Columbia University Press.

Dramstad, W. E., J. D. Olson, and R. T. T. Forman. 1996. *Landscape Ecology Principles in Landscape Architecture and Land-Use Planning.* Washington, D.C.: Island Press.

Forman, R. T. T. 1995. *Land Mosaics: The Ecology of Landscapes and Regions.* New York: Cambridge University Press.

Meffe, G. K., and C. R., Carroll. 1994. *Principles of Conservation Biology.* Sunderland, Mass.: Sinauer.

Naiman, R. J. 1996. "Water, Society, and Landscape Ecology." *Landscape Ecology* 11: 193–196.

Thompson, G. F., and F. R. Steiner, 1996. *Ecological Design and Planning.* New York: Wiley.

Index